Discarded

FLYING THE FLAG

THE UNITED KINGDOM IN EUROVISION

A celebration and contemplation

Andy Roberts

authorHOUSE®

AuthorHouse™ UK Ltd.
500 Avebury Boulevard
Central Milton Keynes, MK9 2BE
www.authorhouse.co.uk
Phone: 08001974150

First published by AuthorHouse 6/29/2009

ISBN: 978-1-4389-5642-8 (sc)
ISBN: 978-1-4389-5643-5 (hc)

Printed in the United States of America
Bloomington, Indiana

This book is printed on acid-free paper.

Contents

ACKNOWLEDGEMENTS

Researching the Eurovision Song Contest from a United Kingdom perspective has been great fun.

Although I have to admit that my prevailing fondness for this musical institution has been somewhat lost on my partner Alison and the rest of the family.

The long hours of study provoked expressions of incredulity bordering on pity as the musical merits from Albania to Armenia and Macedonia to Moldova were etched onto the computer screen. It can't have been easy for them, with me in Eurovision mode, and I thank them for their tolerance and patience and, not least, their support.

Also my mum Leoni, who I'm sure was present at my Bathtime With Abba 'arrival' and who has been left bemused and bewildered ever since.

There are many people to thank for making this book possible and making it such an enjoyable journey over the last couple of years.

Top of the shop must be Sir Cliff Richard, Katrina Leskanich, Lee Sheriden and Bobby Gee for granting interviews, and to Gill Snow (Sir Cliff), Sherry Bendle (Katrina) and Derek Royall (Bucks Fizz) respectively for making the arrangements.

In the same breath, thanks also to Svante Stockselius, the European Broadcasting Union 'Mr Eurovision' and Kevin Bishop and Dominic Smith of the BBC for their views on all things Eurovision and also the authorisation of the use of ESC logos.

I am also grateful to Shavian for access to material published on the Sandie Shaw website and again to the BBC for use of their post-contest interview with Scooch.

Eurovision fans from all over the globe responded to my demands for their views on favourite songs and years and many thanks to all those who did so – the book could not have taken shape the way I wanted it to without these contributions.

Martyn Clarke (OGAE UK), Christian Dufresnes (OGAE France) and Peter Goessnitzer (OGAE Austria) in particular did much to rally their troops to the cause – your help was very much appreciated.

Many of the photographs in this book were provided by Christian and my oldest Eurovision friend, Patrick Racine, so a true Anglo-French collaboration in marrying words to pictures!

The research took up far too much of my time but I am indebted to several reference books and websites for much of the background.

Essentially, the magazines produced by OGAE (UK), the Eurovision Song Contest History by John Kennedy O'Connor and the late Hamish Bruce's Escofile proved invaluable. Online sources I relied on were the official Eurovision Song Contest website, also Esctoday and Wikipedia.

Finally, thanks to Ross Thomson and all the crew at Authorhouse, both in the UK and the States, for putting up with me and keeping the dream alive. Boom bang a bang!

Andy Roberts pictured with his family, partner Alison and the boys Harry, Jake and Zach

BATHTIME WITH ABBA

MY fascination with the Eurovision Song Contest goes back a long way and the defining moment, all too predictably, involved Abba and the smash hit Waterloo.

As an adventurous 11-year-old, Saturday night used to be Andy's deep bath night and with it came the weekly blue riband event, the race between the fat red boat and the thin green boat for plughole glory.

For the record, the fat red boat usually won but I have no recollection if that was actually the case on the evening of 6 April 1974.

On that occasion, my attention was distracted by the sound of sweet music from the wireless which was crackling its way to my bathroom in Northampton in the English Midlands all the way from Brighton, a fabulous resort on the south coast which ranks as one of my favourite places in the whole kingdom.

It was the lush sound of a Swedish super-group in the making. Abba were about to re-write that history book on the shelf, in terms of Eurovision and the world of popular music, and it would certainly be repeating itself in the decades that followed.

Abba's popularity, to this day, is undiminished and the quartet is revered by young and old alike.

Of course it was never like that in the early days. Admitting in the school playground to a fondness for Abba was just about as naff, or as gay, as you could possibly get.

It was far more comfortable to nail your colours to the mast of one of the more vibrant and thrusting punk and new wave pubescent offerings around at the time from the likes of the Sex Pistols and Blondie.

Abba was definitely fringe but the staunch band of Swedish glam enthusiasts at Northampton School For Boys, all three of us, consoled ourselves on our exclusion from the mainstream by maintaining that the music of Abba would live on a lot longer than that of their cooler contemporaries.

Yes we were shouted down but then the daft punk extremists in particular weren't able to recognise a melody or harmony if it clouted them round the ears.

And we were ultimately proved right. Mamma Mia, the musical and the film, has proved a worldwide sensation while tribute band Bjorn Again has enjoyed a career spanning 25 years and must surely sprout its own Rebjorn Again tribute before too long.

Then of course there is Abba Gold's omnipresence in the music charts to add to covers by Erasure and a Gimme Gimme Gimme sample by Madonna in her song Hung Up. All this, together with the arrival of Singstar and an abiding air of mystery, has helped keep the Abba brand alive.

The beauty of Abba, Agnetha Faltskog aside, has even launched a university thesis or two.

Waterloo changed the face of Eurovision and Abba went on to change the face of popular music. A point worth making the next time you hear someone complacently deriding the Eurovision Song Contest as a complete waste of time and space?

Bath nights were never quite the same after Abba's victory but you will be re-assured to hear that, at the age of 46, I have long since grown out of racing my boats in the bath on a Saturday night.

They now race on Thursday nights! Only joking.... but more surprisingly and not least disturbingly, I have yet to shake my addiction to the annual ritual that is Eurovision.

There are many in the UK who can never quite bring themselves to admit the fact that they actually watch the contest.

I am sure there are a number of examples within your own social circle. They proclaim that all the songs are rubbish and that the United Kingdom entry is only marginally less rubbish than the others.

They ritually repeat Sir Terry Wogan's anecdotes and can never ever believe the outcome of the voting, an aspect which in recent years has sent them into a state of apoplexy. All this and they have never watched the darned thing! Sorry, they only watched the voting!

So come on you lot who are in denial out there, there really is no need to worry. Shout your love for the contest from the rooftops. Be out and be proud, you know you want to!

No-one will think any the less of you and, if this book serves any purpose at all, I hope it at least makes it quite plain that by watching Eurovision you are doing nothing wrong or anything to be ashamed of.

The voting patterns since the Millennium have rightly brought into question the United Kingdom's continued participation in the contest but I should point out that the televising of Eurovision has seemingly been under perennial threat from the days the fat red boat first set sail and possibly even long before that.

However, the perversity of the recent viewing figures, which mischievously have held up well thanks in no small part to the views of Sir Terry Wogan, now retired, has helped preserve the status quo.

The axe scenario puts me in mind of that other European institution Jeux Sans Frontieres, a kind of Eurovision Slapstick Contest.

I was in my mid-teens when the powers-that-be took Jeux Sans Frontieres off the UK small screen and I have never quite recovered.

Forty-something UK viewers will remember this as the international arm of It's A Knockout.

I still retain plenty of fond Friday night memories of Guido and Gennaro in an exotic European location; Stuart Hall, Eddie Waring and Arthur Ellis slumming it in a blustery British seaside resort; Hall's uncontrollable laughter at the sliding penguins in search of water from the fountain; the Fil Rouge, my first introduction to the French language; and all-conquering Ely, the JSF equivalent of Katrina and the Waves.

In the same year that Abba won Eurovision, Jeux Sans Frontieres actually came to Northampton's Racecourse which was a bit of a turn-up as Northampton tends to miss out on international fixtures.

The theme was the Wild West. I have never been able to work out why as Northampton is not in the west (it's in middle England) and it is certainly not wild.

Apart from producing world-famous shoes, which gives the town's football club the best nickname in the country – The Cobblers - Northampton has always struggled to shape any sort of identity.

It tends to specialise in the mediocre and frustratingly lives in the shadow of nearby Milton Keynes, which has laid a strong claim to city status on the back of superior sporting, shopping and transportation facilities.

Northampton even managed to turn down an IKEA - which alongside Abba, Volvo and Nokia ranks as Sweden's most famous export - and Milton Keynes quickly snaffled up the opportunity.

Although I love the place dearly, Northampton is that sort of town and it frustrates the hell out of me. So in the absence of any other discernible theme, the Wild West it would have to be!

All too predictably, the German team from Kempten won the Northampton contest, although a spot of sabotage was suspected when a wheel fell off their wagon.

Typical German efficiency was much in evidence, although Eurovision has amazingly so far resisted the Teuton grip.

I cannot accurately recall though whether the Italians were taking part that night. Their involvement tended to be hit and miss, pretty much as is the case in the Eurovision.

Back to the contest, a video machine had to be close at hand if I happened to miss the live transmission and, while I know you must be shaking your heads at this point, please consider the following important statement.

Eurovision remains the most entertaining televisual feast of the year, well worth the BBC's licence fee alone and in the modern age represents an especially welcome departure from the stodgy diet of never-ending reality shows, home improvement programmes, cookery, gardening and sitcom repeats.

Although Wogan ritually poked fun at the event he loved it really, even if the make-up of the voting of late clearly drove him to despair and the odd beverage or two during the night of the final..

It remains the nearest thing that we now have to a shoot-out with our European brethren and the UK has traditionally had to settle for second place, initially behind France and Luxembourg and more recently in the wake of neighbours Ireland.

Since the turn of the Millennium though, we are happy to settle for second from bottom.

For a folksy Swedish four-piece to emerge from Eurovision and challenge the supremacy of the Beatles was unthinkable but the contest did make it happen, and it remains a showcase for many a hopeful artist living the dream.

Canadian diva Celine Dion, who represented and won for Switzerland in 1988, didn't do too badly in the aftermath of Eurovision either!

Competition rules currently decree that you don't have to be a native of the country you represent and participating nations currently have a free choice of language at their disposal.

The smaller nations have tended to be the greatest poachers – Luxembourg, now a fond but distant memory, has in the past boogied along with Spain's Baccara and Euro punked along with a famous Belgian, the distinctive Plastic Bertrand.

Norway's Eurovision story is the stuff of legend – after years of dreadful dirges and scoring 'nul points' more times than anyone else, they now form part of the acceptable mainstream and Finland, also after long years of toil, have also come in from the cold.

Eurovision never fails to deliver the fun factor and it helps to have a sense of humour.

The lyrics can be quite spectacular… La La La from Spain's Massiel in 1968, Ding Dinge Dong from Teach In, representing the Netherlands in 1975, and Diggi-Loo-Diggi-Ley from Sweden's Herreys in 1984…. and yes folks, all these songs won!

It was The Herreys who brought Sweden their second victory but the boys with the golden boots plummeted as rapidly as Agnetha, Frida, Bjorn and Benny soared.

Ireland's Johnny Logan became the first artist to win the Eurovision twice, Hold Me Now in 1987, following up the classy triumph of What's Another Year? in 1980.

Johnny's career did not take off on the back of those victories but his name remains synonymous with the contest, truly Mr Eurovision after also penning Linda Martin's winner – Why Me? – to register another victory for the question mark in 1992.

Rumours persist that Johnny may yet make a third appearance on the Eurovision stage. If that turns out to be the case, then the UK should bring back Sir Cliff Richard without fail!

Eurovision presents a heady mix of songs, dances, gimmicks, fashions, voting and politics; the good, the bad and the horrible, the all-round entertainment package!

And there are always the inevitable language problems, notably in Zagreb in 1990 when the jury representative from Yugoslavia – a short distance away from the contest venue – struggled to communicate with the show's presenter.

The voting is often the best part of the night but now that we are unable to see Yugoslavia, never mind hear her, that element has lost a lot of its dramatic sparkle.

So why does anyone in the UK actually bother to tune in to something which is regarded as little more than a joke? Discuss.

The debate is varied and interesting but the fact is that we do bother and we do watch the thing again no matter what might have happened the year before.

Why? Because the Eurovision is much, much more than a song and entertainment show.

It is an institution that has stood the test of time and continues to spread its tentacles across forgotten nations of Europe and beyond.

And if it disappears from our screens, I might very well cry.

PUPPET

AS with any other notion around the celebration of European togetherness, perish the thought, the United Kingdom had to be dragged kicking and screaming to the party.

The Common Market? Eventually. The Euro? Not yet. The Eurovision Song Contest? Not at first.

That was the clear impression as the UK Cinderella missed the deadline for attending the Eurovision ball in 1956.

The inaugural contest – in Lugano on 24 May – was hosted and won by Switzerland, appropriately enough the land of cheese. The Swiss have only taken top spot once since.

Each country contributed two songs and there was no time limit on the length of the song.

Lys Assia's Refrain won the Grand Prix and the other inaugural entrants to the festival were Belgium, France, Germany, Italy, Luxembourg, the Netherlands and Switzerland.

Feeling brave, the UK took the plunge the following year…

1957

Frankfurt-am-Main, Germany
3 March
New entrants: Austria, Denmark, United Kingdom
United Kingdom entry: All by Patricia Bredin
UK position: 07
Format: Each country entered one song and duos were allowed to participate
Winning song: NET ALS TOEN by Corry Brokken (Netherlands)
Bottom marker: Austria
UK maximum: Austria, France, Italy
Stat: Austria the first confirmed bottom marker in a contest

The first UK participant was Patricia Bredin, from Hull, a little-known star of the London stage.

The operatics failed to strike a chord with the nine fellow competitors and the cause wasn't helped by Bredin's seeming hostility towards 'chef d'orchestre' Eric Robinson, who started conducting before the singer had even readied herself on stage.

Bredin's song was a mere one minute 52 seconds in length – entitled 'All', it amounted pretty much to 'nothing'. It was the first song in English sung at the Eurovision.

Compare that to the excesses of the Nunzio Gallo's Italian song which meandered on for more than five excruciating minutes. To date, this is the longest-ever Eurovision song and though it sparked strong protests from the rest of the field it wasn't disqualified.

But the disquiet was enough for the EBU to impose an upper time limit of three minutes for Eurovision songs, a restriction still in place today.

The Swiss entrant was again sung by Lys Assia, unable to 'refrain' her winning song from the previous year.

The baton passed to the Netherlands with the song Net Als Toen from Corry Brokken who, co-incidentally, had also appeared in Lugano.

Denmark also made her Eurovision bow alongside the UK and Austria, and caused considerable offence with a naughty nautical offering.

No matter, the juries loved it and the Danes finished in a healthy third place, a placing not bettered by a debutant until 1994, when Poland's Edyta Gorniak hit the ground running.

It was established in Frankfurt that the winning nation would host the following year's contest, which ensured the hills (or more accurately the flatlands) of Hilversum would soon be alive with the sound of music.

UK OK? Patricia Bredin could muster only six points from the first run out in the song fest, a disappointing debut.
Belgium, the Netherlands, Luxembourg and Austria mustered up a point each for Bredin, but it was left to generous Switzerland to really show willing with two. Denmark, Germany, France and Italy gave nothing.
The UK felt benevolent and cast its net wide with two-point awards going to France, Italy and Austria.

EUROVISION JURY TOP 5

1	Net Als Toen (Corry Brokken)	NET
2	La Belle Amour (Paule Desjardins)	FRA
3	Skibet Skal Sejle I Nat	
	(Birthe Wilke and Gustav Winckler)	DEN
4	Telefon Telefon (Margot Hielscher)	GER
5	Tant De Peine (Daniele Dupre)	LUX

The UK quickly opted out of the Eurovision experience in 1958, when the Dutch hosted the contest and the French clinched the first of many early successes.

In so doing, the UK actually became the first nation to withdraw from the contest! Luxembourg and the Netherlands finished the bottom markers.

Andre Claveau's Dors, Mon Amour won in Hilversum on 12 March, with Sweden entering the fray. And songs were now limited to three minutes apiece.

The Italian song from Domenico Modugno was entitled Nel Blu Dipinto Di Blu. It became better known as Volare and soared to become a massive international hit.

Not for the first time, this accolade was bestowed upon a song that didn't actually top the Eurovision bill, Volare came third. The song became the first Eurovision entry to chart in the UK and made it all the way to the top ten.

The success of Nel Blu Dipinto di Blu however demonstrated the clear potential of the contest.

Back came the UK in 1959, with a strong song and hopes extremely high...

1959

Cannes, France
11 March
New entrants: Monaco
Return: United Kingdom
Withdrawal: Luxembourg
United Kingdom entry: Sing Little Birdie by Pearl Carr and Teddy Johnson
UK position: 02
Winning song: EEN BEETJE by Teddy Scholten (Netherlands)
Bottom marker: Monaco
UK maximum: Switzerland
Maximum to UK: Monaco, Netherlands, Switzerland
Stat: First winning Eurovision double for Netherlands and songwriter Willy van Hemert.

Domenico Modugno, later to become a member of the Italian parliament, was back for Italy on the French Riviera, although his parade was once again rained upon when Piove could only make sixth.

Once again, he was clearly peeved by the result. But, once again, he gave the song a makeover – recording it as Ciao, Ciao Bambina - and went on to record another global hit.

The UK entry was Sing Little Birdie by Pearl Carr and Teddy Johnson and bore little resemblance to what was actually happening musically in the UK at the time.

The husband-and-wife team were both popular TV and radio stars, the Posh and Becks of their day, and a finger puppet was used to represent the little bird in the song title.

To this day, Teddy remains convinced that it was Italian espionage that forced them into second place.

The song led for long periods but was finally pipped at the post by the Dutch, who came through with Teddy Scholten's Een Beetje. Teddy in this case being a woman!

Monaco made its debut in the competition and embarrassingly came in last with Mon Ami Pierrot, sung by Frenchman Jacques Pills.

UK OK? Much better, with a second-place finish (the first of 15 runners-up slots) with 16 points.

A big five came from the Netherlands and three from Switzerland. Two points came from Belgium, France and Monaco.

In return, the UK's main five points went to Switzerland with Belgium and Denmark (two) and the Netherlands (one) also in favour.

EUROVISION JURY TOP 5

1	Een Beetje (Teddy Scholten)	NET
2	Oui, Oui, Oui, Oui (Jean Phillipe)	FRA
3	Irgendwoher (Christa Williams)	SWI
4	Uh-Jeg Ville Onske Jeg Var Dig (Birthe Wilke)	DEN
5	Piove (Domenico Modugno)	ITA

1960

London, England
29 March
New entrants: Norway
Return: Luxembourg
United Kingdom entry: Looking High High High by Bryan Johnson
UK position: 02
Winning song: TOM PILLIBI by Jacqueline Boyer (France)
Bottom marker: Luxembourg
UK maximum: France
Maximum to UK: Austria, Luxembourg, Netherlands, Switzerland
Stat: French again emerges as the winning language of Eurovision

London hosted Eurovision for the first time, and for the last time there was a midweek date for the contest.

The Royal Festival Hall was the largest venue to date and, the acts apart, the stage was dominated by presenter Katie Boyle – the 'grande dame' of the Eurovision.

Our Katie ruled with a rod of iron, snapping at the audience who dared to welcome any votes for Bryan Johnson too enthusiastically!

Bryan was the brother of Teddy, who had represented the UK in 1959. He trained as a classical actor and the baritone's song Looking High High High couldn't quite manage to look high enough all the way up to the summit.

Second slot was achieved with 25 points, strangely enough a higher points total than that which went to Teddy Scholten's winner in Cannes – although it has to be said that there were two additional competing countries on this occasion.

Our friends from the other side of Le Manche – la France – were winners in Londres, and they would be again down the line in 1977.

And it was Scholten who presented the awards to the victorious French at the end of a frenetic evening.

Jacqueline Boyer's Tom Pillibi, together with the Italian offering, Renato Rascel's Romantica, were to become big hits across Europe.

Boyer, the sister of Jacques Pills who finished last for Monaco the year previously, won from the position of final song.

There were a few oddities among the ranks of the other competing songs, with the entry from Luxembourg actually sung in Luxembourgois.

The entry from Austria suggested that the boys and girls from the mountains were struggling to get the knack of Eurovision.

And Germany doffed their caps westwards by presenting a song with a French title. Little good it did them, although Wyn Hoop did manage a pretty respectable finish!

UK OK? Second place again, this time with a grand total of 25 points with the big points coming from Luxembourg and the Netherlands.

The reliable Swiss chipped in with four, Austria supplied three while debutants Norway and Italy (its first points award to the UK) provided two. A first point from Sweden..

In return, the UK gave the winning French song a high five, so much for the entente cordiale! Austria (two), Denmark, Monaco and Norway (one apiece) were also in favour.

EUROVISION JURY TOP 5

1	Tom Pillibi (Jacqueline Boyer)	FRA
2	Ce Soir-la (Francois Deguelt)	MON
3	Bonne Nuit, Ma Cherie (Wyn Hoop)	GER
4	Voi Voi (Nora Brockstedt)	NOR
5	Mon Amour Pour Toi (Fud Leclerc)	BEL

1961

Cannes, France
18 March
New entrants: Finland, Spain and Yugoslavia
United Kingdom entry: Are You Sure? by the Allisons
UK position: 02
Format: The stage was much bigger and it had a floral backdrop
Winning song: NOUS LES AMOUREUX by Jean-Claude Pascal (Luxembourg)
Bottom marker: Austria and Belgium
UK maximum: Finland, France and Switzerland
Maximum to UK: Luxembourg, Netherlands, Spain and Switzerland
Stat: Luxembourg's first win, from last the year before!

It was back to the French Riviera for Eurovision and this time, for the first time, it enjoyed the attendant glitziness of a Saturday night transmission.

The jury members across Europe were allowed to fling their votes far and wide and three newcomers boosted the contest entry to a record 16.

Protests were made against the controversial regimes of Belgium, Spain and Yugoslavia, deemed not politically correct.

Finland made their debut this year, to embark on one of the most barren runs in Eurovision history.

The Finns enjoyed no win in the contest – not even a place in the top five – until Lordi stormed home in Athens in 2006.

Luxembourg notched their first victory at the concours with a lullaby – Nous

Les Amoureux - from French actor Jean-Claude Pascal, who at the turn of the Eighties once again represented the Grand Duchy.

It didn't register a single vote from the UK jury, who instead went for the old favourites of France and Switzerland and also debutants Finland.

The UK once again chased home the winner with a song from 'brothers' The Allisons, who caused an outrage when it was revealed that they weren't brothers at all!

They were in fact two chaps called Bob Day and John Alford who in future years would fade away from the music scene, blaming their fate on the emergence of a certain group called The Beatles.

Elsewhere in the contest, a flamenco entry from Spain proved several steps too far for the judges.

The biggest star of the night was Germany's Lale Anderson, formerly forces sweetheart Lily Marlene of the Desert War.

Austria was represented by Greek Jimmy Makulis, the Eurovision knack continuing to desert them with a second-from-bottom finish.

And Jean-Paul Mauric's song for France, Printemps, saw him bouncing across the stage singing 'bing a bong'. The Eurovision trademark was born!

UK OK? Second again, this was getting tedious! More than a third of the UK points came from Luxembourg who sent across a whopping eight and Switzerland were not far behind with seven. The Netherlands and debutants Spain, in a fit of enthusiasm, contributed three each.

The UK jury spreads its votes thinly far and wide with Finland, France and Switzerland copping a two-point maximum. The remaining four singles went to Austria, Monaco, Spain and Yugoslavia.

EUROVISION JURY TOP 5

1	Nous Les Amoureux (Jean-Claude Pascal)	LUX
2	Nous Aurons Demain (Franca di Rienzo)	SWI
3	Printemps (Jean-Paul Mauric)	FRA
4	Angelique (Dario Campeotto)	DEN
5	Al Di La (Betty Curtis)	ITA

1962

Luxembourg

18 March

United Kingdom entry: Ring-A-Ding Girl by Ronnie Carroll

UK position: 04

Format: Introduction of 3-2-1 voting restriction for juries

Winning song: UN PREMIER AMOUR by Isabelle Aubret (France)

Nul Points: Austria, Belgium, Netherlands and Spain

UK maximum: Finland

Maximum to UK: Finland

Stat: The first 'nul points' and Norway not amongst them!

What is now regarded as one of the dullest contests on record rolled out in Luxembourg, with all nations from the previous year making a return.

This was to be the last midweek contest and once again the French language and style held sway.

Isabelle Aubret's hypnotic ballad entranced the watching continent and won with double votes of its nearest challenger, France's little sister Monaco.

A greater restriction on jury voting meant a limited spread of votes and inevitably it would mean that some countries would not register a single point.

With weak songs towards the top of the card, four countries in fact failed to get off the mark as the era of 'nul points' set in.

The dubious honour of becoming the first nation to zero, courtesy of the song order, went to Belgium with Fud Leclerc's fourth song for his country (1956, 1958, 1960 and 1962 no less) suggesting that, for the rest of Europe at least, enough was enough!

The Yugoslavian song was a bit of a drag, only in as much that it actually glamorised smoking with both singers puffing away. Can you imagine that taking place nowadays?

The German song Zwei Kleine Italiener, while not faring all that well at the contest, still remains popular to this very day.

The UK was represented by Ronnie Carroll, the first of two consecutive appearances from the cruise ship singer.

His song did not set Luxembourg alight and Carroll had to settle for tied fourth with Yugoslavia's Lola Novakovic.

There wasn't much zing to this particular concours and France, on the back of a third victory, feigned disinterest in hosting the following year's bash.

With Monaco, Luxembourg and Yugoslavia not rushing forward to grasp the baton, the UK stepped into the breach with the firm intention of shaking the beast from its slumber.

UK OK? A slip to equal fourth place this year and only 10 points to celebrate, a big three coming from Finland. Denmark, Switzerland and Yugoslavia awarded two points apiece and there was also one point from Spain.

The UK returned the favour by giving their top three-point award to Finland, an unlikely liaison in the early years of the contest.

EUROVISION JURY TOP 5

1	Un Premier Amour (Isabelle Aubret)	FRA
2	Dis Rien (Francois Deguelt)	MON
3	Petit Bonhomme (Camillo Felgen)	LUX
4	Ne Pali Svetla U Sumrak (Lola Novakovic)	YUG
5	Zwei Kleine Italiener (Conny Froboess)	GER

1963

London, England
23 March
United Kingdom entry: Say Wonderful Things by Ronnie Carroll
UK position: 04
Format: Now a 5-4-3-2-1 voting system!
Winning song: DANSEVISE by Grethe and Jorgen Ingmann (Denmark)
Nul Points: Finland, Netherlands, Norway and Sweden
UK maximum: Switzerland
Maximum to UK: Norway and Spain
Stat: Two wins and two zeroes now for the Netherlands – and the first for Norway!

This was Saturday night at the new BBC Television Centre in Shepherd's Bush, London and the Eurovision Song Contest was dragged wailing and whirling into the swinging Sixties!

The same 16 countries lined up in town to fight out an innovative and controversial contest.

For starters, the audience, hostess Katie Boyle and the scoreboard were in studio one.

The orchestra and the performers were based in studio two, with the stage and set changing quickly between performances.

This gave rise to claims that some of the event had been pre-recorded or arranged, but both the BBC and the European Broadcast Union have always strongly rejected them.

But the whole affair was refreshing, from the sets and visuals, to the irrepressible hostess, from the variety of the songs to the controversial finish and the relaxation of the French language stranglehold.

The UK's Ronnie Carroll however did not benefit from this refreshment, fourth again with his song and fingers pointing at his lip-synching backing singers!

The entry from Austria provided plenty of intrigue – it was sung by Israeli-born Carmela Corren and switched from a German to an English lyric, a useful trick to have up your sleeve!

A more expansive voting system produced a close finish and, thanks to the Norwegian jury and some expeditious neighbourly voting, a controversial winner.

Norway were the fifth jury to give their votes and had awarded three points to Switzerland and two points to Denmark when hostess Katie Boyle challenged the way the votes were being presented.

The Norwegian spokesman, somewhat discomfited, asked Katie if he could re-present the votes at a later stage.

Katie agreed and called Norway back at the death – at which juncture they gave Switzerland one point and Denmark four, which enabled Denmark to sneak to victory by two points? Unsurprisingly, the Swiss have been spitting feathers ever since!

UK OK? It was fourth place again for Ronnie but an improvement this time round in that there were 28 points and no equals sign getting in the way.

Norway and Spain both gave five points. There were a flurry of threes from the Netherlands, Finland, Denmark, Yugoslavia and France.

The UK awarded their 5-4-3-2-1 to Switzerland, Austria, winners Denmark, Italy and Monaco.

EUROVISION JURY TOP 5

1	Dansevise (Grethe & Jorgen Ingmann)	DEN
2	T'En Vas Pas (Ester Ofarim)	SWI
3	Uno Per Tutte (Emilio Pericoli)	ITA
4	Elle Etait Si Jolie (Alain Barriere)	FRA
5	L'Amour S'En Va (Francoise Hardy)	MON

1964

Copenhagen, Denmark
21 March
New entrants: Portugal
Withdrawals: Sweden
United Kingdom entry: I Love The Little Things by Matt Monro
UK position: 02
Format: And now a 5-3-1 voting system!
Winning song: NON HO L'ETA by Gigliola Cinquetti (Italy)
Nul Points: Germany, Portugal, Switzerland and Yugoslavia
UK maximum: Italy
Maximum to UK: Norway and Switzerland
Stat: 16-year-old Gigliola's winner was a big hit in the UK

Scandinavia's first contest success took Eurovision to Copenhagen although Sweden did not make the short journey. A debut for Portugal made up the numbers.

However, the voting system once more was restricted and, once again, the nul points kept coming thick and fast.

Two of the zeroes were reserved for Portugal (who were not to be deterred) and Switzerland, whose delegation members, after the previous year's controversy, were probably looking for a large mountain to throw themselves off.

There were three main talking points, first off being that Norway, Denmark and Finland all voted for each other in the first real manifestation of bloc voting. It was not enough to secure another victory for Scandinavia.

Secondly, a protester burst onto the stage following the Swiss entry to encourage a boycott of the regimes of Franco and Salazar in Spain and Portugal respectively.

Last, but by no means least, Italy stormed to their first victory with a convincing win by 16-year-old Gigliola Cinquetti who sung Non Ho L'Eta (I Am Too Young).

The song was not only the best but almost the most commercial and it reached number 17 in the UK charts in its native language, a considerable feat.

Matt Monro's UK entry, I Love The Little Things, was the only English language song of the night.

Monro was a ballad singer who enjoyed a 30-year career and finished second to Gigliola, although some distance behind the youngster who amassed a staggering 65 per cent of the total vote.

His song was written by Tony Hatch, who penned many hits including Downtown for Petula Clark.

And a future number 4 UK chart hit called Walk Away was actually an anglicised version of the Austrian entry, written and sung by the aforementioned Udo Juergens – the first of his three contest appearances.

UK OK? Matt Monro took the UK back up to second spot but way behind runaway winners Italy. Maximum fives came from Norway and Switzerland and a second-choice three points came from Finland.

The UK gave five to Italy (who picked up eight maximums with the minor awards going to Finland (three) and the Netherlands (one).

EUROVISION JURY TOP 5

1	Non Ho L'Eta (Gigliola Cinquetti)	ITA
2	Des Que Le Printemps Revient (Hugues Aufrey)	LUX
3	Ou Sont-Elles Passees? (Romuald)	MON
4	Le Chant De Mallory (Rachel)	FRA
5	Warum Nur Warum? (Udo Juergens)	AUS

1965

Naples, Italy
20 March
New entrants: Ireland
Return: Sweden
United Kingdom entry: I Belong by Kathy Kirby
UK position: 02
Format: Belgium somehow awarded 6 points to the UK – the maximum should have been five!
Winning song: POUPEE DE CIRE, POUPEE DE SON by France Gall (Luxembourg)
Nul Points: Belgium, Finland, Germany and Spain
UK maximum: Monaco
Maximum to UK: Belgium, Denmark, Spain and Switzerland
Stat: An innocent victory for France, singing for Luxembourg.

This was the debut year for Ireland and the Emerald Isle quickly made it clear that they would be seriously challenging Blighty all the way for the top honours in Eurovision.

The Irish brought with them another English language song to the contest – and this year so did the Swedes!

The latter's departure was duly noted by the organisers, who did not take to the move too kindly.

Ireland and the United Kingdom ignored each other in the voting stakes, so bucking the presumed neighbourly favouritism which produced votes from

Monaco for France and a healthy return from Sweden for Denmark.

This was the first contest involving Intervision, which broadcast Eurovision to the east of Europe, boosting the viewing figures to circa 150 million.

The winning song was a refreshing number from Luxembourg, sung by French teenager France Gall.

She belted out the number, Poupee De Cire Poupee De Son, with a youthful innocence which belied the sub-text of Serge Gainsbourg's lyrics – English title translation Wax Doll Singing Doll.

Gainsbourg of course would have chart success in years to come with the controversial Jane Birkin collaboration Je T'Aime.

The United Kingdom was represented by the stylish television celebrity Kathy Kirby, a popular favourite rated, according to one poll, more positively than Cilla Black, the late Dusty Springfield and Petula Clark.

She took to the stage in a shimmering black gown which dramatically offset her blonde hair and her lip gloss glamour.

Her song, I Belong, scored strongly but once again the UK had to make do with 'deuxieme place'.

Spain, Finland, Germany and Belgium all failed to get off the mark as Eurovision celebrated its tenth anniversary.

In the case of Spain, Conchita Bautista, having a second go, flopped but Austria's Udo Juergens, sixth the year before, lifted himself up too fourth place. His best was yet to come!

UK OK? The seemingly inevitable runners-up spot was achieved with 26 points, courtesy of an 'illegal' six from Belgium who, instead of voting 5-3-1 opted for 6-3 – the three going to Italy. That's how it was recorded! Legal fives came from Spain, Denmark and Switzerland.

The UK plumped for Monaco with its five, Austria (three) and Italy (one) also currying favour.

EUROVISION JURY TOP 5

1	Poupee De Cire, Poupee De Son (France Gall)	LUX
2	N'Avoue Jamais (Guy Mardel)	FRA
3	Sag Ihr, Ich Lass Sie Gruessen (Udo Juergens)	AUS
4	Se Piangi, Se Ridi (Bobby Solo)	ITA
5	I'm Walking The Streets In The Rain (Butch Moore)	IRE

1966

Luxembourg
5 March
United Kingdom entry: A Man Without Love by Kenneth McKellar
UK position: 09
Format: The language rule is enforced after Sweden's English lapse.
Winning song: MERCI CHERIE by Udo Juergens (Austria)
Nul Points: Italy and Monaco
UK maximum: Yugoslavia
Maximum to UK: Ireland
Stat: Third time lucky for Austria's Udo Juergens

This was a good year for English football, but a very disappointing Eurovision year for the United Kingdom.

Scots tenor Kenneth McKellar, in a tartan kilt, contributed a maudlin offering which found little favour with the good burghers of the continent.

Only the Irish resonated with its Celtic tone and, ironically, weighed in with maximum points.

McKellar slumped to ninth out of 18 entrants, his song neither connecting with its target audience or, indeed, with the musical scene back home.

This was a mistake, and big enough to persuade UK organisers to get back to the old drawing board.

But they could surely draw inspiration from Austria, for whom the old adage of 'If at first you don't succeed try, try again' certainly held true.

Udo Juergens, sixth in Copenhagen and fourth in Naples, now roared to victory in Luxembourg with a song which had a French title but which was sung in German.

German songs do not fare well in Eurovision – the only other song to pull it off was Nicole's triumph for the Fatherland in 1982.

Merci Cherie secured almost double the votes of second-placed Sweden and proved a popular winner for the respected singer.

But spare a thought for Italian veteran Domenico Modugno who could not make the quantum leap that Juergens achieved.

Modugno fell out with the orchestra and his song, although a hit for Giglio Cinquetta in later years, joined Monaco on nul points.

Competing nations were instructed to deliver songs in their native language and the contest saw the final appearance for Denmark for quite some time – the Danes would eventually return in 1978.

Netherlands singer Milly Scott became the first black singer to compete in Eurovision and also the first to use a hand mike (great for artist movement!). The hand mike didn't catch on though and only one singer used it the following year. No prizes for working out who that may have been!

*UK OK? Oh dear, Kenneth McKellar's tartan kilt put off Europe and we slumped
to a worst-ever ninth finish, mustering only eight points along the way.*

*Only two nations deigned to give the UK any points, good old Ireland appreciating
the Celtic touch with a bumper five and Luxembourg demonstrating support with
three.*

*The UK gave Yugoslavia five points top marks with Spain (three) and Netherlands
(one) making up the votes.*

EUROVISION JURY TOP 5

1	Merci Cherie (Udo Juergens)	AUS
2	Nygammal Vals Eller Hip Man Svinaherde (Lill Lindfors and Svante Thuresson)	SWE
3	Intet Er Nytt Under Solen (Ase Kleveland)	NOR
4	Un Peu De Poivre, Un Peu De Sel (Tonia)	BEL
5	Come Back To Stay (Dickie Rock)	IRE

1967

Vienna, Austria
8 April
Withdrawals: Denmark
UK position: WINNER
**Format: A wider voting spread, artist reaction and on-screen
translations!**
**Winning song: PUPPET ON A STRING by Sandie Shaw (United
Kingdom)**
Nul Points: Switzerland
UK maximum: France, Ireland and Luxembourg
**Maximum to UK: Austria, Belgium, France, Luxembourg, Monaco,
Norway and Switzerland**
Stat: The start of the long goodbye for Denmark

Yes, Sandie Shaw was that artist with the hand mike and, again just to be
different, she sang her entry, Puppet On A String, in bare feet.

Just to be different, the song was unlike one that Eurovision had ever heard
before.

And, just to be different, the United Kingdom did not finish in second place!
Kenneth McKellar's ninth-place finish became a distant memory as Shaw
swept to a memorable win.

Her nearest rivals, in a distant second place, were Ireland and the song became a monster smash all over Europe and out-sold every single in the UK that year.

The song however was distinct irritation to the singer who bemoaned its 'stupid cuckoo clock tune'. Heaven knows what the Swiss made of that remark?!

The first note of the song was lost because of a technical fault but no matter, Shaw admitted later that knew she had won the contest before she had even opened her mouth.

After a period of disaffection with the contest, Shaw took to the Song For Europe stage in 2005 to present Javine with her winning ticket to Kiev.

Shaw's success came in the year that the Beatles hit the big time with Sergeant Pepper's Lonely Hearts Club band album.

But, as has always been the case, Eurovision in Vienna chugged along very much in its own little space bubble.

In the years that followed, many nations felt that imitation was the sincerest form of flattery and tried to emulate the Shaw style.

It is never really a successful gambit and plenty of inferior imitations dragged the contest down.

However, technological advances did move the contest forward and cameras were allowed into the Green Room for the first time to gauge artist reaction to the voting – enough to make you cringe but a quirk that has remained ever since.

As the Seventies, in glorious and gaudy technicolour, beckoned, both the United Kingdom and the Eurovision found themselves on the up.

But it would certainly be difficult for the UK to follow Shaw's success on home turf the following year.

She was a hard act to follow. Could they pull it off? Very nearly, as it turned out. The late Sixties certainly belonged to the United Kingdom.

UK OK? A UK win, at long last, with only Spain and Yugoslavia NOT registering a vote for Sandie Shaw's Puppet!

The song completely won over Austria, Switzerland and Norway who each gave seven points and Luxembourg were not far behind with five.

The UK gave two points to Luxembourg, France and Ireland and one each for Netherlands, Belgium, Germany and Italy.

EUROVISION JURY TOP 5

1	Il Doit Fair Beau La-Bas (Noelle Cordier)	FRA
2	If I Could Choose (Sean Dunphy)	IRE
3	L'Amour Est Bleu (Vicky Leandros)	LUX
4	Boum-Badaboum (Minouche Barelli)	MON
5	Hablemos Del Amor (Raphael)	SPA

CONGRATULATIONS!

THE late Sixties was a golden era for the United Kingdom in the Eurovision Song Contest, with three of the nation's international stars dominating the contest stage.

Sandie Shaw lay down the gauntlet with the irrepressible Puppet On A String in 1967 and Lulu's Boom Bang-A-Bang shared the Grand Prix honours with three other countries two years later.

Wedged in between, Sir Cliff Richard's Congratulations established itself as a Eurovision anthem although the song finished second behind Spain's Massiel, who controversially claimed the title with La La La.

The result left Cliff wounded but this stain on such an illustrious career may yet be removed.

An investigation in Spain has uncovered some skullduggery which apparently shows that the dictator at the time, Francisco Franco, had the vote rigged - ensuring that the Cliff never had a chance of winning.

Cliff said: "I've lived with this number two thing for so many years, it would be wonderful if an official from the contest turned around and said that I had won the darn thing after all."

His cause for hope has come in the form of a new Spanish documentary, which claims that Franco was determined to claim Eurovision glory for his own country.

The investigation details how El Generalissimo was so keen to improve Spain's international image that he sent corrupt TV executives across Europe to buy goodwill in the run-up to the contest.

The documentary director claimed: "Massiel's win was fixed. It's in the public domain that Television Espanola executives travelled around Europe buying series that would never be broadcast and signing concert contracts with odd, unknown groups and singers.

"These contracts were translated into votes. It was these bought votes that won Eurovision for Massiel. The regime was well aware of the need to improve its image overseas.

"When you look at all the parties they organised and how Massiel was transformed into a national heroine, you realise it was rather over the top for a singing competition. It was all intended to boost the regime."

Cliff added: "If, like they say, they believe there is evidence that I was the winner, there won't be a happier person on the planet.

"It's never good to lose, never good to feel a loser. When I went on that night I said to the band that there would be 400 million people watching and that it would be a massive plug for our song. And it was. I think we sold a million singles. But we really wanted to win."

Indeed, being crowned victor would dovetail nicely with Cliff's own golden jubilee celebrations.

Sir Cliff Richard, for whom Eurovision nowadays is a joke – but a good one!
www.cliffrichard.org

Although he conceded that opening an official investigation into the rigged vote "might not be worth the trouble", the belated verdict would mean a lot to him.

He said: "I'd be quite happy to be able to say I won Eurovision 1968. It's an impressive date in the calendar these days.

"But I will remain philosophical. I don't hold Massiel accountable for the vote 40 years ago and, if the adjudication is reversed, I will gladly send her a signed copy of Congratulations!"

While La La La disappeared without trace, Congratulations has lived on the world over.

The song title even lent itself to the event which marked Eurovision's 50 years bash in Denmark in 2005.

Cliff went on to confirm his status as Britain's most successful vocalist, with millions of sales worldwide.

But one of Eurovision's few household names now regards the contest as a joke.

Cliff, who narrowly missed out on the Eurovision crown a second time when Power To All Our Friends finished third in 1973, believes the contest has become a musical let down.

He said: "As a genuine musical competition, the Eurovision Song Contest has become a joke – but quite a good joke!

"I had hoped that the Eurovision would become a presentation of the very best of pop rock in Europe but sadly that hasn't been the case in recent years.

"I don't think the United Kingdom's credibility has been damaged by not putting forward a big name.

"That is definitely not the case. In the old days, the UK did put up major names – Lulu, The Shadows and Sandie Shaw for example – in the hope, and assumption, that the competition would become musically important.

"Sadly it hasn't, and today no major artist in the United Kingdom would want to be identified with it."

Cliff's musical highlights from Eurovision see Abba's barnstorming Waterloo and Sandie Shaw's Puppet On A String at the forefront.

Jostling these two songs for his favour is the Italian song Marianne, sung by Sergio Endrigo, which competed against Cliff's Congratulations in London in 1968, finishing tenth.

Cliff added: "I would consider entering the competition for a third time but only if the competition was radically changed and the entries were generally representative of the country's musical talent.

"I understand Sir Andrew Lloyd Webber asked if I'm available. It was nice of him to consider me.

"But for me, Eurovision has lost its credibility and in its present form I wouldn't want to be associated with it."

Sandie Shaw has also distanced herself from Eurovision following her emphatic success in 1967.

At one stage she could not bear to be associated with her stand-out hit Puppet On A String but nowadays she is more accepting of her participation and its significance.

OH Vienna! Forty years after the triumph – and on a trip specifically designed to celebrate her 60th birthday – Sandie Shaw once more found herself in the Austrian capital.

And it is fair to say that on this occasion she felt more at ease in the city of cream cakes and waltzes than she did in the Wiener Hofburg palace back on 8 April 1967.

The much-loved Essex girl felt that she very much personified the Puppet On A String she was singing about.

At the time, she was experiencing considerable trauma in her private life and really didn't want to be singing her heart out for a Eurovision audience.

But events had moved beyond her control – her strings were being pulled, and she didn't much care for it.

Accordingly, it took some considerable time for Sandie to come to love her Eurovision song which helped make her name and, not least, quite a bit of money.

She is now reconciled to it – in fact, she re-recorded it as a bluesy ballad as a 60th birthday gift to her legion of fans.

Born Sandra Ann Goodrich in Dagenham, the daughter of a welder and an insurance clerk, her ordinariness marked her out as she drifted through school, daydreaming about stardom.

Sandra was so convinced of her own destiny - a hazy notion of being a model, a singer or an actress - that she skipped sitting the last of her O Levels at the age of 16 and chugged off on the back of her boyfriend's Lambretta.

For anyone else in Dagenham, it would have been the start of a journey into oblivion.

At this point, the common mythology is that Essex's very own Cinderella, an Adam Faith devotee, blagged her way backstage, demanded an audition, met legendary showbiz manager Evelyn Taylor, and - re-christened Sandie Shaw - hit the big time.

Only this Cinderella avoided any problems with glass slippers. Probably because she never ever, it seemed, wore shoes.

Throughout the decade, Sandie recorded in French, German, Spanish and Italian and parallel careers in Europe, South America and Australasia spared Sandie the ignominy of a summer season in a seaside resort.

But her huge initial success had stalled on the back of a divorce scandal, in which she was named as a co-respondent.

Through one twist of fate after another, the singer, who just three years earlier had been tipped by the style cognoscenti as the female answer to The Beatles, gambled her career and credibility on a two-minute-twenty pop song that for her conveyed absolutely no truth whatsoever.

Faced with the very real prospect of a slow drift into obscurity, as just another of the class of 1965 who failed to make the grade, Sandie decided that she was going to win the contest in a way that no-one had ever won before.

Mentor Evie passed on the message from the BBC that either Sandie did Eurovision or she didn't work for them again.

Senior BBC figures, who ought to have known better, argued that Eurovision could 'rehabilitate' her public image.

Four candidate songs for Sandie's performance in Vienna, including Tell The Boys, were chosen from a shortlist whittled down by the Music Publishers Association.

A fifth, Had A Dream Last Night, written by Chris Andrews, was given a 'bye' into the final round.

Sandie performed each song on the Rolf Harris Show, praying that the public would prefer either Tell The Boys or the Andrews creation over a song about women dancing around men like puppets.

Puppet On A String was so awful, she reasoned, it had absolutely no chance of being chosen. But her reasoning was out.

By the time Sandie arrived in Vienna, the atmosphere that Evie had managed to engineer between Sandie, the BBC and Rolf Harris and his entourage was so toxic that no-one was on speaking terms.

Everyone avoided Sandie, who in turn kept her distance, warned by Evie that they were out to destroy her. Bewilderingly unaware of Sandie's high profile on continental Europe, the attention Sandie attracted in Vienna mystified the BBC.

As she walked on stage, Sandie knew she was going to win. The applause started from the moment her name was announced, and continued long after she had stopped singing.

On stage, in a heart-stopping moment, the microphone failed; back home, people put it down to a plot by continentals out to sabotage 'our Sandie'.

France, Switzerland and Norway gave her maximum points. The Spaniards couldn't see it our way, with a miserly zero.

Not that their votes mattered, because after six of the sixteen voting nations had spoken, Sandie was beyond the reach of the runner up, Ireland's Sean Dunphy.

Commercially, 'Puppet On A String' was a triumph. Advance orders from Germany alone on the night of the contest topped 500,000 copies.

The single hit Number 1 in practically every country where the contest was shown, and beyond.

But the Eurovision brand wore Sandie down and Puppet got a brand new string in 2007.

Sandie says on her website www.sandieshaw.com: "Puppet On A String is a song which has been the source of much grief, hilarity, circumspection and I have to admit, financial reward for many years.

"But the new version is like you have never heard it before. Courtesy of my very good friend, Howard Jones, who spends much time locked up in a recording studio with his vast array of technology nowadays, I have completely turned everything around.

"So much so, that I am really proud of my efforts. It actually sounds super cool. I went to visit Howard one day and he was sitting at his keyboards playing around with some really beautiful chords and he started humming a bit of a soulful melody over it.

"I told him that it sounded nice and he asked me to try it. I did and it felt really good. I suddenly realised that this was the dreaded Puppet.

"He urged me not to lose my nerve and coaxed me to see if I could change my karma. So we finished it off, recorded it and sent it to a young, hip producer/mixer, Andy Gray, who re-arranged and mixed the track and voila! I am cured! "I really love it and I made it available to my fans as an extra special 60th birthday present."

Oh Vienna. A beautiful city where Sandie Shaw became the first artist to win the Eurovision for the United Kingdom.

Sandie is now happy to acknowledge her place in the history book but, like Lulu – a joint winner in 1969 – she would like the whole Eurovision thing kept in perspective.

Eurovision has its place – but winning the contest isn't really what she wants to be remembered for.

THE HISTORY BOOK ON THE SHELF

1968

London, England
6 April
United Kingdom entry: Congratulations by Cliff Richard
UK position: 02
Format: The contest transmission was in colour!
Winning song: LA LA LA.... by Massiel (Spain)
Bottom Marker: Finland and Netherlands
UK maximum: Germany
Maximum to UK: France, Monaco and Switzerland
Stat: Irish singer Pat McGuigan was the father of boxer Barry
McGuigan

London welcomed back Eurovision and Cliff Richard took the home stage
with a song which will be very familiar.

Congratulations is still played at parties and awards ceremonies to this very
day and remains one of Eurovision's most memorable songs – similar to
Volare, and, like Volare, it didn't win!

Richard – born Harry Rodger Webb in Lucknow, India on 14 October 1940
– locked himself in the toilet as the voting unfolded because he could not face
up to the tension and the drama.

He was beaten to the post by Spain's Massiel with the quintessential Eurovision
refrain of La La La.

This song incidentally was originally advanced by another artist singing in
Catalan. That approach was considered too risky for the Eurovision stage,
Spanish singer Massiel took up the baton and beat our man by a single point.

Richard, however, had the last laugh as Congratulations rocketed to worldwide
success, even charting in the United States – albeit at 99!

The song has been recorded in many different languages and was even sung
by Richard at the Lawn Tennis Championships in Wimbledon during a rain-
break in 1997.

Many still believe Richard was denied a rightful victory by a little vote-rigging
on the part of Yugoslavia. The last jury to vote, the Slavs gave zero points to
both Spain and the United Kingdom and Massiel hung on for victory.

Ireland were represented by Pat McGuigan, whose rendition of 'Danny Boy' ringside was to be heard years down the line when son Barry prepared for world title boxing action.

All said, the result was a universal disappointment and Eurovision's credibility was under threat. Worse, however, was to follow.

UK OK? Many people think that Cliff Richard actually won the Eurovision for the UK, but this was the first of two top three placings – second and just a point behind Spain.

Congratulations became a classic song of celebration and attracted votes from all but four countries – Austria, Norway, Spain and Yugoslavia did not oblige.

The UK's top mark of five went to Germany and we also gave points to Sweden (two), Belgium, Luxembourg and Monaco.

EUROVISION JURY TOP 5

1	La La La (Massiel)	SPA
2	La Source (Isabelle Aubret)	FRA
3	Chance Of A Lifetime (Pat McGuigan)	IRE
4	Det Borjar Verka Karlek Banne Mej (Claes-Goran Hederstrom)	SWE
5	Ein Hoch Der Liebe (Wenche Myrhe)	GER

1969

Madrid, Spain
29 March
Withdrawals: Austria
United Kingdom entry: Boom Bang-A-Bang by Lulu
UK position: EQUAL WINNER
Format: This was the beginning of the end for the 'one jury member, one vote' system
Winning songs: UN JOUR, UN ENFANT by Frida Boccara (France); DE TROUBADOUR by Lenny Kuhr (Netherlands); VIVO CANTANDO by Salome (Spain); BOOM BANG-A-BANG by Lulu (United Kingdom)
Bottom Marker: Norway
UK maximum: France
Maximum to UK: Luxembourg and Sweden
Stat: The Madrid Madhouse – the only occasion that a Eurovision year has produced no less than four winners. On top vote count back, the gong would have gone to France or Spain.

Welcome to Madrid and a never-to-be-forgotten Eurovision, where Lulu – another established solo artist – gave it up for the United Kingdom.

La La La won it for Spain the year previously and here was the Scottish songstress delivering what has become the Eurovision call sign, Boom-Bang-A-Bang.

And it won, although the UK had to share the title with three of their European neighbours.

Nowadays, while most people think that Cliff was a Eurovision winner, they naturally struggle to put Lulu – born Ann-Marie Laurie on 3 November 1948 - in the same bracket.

Lulu, like Sandie Shaw before and Olivia Newton-John to follow, didn't much care for the song she had been landed with.

You could forgive her for having been distracted because, a matter of days before she flew out to Madrid, she married Maurice Gibb, a member of the Bee Gees.

But, the trouper that she is, she gave it her all and even ended the rendition with an 'Ole' which melted many a Spanish heart.

Banal though the song was, the juries loved it and it gave Lulu her biggest hit – she had to wait until 1993, and the collaboration with boy band Take That, to top it.

The organisers, presented with four winning songs and no rule to separate them, frantically searched for four winning medals to present to the winning artists.

They managed it, only because they had four medals struck for a winning artist and backing group – who knows what would have happened had it been a five-way tie?

The farcical outcome had the Scandinavian countries in uproar and the disquiet was deafening.

The EBU were forced to go back to the rulebook and, with Eurovision's stock at an all-time low, the Dutch won the ballot to host the 1970 gathering.

A poisoned chalice if ever there was one and Amsterdam 1970 had plenty of work to do!

UK OK? The mayhem in Madrid saw the top four each on 18 points with Lulu's total boosted by a weighty five from Sweden.

Luxembourg also liked it and there was a notable three points from Italy although we did not get as many top votes as either France or Spain.

The UK spread its votes in descending 4-3-2-1 style, the most going to France with Belgium, Switzerland and Ireland respectively also featuring.

EUROVISION JURY TOP 5

1	Vivo Cantando (Salome)	SPA
2	Un Jour, Un Enfant (Frida Boccara)	FRA
3	The Wages Of Love (Muriel Day & The Lindsays)	IRE
4	De Troubadour (Lenny Kuhr)	NET
5	Bonjour, Bonjour (Paola Del Medico)	SWI

1970

Amsterdam, Netherlands
21 March
Withdrawals: Finland, Norway, Portugal and Sweden
United Kingdom entry: Knock Knock (Who's There?) by Mary Hopkin
UK position: 02
Format: Still 'one jury member one vote' – the votes were telephoned in.
Winning song: ALL KINDS OF EVERYTHING by Dana (Ireland)
Nul Points: Luxembourg
UK maximum: Ireland and Yugoslavia
Maximum to UK: Germany, Ireland, Monaco and Yugoslavia
Stat: Belgium's nine-point whopper for Ireland swung the contest the Emerald Isle's way

With a huge amount of trepidation, Eurovision in the 1970s was ushered in over in Amsterdam.

The backlash had materialised with a whole host of countries refusing to enter songs, believing that the contest was on the way out.

Indeed with only 12 nations taking part, it was difficult to picture any sort of future for the event.

Eurovision needed a change of direction and Ireland's Dana – Rosemary Brown from the Bogside, Derry, Northern Ireland and a British citizen – provided it with a sweet winner.

In a Celtic flavour to the proceedings, the United Kingdom was represented by Welsh lass Mary Hopkin singing Knock Knock (Who's There?)

Her song delivery was crystal clear and this time the United Kingdom had to content itself with another second place behind the Emerald Isle, celebrating its first victory – the first of many.

Dana's was a 'sit down' victory and, Mary Hopkin aside, she had a few other heavyweights to see off.

Among them was a certain Julio Iglesias, who sang Gwendolyne for him Spanish homeland.

And rising star Katja Ebstein was belting out the German entry Wunder Gibt Es Immer Wieder.

Dana left them all in her wake, wedged among them in the top five being the eurosong Retour from Switzerland.

The stage design in Amsterdam was swish and the technical aspect of the show helped to restore the contest's tarnished image.

Ireland won by six points, so no dead heat horror shows, and Dana's triumph was broadcast to South America where both Brazil and Chile took on the transmission live by satellite.

At the end of the show it was job done – a popular winning song and artist and one of the most successful contests ensured that Eurovision was back on track.

The Seventies would prove to be a landmark decade for Eurovision. The only way would be up!

UK OK? The nation was running hot in Eurovision and Mary Hopkin's second place was six adrift of Ireland's Dana.

A low turnout in Amsterdam, with only two of the eleven potential voters – Belgium and Spain – ignoring Hopkin's claim. Ireland did us proud, awarding the UK and also France its top mark of three.

The UK maximum went to the Irish winner and also Yugoslavia, the four points from the UK were Yugoslavia's only points!

EUROVISION JURY TOP 5

1	All Kinds Of Everything (Dana)	IRE
2	Wunder Gibt Es Immer Wieder (Katja Ebstein)	GER
3	Retour (Henri Des)	SWI
4	Gwendolyne (Julio Iglesias)	SPA
5	Marie Blanche (Guy Bonnet)	FRA

1971

Dublin, Republic of Ireland
3 April
New entrants: Malta
Return: Austria, Finland, Norway, Portugal and Sweden
United Kingdom entry: Jack In The Box by Clodagh Rogers
UK position: 04
Format: A modified scoring system was introduced to try and avoid the fiasco of 1969 and refresh the contest
Winning song: UN BANC, UN ARBRE, UNE RUE by Severine (Monaco)
Bottom Marker: Malta
UK maximum: Finland
Maximum to UK: Malta
Stat: The jury mark was split, with half the award coming from a member who had to be under 25 years of age. No chance of nul points for anyone, Malta who were bottom scored 52!

Once again the United Kingdom entry went to another part of the kingdom with Northern Ireland's Clodagh Rogers selected for the contest, which this year came from the southern Ireland capital of Dublin.

This followed the selections of Lulu (Scotland) and Mary Hopkin (Wales) in the two previous years.

The selection was diplomatic, in the wake of the prevailing difficulties between Ireland's north and south communities.

Rogers had first charted in 1969 but Jack In The Box was to become her best-known song.

She took to the stage in an eye-catching outfit but could only manage fourth place, a disappointment for the UK judged against the high standard of entries that had gone before.

It meant that for the first time since 1966, the UK had failed to finish in either first or second place.

No matter, Rogers went on to become a household name in the decade and quite recently appeared on the musical stage in popular Blood Brothers.

The Dublin contest chalked a first on a number of fronts, the final result containing no nations with equal votes.

It also allowed groups to enter the competition for the first time, as opposed to solo artists and duos with backing singers.

The first group to take the Eurovision stage were Switzerland's Peter, Sue and March – the first of four appearances the group were to make in the contest, with follow-ups coming in 1976, 1979 and 1981.

Finally, each act was introduced by a preview video which, in some shape or form, persists to this very day.

Malta endured a tough baptism, with their artist Deo Grech having the misfortune to be drawn second and finishing bottom of the pile below Norway.

Monaco's winner from Severine was the pick of the night, Un Banc, Un Arbre, Une Rue landing the Principality's one and only Grand Prix success.

UK OK? The voting all of a sudden got horrendously complicated and there were massive scores on offer.

Everyone was able to vote for everyone and Clodagh Rogers received solid scores from Belgium, France, debutant Malta and Monaco.

Going the other way, a big 10-point maximum went to eighth-placed Finland and we also quite liked the winner from Monaco.

EUROVISION JURY TOP 5

1	Un Banc, Un Arbre, Une Rue (Severine)	MON
2	Diese Welt (Katja Ebstein)	GER
3	En Un Mondo Nuevo (Karina)	SPA
4	L'Amore E Un Attimo (Massimo Ranieri)	ITA
5	Vita Vidder (The Family Four)	SWE

1972

Edinburgh, Scotland
25 March
United Kingdom entry: Beg, Steal Or Borrow by The New Seekers
UK position: 02
Format: The UK stepped in again to host the contest, with the Scottish capital city Edinburgh hosting on this occasion.
Winning song: APRES-TOI by Vicky Leandros (Luxembourg)
Bottom Marker: Malta
UK maximum: Luxembourg
Maximum to UK: France, Monaco and Norway
Stat: This contest was notable, if for no other reason, that there were no tied places in the final order of merit.

The United Kingdom took advantage of the new group rule to enter the well-known New Seekers on the Edinburgh stage.

The catchy Beg Steal Or Borrow went down a treat with the juries across the continent.

But the New Seekers had the misfortune to be pitched against one of the barnstorming Eurovision ballads of all time and Vicky Leandros, singing for Luxembourg, won a deserved victory.

Thousands of viewers in the UK were unable to watch the New Seekers winning the selection as a power cut interrupted the transmission – oh the good old days of the early Seventies!

The New Seekers had been formed out of The Seekers and sold 35 million records in 1972 alone.

They are probably best remembered – well by me at least – for the uplifting I'd Like To Teach The World To Sing, the theme tune for Coca Cola.

Paul Layton remained the lead singer of the group, surviving the transition from old to new, and group member Danny Finn would later maintain the Seekers influence in Eurovision by fronting Prima Donna in 1980.

Edinburgh's Usher Hall was the host venue, Monaco decreeing there was nowhere on their patch to stage the contest.

And for the first time the Eurovision was broadcast across Asia, spreading its message of technological development like never before.

Malta's woe continued, the islanders again finishing bottom of the pile, this time depriving Belgium of the wooden spoon.

Mary Roos represented Germany and her song, Nur Die Liebe Laesst Uns Leben, saw off the Netherlands challenge to take third place.

But the rave reviews were for Leandros, whose song, translated into several languages, has stood the test of time.

It was penned by Yves Desia, who had also written Monaco's winner the previous year and so he became the only person to pen two Eurovision winners in successive outings.

UK OK? The New Seekers took the UK back up to second place behind one of my favourite Eurovison songs, the classy Apres-Toi from Vicky Leandros.

Norway gave the UK a big ten points and France, Monaco and Yugoslavia were only a point behind.

The UK jury recognised class, sending the top ten Luxembourg's way and also approving of France and the Netherlands (nine apiece).

EUROVISION JURY TOP 5

1	Apres Toi (Vicky Leandros)	LUX
2	Nur Die Liebe Lasst Uns Leben (Mary Roos)	GER
3	Als Het Om De Liefde Gaat	
	(Sandra & Andres)	NET
4	Falter Im Wind (The Milestones)	AUS
5	I Giorni Dell'Arcobaleno (Nicola di Bari)	ITA

1973

Luxembourg
7 April
New entrants: Israel
Withdrawals: Austria and Malta
United Kingdom entry: Power To All Our Friends by Cliff Richard
UK position: 03
Format: Israel in Europe? – no! Israel in the European Broadcasting Union? – yes!
Winning song: TU TE RECONNAITRAS by Anne-Marie David (Luxembourg)
Bottom Marker: Belgium
UK maximum: Luxembourg
Maximum to UK: Finland, Israel, Luxembourg, Netherlands and Sweden
Stat: Luxembourg became the first nation to win the contest outright for two successive years.

Cliff Richard made his second appearance on the Eurovision stage by winning the selection to represent the UK in Luxembourg.

He was hoping to go one better after being squeezed into second place in London back in 1968 but instead he was pushed down one place in the Grand Duchy, behind the hosts and the Netherlands.

The winner from Luxembourg by Anne-Marie David is regarded as the strongest-ever Eurovision winner, with the highest points percentage recorded of all songs that have won the contest.

Once again, Richard made an impression with his choice of costume, a dashing red-and-black ensemble.

And the in-your-face choreography remains a popular clip on the flashback highlights.

His career was certainly not blighted by his experience, going on to celebrate number one singles in five successive decades which is an outstanding achievement.

This contest saw the introduction of Israel, to the consternation of many observers around the continent.

With the horrors of the Munich Olympics still vivid from the previous year, security around the contest venue was heightened.

Israel put in a strong debut but Richard's offering aside, the big commercial hit belonged to Spain's Mocedades and the song Eres Tu although it was plagued by claims of plagiarism.

The Swedish entry also drew criticism as it contained mention of breasts and Patrick Juvet, replete with purple eye shadow, flew the flag for Switzerland.

This contest also allowed competing nations to choose the language for their song, a rule that remained in place until 1976.

From 1977, nations once again had to sing in their native tongue but the choice factor was re-introduced in 1999 and has remained in place since.

UK OK? Cliff Richard was down in third in a very tight finish which saw Luxembourg win twice on the spin.

Luxembourg and Netherlands powered Cliff along with a ten-point maximum with Finland, Ireland, Israel and Sweden just a point behind on nine each.

Once again the UK maximum went to the Duchy hosts, Finland the only nation coming remotely close (nine).

EUROVISION JURY TOP 5

1	Tu Te Reconnaitras (Anne-Marie David)	LUX
2	Eres Tu (Mocedades)	SPA
3	Ey-Sham (Ilanit)	ISR
4	You're Summer (The Nova & The Dolls)	SWE
5	Tom Tom Tom (Marion Rung)	FIN

1974

Brighton, England
6 April
New entrants: Greece
Withdrawals: France
United Kingdom entry: Long Live Love by Olivia Newton-John
UK position: 04
Format: Katie Boyle was once again the contest commere and a certain Terry Wogan made his debut as the UK television commentator. And it was back to one jury member one vote!
Winning song: WATERLOO by Abba (Sweden)
Bottom Marker: Germany, Norway, Portugal and Switzerland
UK maximum: Italy
Maximum to UK: Germany, Italy and Yugoslavia
Stat: Sweden's first victory with the song that changed the face of Eurovision – and the UK gave Waterloo a big fat zero?!

1974. Brighton. Abba. Waterloo. The song that changed the face of Eurovision. Enough said!

Well not quite, because it would be most remiss to gloss over the contribution of English-born Olivia Newton-John, who was raised in Australia, and her song Long Live Love, a Salvation Army tribute (as was Love Shine A Light by Katrina and the Waves in 1997).

Newton-John was a regular on Cliff Richard's weekly television show and of course she went on to star alongside John Travolta in the 1977 film smash Grease!

Like Sandie Shaw and Lulu before her, Newton-John was not happy with the song chosen by the great British public.

But she belted it out in good style and returned a healthy fourth place for the UK on the south coast.

Newton-John has gone on to promote environmental and breast cancer issues and is regarded as a national treasure.

But at the contest she was sunk by the Abba phenomenon, which blew the rest away with the stand-out Eurovision signature tune that is Waterloo.

Sweden's winner remains one of the contest's most popular songs of all time and it was indeed awarded the top accolade at the golden jubilee celebration in 2005.

Abba had tried to enter the 1973 Eurovision but their offering, Ring Ring, could only finish third at the Melodifestivalen selection. Hasta Manana had also come under consideration as a Eurovision entry.

On the day of the Brighton contest, Abba's Waterloo was rated as a 20-1 win chance by the bookies.

But Agnetha, Frida, Bjorn and Benny won their war and world domination beckoned this super group in the making.

The end result was that they became the biggest-selling group since the Beatles! Who said Eurovision holds you back?!

The evening was not without its challenges for the Swedes however – Abba were required to mix socially with The Wombles, who were the interval act, and Bjorn and Benny were actually turned back by security at The Dome as they made their way to the stage for the winner's presentation!

UK OK? Poor old Olivia Newton-John had the unenviable task of fronting up against Abba and finished equal fourth in the Dome.

Yugoslavia and Italy were our biggest friends and there were two points towards the tally from Germany.

The UK gave their heart to Italy's Gigliola, who could not repeat her 1964 triumph, and there were also two points for Israel and one each for Finland, Ireland and Switzerland.

EUROVISION JURY TOP 5

1	Waterloo (Abba)	SWE
2	Si (Gigliola Cinquetti) `	ITA
3	I See A Star (Mouth & McNeal)	NET
4	Bye Bye, I Love You (Ireen Sheer)	LUX
5	Celui Qui Reste Et Celui Qui S'En Va (Romuald)	MON

1975

Stockholm, Sweden
22 March
New entrants: Turkey
Withdrawals: Greece
Return: France and Malta
United Kingdom entry: Let Me Be The One by The Shadows
UK position: 02
Format: The now standard Eurovision 'douze points' voting system was introduced.
Winning song: DING DINGE DONG by Teach-In (Netherlands)
Bottom Marker: Turkey
UK maximum: Netherlands
Maximum to UK: France, Luxembourg, Monaco, Yugoslavia
Stat: One in, one out and two back took the number of competing countries in Stockholm to 19.

Cliff Richard had had two attempts at the Eurovision crown and this year it was the turn of The Shadows to step out from the shadows and give it a go themselves.

Let Me Be The One scored a runners-up spot in Sweden but was beaten by what is regarded as one of the least-deserving of Eurovision winners.

That viewpoint probably had virtually everything to do with the title of the Dutch winner, Ding Dinge Dong, which did little to advance the contest's credibility cause.

Having said all that, the Teach-In song's singalong style, is fondly recalled by many devotees although it is hard to believe that it actually won! The song may not have been the greatest but the performance was certainly distinctive and the 'triangle' finale an abiding gimmick.

The Shadows were formed to support Cliff Richard in 1958 and, thanks to the presence of Hank Marvin on guitar, went on to have several hits in the 1960s in their own right.

After a split, the group re-formed in 1973 – Eurovision becoming part of their renaissance – and they finally gave up the ghost in 2004 when they embarked on a farewell tour.

John Farrar, linked closely to Olivia Newton-John and Cliff Richard, went on to play an instrumental part in the successes of Xanadu and Heathcliff.

In many respects this was an unremarkable contest, but Finland's Old Man Fiddle reached the dizzy heights of seventh in country-and-western style.

While a top-five slot still eluded the Finns, this offering represented a sound step in the right direction.

And while bombing at the contest, Ein Lied Kann Eine Brucke Sein, by Joy Fleming representing Germany, now has a place in the Eurovision zenith.

The contestants also had to dodge left-wing demonstrations in the Swedish capital, which provided a little unwanted colour.

UK OK? From this year it became more straightforward with the introduction of the 'douze points' voting system we are all now familiar with.

The Shadows finished shy of the dubious winning song from the Netherlands raking in votes from all over Europe with the exception of new boys and girls Turkey.

The first 'douze points' from 'le Royaume Uni' went to 'Le Pays Bas' (yes really!) with ten to Italy and eight to France.

EUROVISION JURY TOP 5

1	Tu Volveras (Sergio Y Estibaliz)	SPA
2	Ein Lied Kann Eine Brucke Sein (Joy Fleming)	GER
3	Seninle Bir Dakika (Semiha Yanki)	TUR
4	Ding Dinge Dong (Teach-In)	NET
5	Era (Wess & Dori Ghezzi)	ITA

1976

The Hague, Netherlands
3 April
Withdrawals: Malta, Sweden and Turkey
Return: Austria and Greece
UK position: WINNER
Format: This contest was watched in 33 countries and broadcast live by 25 national radio stations.
Winning song: SAVE YOUR KISSES FOR ME by Brotherhood Of Man (United Kingdom)
Bottom Marker: Norway
UK maximum: Switzerland
Maximum to UK: Belgium, Greece, Israel, Norway, Portugal, Spain and Switzerland
Stat: France awarded four points to Yugoslavia – but, because this did not come to light until after the transmission, the score was never included in the final scoreboard until some time later when Norway eventually replaced Yugoslavia in last place!

Brotherhood Of Man inevitably earned the tag of the British Abba, their success just two years on from that of the Swedes.

The group's hit singles of Angelo (1977) and Figaro (1978) mingled in with Abba's Fernando (1976). Two chaps and two lasses, one dark and one blonde – it didn't take a genius to suggest that here was a case of imitation being the sincerest case of flattery.

It is a charge that the group vehemently deny, but they certainly struck upon a winning formula and proved unbeatable from the moment they took to the stage to open the contest in The Hague.

They won with the biggest percentage of the total vote for any winning song bar Luxembourg's winner in 1973.

For the first time, Eurovision boasted an illuminated scoreboard and the stage was made up of several moving pieces.

So Brotherhood Of Man really were the first Eurovision winners to see their name up in lights. And this contest also introduced playback, later to be immortalised in song by the Portuguese!

The perennial dance floor classic, Abba's Dancing Queen, hit the top of the charts in late 1976 and it is testament to the mass appeal of Save Your Kisses For Me in that it actually managed to outsell the biggest dance floor hit ever!

So a good Seventies tussle between Abba and Brotherhood Of Man – the Brits won a good battle in 1976 but the Swedes certainly won the war.

UK OK? Brotherhood of Man, clear favourites pre-contest, took The Hague by storm from first place on the running order. The lowest award of three came from Ireland!

Both the UK and runner-up France – a strong display too from Catherine Ferry – scored points from every nation.

The UK's 12 points though went to Switzerland – Ireland got the ten and France's Catherine got eight, which is one more than Brotherhood of Man got from the French.

EUROVISION JURY TOP 5

1	Panaghia Mou, Panaghia Mou (Mariza Koch & Dimitris Zouboulis)	GRE
2	Ne Mogu Skriti Svoju Bol (Ambassadori)	YUG
3	Mata Hari (Anne-Karine Strom)	NOR
4	Un, Deux, Trois (Catherine Ferry)	FRA
5	Toi, La Musique Et Moi (Mary Cristy)	MON

1977

London, England
7 May
Withdrawals: Yugoslavia
Return: Sweden
United Kingdom entry: Rock Bottom by Lynsey De Paul and Mike Moran
UK position: 02
Format: The broadcast dateline was the latest in the year on which any contest, apart from the very first, had ever been held.
Winning song: L'OISEAU ET L'ENFANT by Marie Myriam (France)
Bottom Marker: Sweden
UK maximum: Ireland
Maximum to UK: Austria, Belgium, France, Luxembourg, Monaco and Portugal
Stat: France's fifth win within the first two decades of UK participation – and not a sniff since?

Wembley Conference Centre played host to the 1977 contest but the event was dogged by a strike.

A walkout by technicians meant that the contest had to be postponed for a period of five weeks to the first Saturday in May.

Lyndsey De Paul and Mike Moran represented the United Kingdom with the jaunty piano-jangling Rock Bottom, both singers sitting back to back during the performance.

They were both successful singers in their own right and the chemistry was obviously there, the juries voting the song into second place.

De Paul was the better known artist of the two but Moran, both a musician and producer, went on to enjoy success with a number of compositions.

He penned Freddie Mercury's Barcelona, composed the theme tune for the cult Scots detective series Taggart and, less stunningly, was the inspiration behind Kenny Everett's Snot Rap!

The Wembley show was presented by newsreader Angela Rippon who kept a measured grip on the proceedings.

This was the contest to which the north Africans of Tunisia at first said yes and quickly thereafter said no.

Of those nations who did turn up, the comic relief arrived in the form of the Austrian entry, performed by Schmetterlinge (Butterflies).

Their song was entitled Boom Boom Boomerang (didn't Abba have a song going by a similar title) and that probably told you everything you needed to know.

The routine encompassed a costume change, courtesy of turning round a front-facing ensemble to reveal another combination on the backs of the performers.

Comedy rarely works well on the Eurovision stage and this was to be no exception.

Austria finished second from bottom, with only Sweden's tribute to the Beatles below them!

The win went to France's emotional Marie Myriam, whose song L'Oiseau et L'Enfant – The Bird and The Child – soared to victory.

UK OK? Back to second spot for Lynsey De Paul and Mike Moran, with France claiming victory in a top two reversal from the previous year.

The UK scored very strongly on home turf but this time there was nothing from Ireland, nor Greece or Switzerland for that matter.

No matter, the UK sent 12 points across the Irish sea, with Belgium getting the ten and Germany the eight. France's Marie Myriam picked up six.

EUROVISION JURY TOP 5

1	L'Oiseau Et L'Enfant (Marie Myriam)	FRA
2	It's Nice To Be In Love Again (The Swarbriggs Plus Two)	IRE
3	Une Petite Francaise (Michelle Torr)	MON
4	Mathema Solfege (Pascalis, Marianna, Robert & Bessy)	GRE
5	Swiss Lady (Pepe Lienhard Band)	SWI

SHRUGS AND KISSES

OF course you remember that show-stopping band that took the Eurovision Song Contest by storm in the mid-1970s?

Two girls and two boys, the blonde and the other one, the bloke with the whiskers and the one who was always smiling.

That's right, let's hear it for the trailblazing Brotherhood Of Man.

The four-piece that swept away all the competition with the infectious Save Your Kisses For Me in the Dutch capital, The Hague, back in 1976.

The blonde, Sandra Stevens, from Leeds. The other one, brunette Nicki Stevens, from Carmarthen, living in Dorset, no relation. The bloke with the whiskers, Martin Lee, married to Sandra, living in Weybridge. And the one who was always smiling, Lee Sheriden from Bristol, now living in Beaconsfield.

Opening the contest that year, the group's catchy tune and the endearing dance routine won the hearts of Europe and it reached the number one slot in 33 countries, staying at the top of the charts in the United Kingdom for six weeks.

It remains one of the biggest-selling songs of all time and the band went to enjoy chart success at home and across Europe during the late Seventies.

Brotherhood Of Man appeared at the Royal Command Performance before the Queen in her Silver Jubilee Year in 1977 and the platinum, gold and silver discs kept rolling in.

The writers each won three Ivor Novello awards but the fusion of popular music styles at the start of the Eighties gradually pushed them out of the limelight.

The band split very briefly in the mid-Eighties but reformed in 1986 with the same line-up which survives to this day and the group continues to keep the Seventies experience alive in theatres, clubs and resort venues far and wide.

The Rubettes and Showaddywaddy still retain several original members but possibly only Chicory Tip can match Brotherhood Man's claim of being the real deal after all this time.

The first question aimed at Brotherhood Of Man invariably draws into question their similarity in the Seventies to another super group from Sweden who were also pretty big in Eurovision circles at the time.

You've probably heard of them too. Abba. The blonde one, Agnetha Faltskog. The other one, Anni-Frid Lyngstad. The bloke with the whiskers, Benny Andersson. And the one who was always smiling, Bjorn Ulvaeus.

Brotherhood Of Man, still going strong after all these years
www.brotherhoodofman.co.uk

It's a fair question. Abba won the contest two years before Brotherhood of Man, begging the suggestion that imitation is the sincerest form of flattery.

But Lee Sheriden, who was responsible for the arrangement of Save Your Kisses For Me and who shares the song credits with lead vocalist Martin Lee and producer Tony Hiller, is quick to place the inevitable Abba reference in context.

He said: "People always say we looked and sounded like Abba and were just copying them but this just isn't true. The sound may have been similar but remember this was the musical genre of the time and you write in the mode of the day.

"We certainly didn't set out to look like Abba or imitate them although some people assume the group, like Bucks Fizz, was manufactured specifically for the Eurovision.

"The fact is that we were actually around for quite a while before we took part in Eurovision in 1976 and we were actually the first emerging group to represent the United Kingdom, following on from The Shadows who had taken part the year before.

"All of the present band members were session singers at the time that the existing group Brotherhood Of Man had a hit with United We Stand in 1970, although none of us actually sung on that particular hit.

"But by then we had started doing their sessions and when singer Tony Burrows - together with Sonny, Sue and Roger Greenaway - hit the big time all over the world, we stepped in.

"We began having our own hits around 1972 and 1973 and went on the road before our big Eurovision break came along."

The 1976 contest in the The Hague is an experience that none of the group members are ever likely to forget in a hurry.

The success of 'Kisses' made the band's fortune and, from that day on, it certainly shaped their careers.

Lee added: "We were expected to do well and the whole thing went like a dream. Everyone remembers the dance routine and Martin sung absolutely brilliantly.

"The pizzicato and the glockenspiel smoothed everything along and there was a real chemistry about the whole performance.

"We were also lucky in that we'd had a big hit in Europe with the Barry Blue composition Kiss Me, Kiss Your Baby. It sold a million copies but didn't chart in the UK.

"So we were pretty well known in Europe before we even got up on the stage and that definitely worked in our favour."

The result was a runaway victory, which remains one of the most emphatic successes in Eurovision history to date.

And it was a win from the difficult opening slot which has only been achieved on two other occasions – Teach-in for the Netherlands in 1975 with Ding Dinge Dong and The Herreys for Sweden with Diggi Loo Diggi Ley in 1984. Save Your Kisses For Me is the only sensible song title among them!

Lee revealed that the group actually once appeared on a show in Holland specifically dedicated to Eurovision number ones from the number one position!

Kisses shifted a stack load of singles and it even outsold Abba's Waterloo in that particular market.

Although once you factored in Abba's album sales – which continue apace to this very day – then it is fair to say that their so-called musical rivals did go on to win that particular war.

Brotherhood Of Man went on to have smash hits in Angelo and Figaro which kept them very much in the public eye and the big numbers remain very much in demand on the band's regular tours, primarily around the UK.

Angelo hit the top of the charts a month after the Queen's Silver Jubilee celebrations, a sing-along ditty well known as far afield as Mexico and Walthamstow and following it to the top of the pile, early in 1978, was the catchy Figaro, a personal favourite of mine it has to be said.

However, by the May of that year, the band was to taste its last Top 40 success with Beautiful Lover, which peaked at 15.

Still, more than 30 years on, Brotherhood of Man are still with us and Lee said: "The secret of our longevity I think is that we insist on three months in a year where we just don't do anything.

"We all go away and do our own thing and then get together to do the theatre circuit which is very much our core business now.

"We do a Seventies show called The Seventies Story, which of course has a mock Eurovision section, and we often tour with Bucks Fizz as we have always been very good friends with Bobby G, who is the only one of their 1981 winning line-up still remaining.

"And we have also embarked on a Best of British Variety tour with Cannon and Ball and Paul Daniels which has also been great fun to do.

"We love taking part in the Seventies concerts that we do at Butlins, where we always get a wonderful reception. And of course the trips abroad whenever Eurovision approaches and where we regularly get invited to appear on selection shows.

"We always get a call from the BBC in the run up to the Eurovision selection for the UK but an appearance rarely materialises, although we did make the show a few years back!"

Save Your Kisses For Me finished in the top five of all-time Eurovision faves at the Congratulations event held in Denmark in 2005 to mark the fiftieth anniversary of the contest.

Lee said: "That was also fun to do. Abba's Waterloo was voted the best Eurovision song ever and I think that was always going to be the case.

"It was another opportunity for us to join up with fellow members of our Eurovision winners club who we catch up with at the many events that are organised around the contest.

"We are particularly fond of Dana, John Logan and Katrina, who delivered a superb victory for the United Kingdom with Love Shine A Light.

"When we worked with Katrina for the first time in Newcastle with Bucks Fizz a few years back we did not know what to expect of her.

"However, she went out in front of a big crowd miming to her records and totally pulled it off. By the end of her set, she had the crowd eating out of her hand.

"She is a tremendous performer and has a great presence about her. I am full of admiration for her."

Brotherhood Of Man remain committed advocates of the Eurovision Song Contest and won't have a word said against it.

Lee added: "It's fashionable to knock it but I would never do so. It has been exceptionally good to me and the rest of the band.

"We watch all the heats and the final and always make sure we record it if we happen to be in concert that particular night.

"My personal Eurovision favourite, after Kisses of course, is Milk and Honey's Hallelujah which won for Israel in 1979. What a lovely song, superbly delivered. And I liked the Bonaparti top hats song from Latvia in Helsinki. I think that deserved a much better placing."

My first meeting with Lee was in the Nottinghamshire town of Newark back in 1992, a few weeks before Michael Ball was set to step out for the United Kingdom in Malmo.

At that point, Lee felt the BBC's quest to put an established artist on the Eurovision stage would bring long-overdue success back to the UK.

Lee said at the time: "Michael Ball was a very good choice and I think they had to do that because up until then it hadn't been very inspiring.

"The format did need a change and the general feeling was that better artists had to be attracted to represent the UK in the contest.

"With 600 entries that year alone for consideration, it shows there is still tremendous interest in the event.

"But the media don't like it and the public love to hate it. I think we should always take part in Eurovision, especially as we are now becoming more European in our outlook."

The intervening years have seen the BBC row back from chasing established artists, on grounds of cost and practicality.

The UK results had admittedly not been good back then but, in terms of points, they represented veritable riches compared to the more recent offerings.

Winding forward again to today, interest in the event continues unabated, the media still shun it and the general public still professes to 'only watch the voting'.

Sir Terry Wogan remained the high priest of Eurovision commentators until his recent retirement.

1992 of course was the year of the Maastricht Treaty, drawing the United Kingdom ever closer to our friends across the English Channel. But, in the 21st century, have the Brits really become more European in their outlook?

Lee reflected: "It was worth a try putting forward established artists for Eurovision but then things have changed quite a lot in the music business.

"I couldn't believe it when the BBC took Top of the Pops off the air. I miss the programme dreadfully because I still keep up to date with the charts. I tape the Charts Show every week.

"And of course Eurovision has changed. With so many more countries from the east competing it is becoming harder and harder for a country from the west to win the contest.

"I loved the Scooch entry and I thought it would do a lot better. They went well at the contest and seemed really up for it."

So would Kisses have won at The Hague if the participating nations were of today's proportions and with televoting, rather than juries, in place?

It's an interesting thought. I reckon they would have done. But it would probably have been a very close call.

HERE'S JOHNNY!

1978

Paris, France
22 April
Return: Denmark and Turkey
United Kingdom entry: The Bad Old Days by Co-Co
UK position: 11
Format: A 'laissez-faire' production on the one and only occasion in the French capital
Winning song: A-BA-NI-BI by Izhar Cohen and Alpha Beta (Israel)
Nul Points: Norway
UK maximum: Belgium
Stat: Jahn Teigen became the personification of 'nul points' with his zero for Mil Etter Mil

After the high finishes of previous years, this year's offering from Co-Co, The Bad Old Days, was prophetic.

The line-up missed out on Eurovision selection two years previously but the Slater/De Sykes composition had high hopes for a good placing in Paris.

The UK however finished in eleventh place (out of twenty), the worst standing ever, a distinction they would hold for another nine years.

Cheryl Baker was a member of the Co-Co line-up, with a fond 'Hello Mum' for the camera, and for her the Eurovision story wasn't over.

She would soon be joining the likes of Ronnie Carroll and Sir Cliff Richard by twice representing the UK in the final.

This year would be remembered, above all, not for the song that came first but for the one that finished bottom of the pile.

The garishly fun persona of Norway's Jahn Teigen scored a big fat zero and probably a rip in his trousers with that iconic split jump at the end of his song, Mil Etter Mil.

No matter, his home country took Teigen to their hearts and his notoriety ensured a big hit in Norway.

Victory went to a country that wasn't even in Europe as Israel notched their first Eurovision success.

What is now regarded as a comic interlude was called A-Ba-Ni-Bi (a Polar Bear?!) and was drawn from a craze among Israeli schoolchildren to speak in a 'B' language.

Luxembourg awarded twelve points to the winner which was something of a novelty as, together with Cyprus, they usually had great difficulty chiming with the popular choice!

UK OK? Co-Co proved to be clowns as far as an eleventh place finish went and, for the first time in the history of the UK participation, no-one sent the maximum our way.

This was the start of the Bad Old Days and the highest mark actually came from Germany who submitted eight points. Four countries missed us out – Denmark, Italy, Finland and Norway.

The UK maximum went the way of Belgium's Jean Vallee who finished comfortably adrift of the Israeli winner – which got just five from the UK.

EUROVISION JURY TOP 5

1	Parlez-Vous Francais (Baccara)	LUX
2	Questo Amore (Ricchi E Poveri)	ITA
3	A-Ba-Ni-Bi (Izhar Cohen & Alpha Beta)	ISR
4	Il Y Aura Toujours Des Violons (Joel Prevost)	FRA
5	Les Jardins De Monaco (Caline & Olivier Toussaint)	MON

1979

Jerusalem, Israel
31 March
Withdrawals: Turkey
United Kingdom entry: Mary Ann by Black Lace
UK position: 07
Format: Six countries put forward song teams consisting of a lead singer and a group of backing singers
Winning song: HALLELUJAH by Gali Atari with Milk and Honey (Israel)
Bottom Marker: Austria and Belgium
UK maximum: Israel
Stat: Spain's Betty Missiego led by one point from Israel going into the final round of voting – but it was the Spanish jury who gave ten points to Israel.

Black Lace flew the flag for the UK in Jerusalem and went on to become one of the most interesting acts to have represented their country in Eurovision.

The quartet, which many felt were a Smokie rip-off, presented Mary Ann to the faithful and it never really got going.

It was to be the group's first and last hit until 1983 when they were to find a niche in the popular music market.

They re-emerged in the 1980s as a duo with the song Superman, also known as Gioca Jouer.

Black Lace are best known for the nonsense summer hit Agadoo (push pineapple, shake the tree) which accorded them legendary status on dance floors across the continent.

Agadoo was actually voted the worst song of all time by Q magazine in 2003 although I would like to know whether the vote took place before or after that year's contest in Riga, as surely Jemini would have been in with a shout?

The group, which hailed from Ossett in West Yorkshire, enjoyed a good living from the cabaret circuit.

They appeared in the film Rita, Sue & Bob Too and were honoured by Spittin' Image in 1986 with the Chicken Song which mirrored the nonsense and tune of Agadoo.

And they also linked up more recently with the anarchist collective Chumbawamba.

Original band member Alan Barton joined Smokie but died at the age of 41 following a road traffic accident in early 1995.

Israel's first hosting of the event was a success and the stage backdrop was dominated by a selection of colourful and spectacular concentric rings.

Denmark's Tommy Seebach, on the first of three appearances, seemed to have been watching a bit too much of John Travolta in Disco Tango while Switzerland's entry could only be described as trash bizarre.

Anne-Marie David returned to the contest, this time representing France, and the deserved winner was the lilting melody of Gali Atari with Milk & Honey's Hallelujah, two on the trot for Israel.

The talking point was Germany's Dschingis Khan by a band of the same name – like it or not, one of Eurovision's most memorable songs and acts!

UK OK? Black Lace fared little better than Co-Co, this in the days before inflicting the dance floor smash Agadoo on an unsuspecting public.

Mary Ann attracted no big backers although Denmark weighed in with a ten, six nations giving us nowt – Belgium, France, Greece, Israel, Luxembourg and Sweden.

This time UK backed the Israeli winner to the hilt with 12 points, a surprising ten going to Luxembourg (who finished 13th) with eight to Dschingis Khan!

EUROVISION JURY TOP 5

1	Hallelujah (Gali Atari with Milk and Honey)	ISR
2	Dschingis Khan (Dschingis Khan)	GER
3	Disco Tango (Tommy Seebach)	DEN
4	Colorado (Xandra)	NET
5	Su Cancion (Betty Missiego)	SPA

1980

The Hague, Netherlands
19 April
New entrants: Morocco
Withdrawals: Monaco and Israel
Return: Turkey
United Kingdom entry: Love Enough For Two by Prima Donna
UK position: 03
Format: The Netherlands were fourth choice to host the contest after Israel declined – Israel did not take part as the day of the contest was a national holy day, so becoming the only country to date that were not in a position to defend their title
Winning song: WHAT'S ANOTHER YEAR? by Johnny Logan (Ireland)
Bottom Marker: Finland
UK maximum: Ireland
Maximum to UK: Sweden
Stat: This was to be Morocco's only tilt at Eurovision – they finished second from bottom

As far as the UK selection was concerned, everything had become a little incestuous at the turn of the 1980s and there were Eurovision family relationships everywhere!

The surprise nomination for the UK was the group Prima Donna, specially formed for the contest.

Once again the Slater/de Sykes combination – which had penned the Bad Old Days for Co-Co in 1978 - came up with the song Love Enough For Two and the band featured Kate Robbins, a second cousin of Paul McCartney no less.

Also in the line-up was Danny Finn, who had performed for the New Seekers at Eurovision, Sally-Ann Triplett – who was to appear again with Bardo in 1982 and Lance Aston, the brother of Jay who represented Bucks Fizz in 1981.

Robbins went on to have limited success with the band Beyond while Triplett was to become a regular on the musical stage.

Prima Donna only made it to The Hague following a sudden death countback at the national final.

They finished third in The Hague behind strong entries from Ireland's Johnny Logan and Germany's Katja Ebstein and provided a firm rebuff for their critics.

The eccentricity came from Turkey and Norway, Greece sung about hitchhikers, Luxembourg about penguins and Belgium quirkily celebrated Eurovision itself courtesy of the wonderful Telex.

In amongst all that was the classy winner from Ireland and the introduction of the Eurovision brand that is Johnny Logan!

UK OK? This was more like it, Prima Donna's twee Love Enough For Two making third place but scoring only one 12-point maximum from Sweden. Ten-point awards came from Denmark and Switzerland.

In return, the UK sent the maximum Ireland's way, deserved recognition for Johnny Logan's classy winner.

Germany's Katja Ebstein, with the foot-stomping Theater, collected ten points from the UK and the eight went the way of Luxembourg's quirky Papa Pingouin!

EUROVISION JURY TOP 5

1	What's Another Year (Johnny Logan)	IRE
2	Amsterdam (Maggie MacNeal)	NET
3	Theater (Katja Ebstein)	GER
4	Cinema (Paola del Medico)	SWI
5	Le Papa Pingouin (Sophie & Magaly)	LUX

1981

Dublin, Ireland
Date: 4 April
New entrants: Cyprus
Withdrawals: Italy, Morocco
Return: Israel, Yugoslavia
UK position: WINNER
Format: A vast set and three separate stage areas set aside in the auditorium
Winning song: MAKING YOUR MIND UP by Bucks Fizz (United Kingdom)
Nul Points: Norway
UK maximum: Switzerland
Maximum to UK: Israel and Netherlands
Stat: Austria and Turkey were one and two on the order respectively for the second year running – the early showings did neither any good.

Ah, 1981! My favourite year for popular music and my favourite Eurovision, courtesy of this win from the Fizz.

The quick-tempo and boppy ditty Making Your Mind Up had enough about it to secure victory at the Simmonscourt Pavilion in Dublin and it made you proud to be British.

It wasn't everyone's cup of tea but it was strong enough to see off the opposition in spite of a pretty mediocre performance on the night.

Bucks Fizz, once again, were specially formed for Eurovision and featured the return of Cheryl Baker (formerly of Co-Co) and Prima Donna's Lance Aston's sister Jay.

The blond lad was Mike Nolan and the line-up was completed by Bobby G (Guppy) who was drafted in because Stephen Fischer (who was to represent Bardo the following year) could not prise himself away from contractual stage commitments to the musical Godspell.

Following the success of Making Your Mind Up, the group went onto enjoy sustained success in the early 1980s but they were bedevilled by poor fortune.

The group was involved in a coach crash in 1984 which left Nolan with serious injuries which resulted in long-standing impairment.

Aston was the first to quit the group and, in time, Baker followed to carve out a niche in television.

Eventually the boys too went their separate ways and two versions of the Bucks Fizz mix went on to do the rounds.

The Eurovision victory was a triumph of choreography and the demand for all-round entertainment, instead of just a song, began to increase.

The Bucks Fizz win resulted in a number of pale imitations hitting the Eurovision stage in the years to follow. The contest was moving on.

Morocco had come and gone, Italy were absent because of diminished interest and Yugoslavia returned with Israel, who didn't take part in 1980 after winning the thing the year before.

Germany, France and Switzerland provided stiff opposition for the Fizz but Finland again struggled with Riki Sorsa's Reggae OK and Yugoslavia entered a song called Leila – a song title repeated by Bosnia & Herzegovina in 2006.

UK OK? The fourth Eurovision win was recorded by Bucks Fizz with a song and routine which was a breath of fresh air for the contest but in the end there was only four points separating the UK and Germany's Johnny Blue, sung by Lena Valaitis.

A close contest produced only two big twelves, with three tens in support from Denmark, Ireland and Yugoslavia. Making Your Mind Up got points from every jury, the least impressed being Finland and Norway (three points).

The UK voters plumped for Switzerland's lilting Io Senza Te which actually picked up five maximums, the four others coming from Finland, Ireland, Norway and Yugoslavia – but it could only finish fourth?!

EUROVISION JURY TOP 5

1	Johnny Blue (Lena Valaitis)	GER
2	Io Senza Te (Peter, Sue & Marc)	SWI
3	Monica (Island)	CYP
4	Het Is Een Wonder (Linda Williams)	NET
5	C'est Peut-Etre Pas L'Amerique (Jean-Claude Pascal)	LUX

1982

Harrogate, England
24 April
Withdrawals: France and Greece
United Kingdom entry: One Step Further by Bardo
UK position: 07
Format: The future of the contest was in question – only 18 nations competed in Harrogate, the lowest number in five years
Winning song: EIN BISSCHEN FRIEDEN by Nicole (Germany)
Nul Points: Finland
UK maximum: Switzerland
Maximum to UK: Austria and Luxembourg
Stat: The only victory for Germany to date, and Jahn Teigen in company with Anita Skorgan returned for Norway... and picked up quarante points, their best result since 1973!

And so to Yorkshire in rural England - Harrogate was the unlikely venue for the UK's silver anniversary participation and newsreader Jan Leeming took on the role of presenting.

Bardo were the duo representing the UK – Sally-Ann Triplett, part of Prima Donna in 1980, and Stephen Fischer who had been sought for Bucks Fizz the year before but was now available for duty.

The song One Step Further actually took the UK several steps back although it still gets a lot of airplay at Eurovision discos. The pair's nerves were betrayed in the dance routine and hopes of another fizzing success were laid to rest.

Triplett followed Ronnie Carroll, Cliff Richard and Cheryl Baker on making a second Grand Prix appearance – she became part of the BBC's Crackerjack children's scene and more recently could be seen as an actress on the London stage. Fischer also did pretty well, in particular as vocalist with the Pasadena Roof Orchestra.

A poor show from Norway in Dublin set the 'Victory For Norway' bandwagon rolling in Harrogate. Much of the town was plastered with mini stickers imploring anyone who would take notice to 'please give Norway a vote'.

But the star of Harrogate was the lass with the stool and the guitar singing about A Little Peace, this at a time when the UK was at war with Argentina over the Falkland Islands.

Nicole Hochloch took the plaudits with a strong performance from the last spot on the bill – a first and only victory for Germany and a triumph for the writing duo of Ralph Siegel and Bernd Meinunger who, in future years, would try several more times to re-create that winning formula.

UK OK? Bardo struggled painfully in the final stages of the voting and slumped to

seventh place, amassing only 20 of their 78 points from the last seven juries.
Austria and Luxembourg's twelve was followed up with a surprising ten from
Turkey and the UK top mark once again went to the Swiss, this time represented
by Arlette Zola.
Germany's Nicole won by 61 points from Israel and picked up nine maximums –
the UK contributed eight; at the bottom end of the scale, neighbours Austria could
only find one point for Germany while Luxembourg declared war on A Little
Peace with nought!

EUROVISION JURY TOP 5

1	Ein Bisschen Frieden (Nicole)	GER
2	Mono I Agapi (Anna Vissi)	CYP
3	Si Tu Aimes Ma Musique (Stella)	BEL
4	Adieu (Jahn Teigen & Anita Skorgan)	NOR
5	Video Video (Brixx)	DEN

1983

Munich, Germany
23 April
Withdrawals: Ireland
Return: France, Greece and Italy
United Kingdom entry: I'm Never Giving Up by Sweet Dreams
UK position: 06
**Format: A long introduction before the songs could get underway and
an imposing display from mistress of ceremonies Marlene Charrell**
**Winning song: SI LA VIE EST CADEAU by Corinne Hermes
(Luxembourg)**
Nul Points: Spain and Turkey
UK maximum: Yugoslavia
Maximum to UK: Sweden
Stat: Luxembourg took an early grip for their fifth and final win
The Germans took Eurovision to Munich but the show was not a spectacular
and is still recalled in the main because of presenter Marlene Charrell's attempt
to hijack it.
Sweet Dreams were the UK representatives in Bavaria and yes, you guessed
it, once again they were specially formed for the experience. Thankfully they
were to be the last of the manufactured groups.
The band wore startling costumes for their performance of I'm Never Giving
Up which came in sixth, edging out Bardo from the previous year by one
place.

Carrie Gray was one of the performers and went on to marry David Grant, latterly of Fame Academy fame.

Bobby McVey went on to pursue a solo career and also enjoyed a stint as a radio presenter.

The inspiration behind Sweet Dreams was Ron Roker, who had written for Barry Blue and Boney M and contributed to Brotherhood of Man's continental hit Kiss Me, Kiss Your Baby.

It was actually the second time he had used a group name of Sweet Dreams to form an act!

Jahn Teigen, buoyed by his success for Norway in Harrogate where he stunned observers with a neat collaboration alongside Anita Skorgan, was back again and this time finished ninth!

The late Ofra Haza did well for Israel but the biggest seller of the 1983 entries was the falsetto yodel of Yugoslavia's Danijel with a swingalong number called Dzuli (Julie).

Danijel was half Belgian and half Montenegrin and brought the Slavs their best Eurovision finish.

But the win went to Luxembourg (it was to be their last and, to date, the final hurrah for the French language) with Corinne Hermes securing victory from last song up, as Nicole had done the year before.

At the time I did not have much time for Si La Vie Est Cadeau but now it is certainly one of my favourite Eurovision songs.

UK OK? Sweden again turned up trumps for the UK's bouncy offering from Sweet Dreams which struggled to hit the heights – Austria supplied ten but there were five fives in the final countdown which marked out a middling course.

The UK liked the high notes from Yugoslavia's Danijel, whose song Dzuli has to be one of the most distinctive Eurovision entries of all time!

The Luxembourg winner from Corinne Hermes, a pleasant enough song, held off Israel for victory but with no help from the UK who did not give it a single point. Just us and Norway in the doghouse!

EUROVISION JURY TOP 5

1	Si La Vie Est Cadeau (Corinne Hermes)	LUX
2	Dzuli (Daniel)	YUG
3	Hi (Ofra Haza)	ISR
4	Framling (Carola)	SWE
5	Ruecksicht (Hoffmann & Hoffmann)	GER

1984

Luxembourg
5 May
Withdrawals: Greece and Israel
Return: Ireland
United Kingdom entry: Love Games by Belle And The Devotions
UK position: 07
Format: A May date set the trend for Eurovision and the most ambitious set to date
Winning song: DIGGI-LOO-DIGGI-LEY by The Herreys (Sweden)
Bottom Marker: Austria
UK maximum: Denmark
Stat: The Herreys became only the third act to win from first up – and the first act to win singing in Swedish!

Tiny Luxembourg presented the contest in what was a year mired in controversy as far as the UK was concerned.

Singing for the nation - although that was a moot point - were Belle And The Devotions with their Motown number called Love Games.

The group was essentially Kit Rolfe (as Belle), who had been an offstage backing singer for Sweet Dreams the year before.

But the entry caused a storm with allegations that the group were not actually singing live, as is a requirement of the contest, but that the singing was being done by a group of backing singers hidden away behind the scenes.

The Dutch in particular were up in arms and led the protests and the British delegation in the Grand Duchy was made to feel distinctly uncomfortable.

Belle and her Devotions found themselves up against it and, against a backdrop of questionable vocals and dodgy garments, it was anything but plain sailing.

After their performance on the night they were booed off the stage – Eurovision audiences are normally pretty polite, the only other occasion I can recall in recent times when this happened was in 2003 when the Russian minxes t.A.t.U were greeted with a chorus of disapproval.

Rolfe later recorded Fly Eddie Fly with Great Britain's Olympic ski-jump hopeful Eddie 'The Eagle' Edwards. Pretty much like Eddie, this struggled to get off the ground.

Ireland's Linda Martin (who hails from the UK) sang a song about Terminal 3 which had words and music from a certain Sean Sherrard – Johnny Logan by another name.

But the glory went to Sweden, the Herreys boys with their golden boots winning from the top of the shop with a song of dubious merit which clearly made a big impression right from the word go.

UK OK? You either loved or hated Love Games and I veered into the latter category – I think it was the costumes and, of course, the controversy surrounding the entry.

In the end, Belle and the crew settled for seventh slot and couldn't manage a maximum from anyone although Italy was bold enough to put down ten points. Sweden's golden boys with the golden shoes, The Herreys, won with the contest's opening song although the UK's twelve went across the water to those Hot Eyes from Denmark – the golden boys got just seven.

EUROVISION JURY TOP 5

1	Det Lige Det (Hot Eyes)	DEN
2	I Treni Di Tozeur (Alice & Franco Battiato)	ITA
3	100% D'Amour (Sophie Carle)	LUX
4	Silencio E Tanta Gente (Maria Guinot)	POR
5	Ik Hou Van Jou (Maribelle)	NET

1985

Gothenburg, Sweden
4 May
Withdrawals: Netherlands and Yugoslavia
Return: Greece and Israel
United Kingdom entry: Love Is by Vikki
UK position: 04
Format: A favourite Eurovision for many observers – hostess Lill Lindfors was a big hit and managed to lose her skirt along the way!
Winning song: LA DET SWINGE by Bobbysocks (Norway)
Bottom Marker: Belgium
UK maximum: Norway
Stat: Norway swung to their first victory with 30 points separating the top five

Vikki Watson saw off the challenge of Seventies star Alvin Stardust in the national final to win her place in Gothenburg.

Her song, Love Is, came in fourth, a sound return for the cabaret artist whose first single, The Poppy Song, was dedicated to the British Legion in the aftermath of the Falklands conflict.

A relaxed Vikki is now a Los Angeles-based artist known as Aeone, drawing on her Celtic roots to write New Age and folk music.

As Aeone, her debut in Zimbabwe saw her singing one song while the band played another and she was almost flattened by the burly Meat Loaf at a gig in the United States.

The 1985 contest remains one of best loved among fans, with host presenter

Lill Lindfors hitting just the right note and stealing the show with a stage routine which resulted in her losing her skirt although it didn't go down too well in some quarters.

Germany was represented by the group Wind - who were to return in the years ahead – while Denmark were represented by the ensemble Hot Eyes for the second year running.

The winners didn't have to travel far, a joyous rock and roll success for Norway who had come a long way since those dark days of Dublin four years previously!

UK OK? Love Is collected 100 points and fourth place, a creditable showing – no maximums but scores from all juries with the exception of Cyprus.

The UK top mark went to Norway's swinging Bobbysocks, La Det Swinge written and arranged by Rolf Lovlund who went on celebrate further success for Norway ten years further down the line.

With the twelve to Norway, the UK's ten went to Austria (eighth) and the eight to Turkey (equal fourteenth) – I doubt that combination will ever be repeated!

EUROVISION JURY TOP 5

1	La Det Swinge (Bobbysocks)	NOR
2	Elakoon Elama (Sonja Lumme)	FIN
3	To Katalava Arga (Lia Vissi Pilouri)	CYP
4	Fuer Alle (Wind)	GER
5	Bra Vibrationer (Kikki Danielson)	SWE

1986

Bergen, Norway
3 May
New entrants: Iceland
Return: Netherlands and Yugoslavia
Withdrawals: Greece and Italy
United Kingdom entry: Runner In The Night by Ryder
UK position: 07
Format: 'Soon We Will Know Who'll Be The Best, In The Eurovision Song Contest' - presenter Ase Kleveland
Winning song: J'AIME LA VIE by Sandra Kim (Belgium)
Bottom Marker: Cyprus
UK maximum: Germany
Stat: Sandra Kim became Eurovision's youngest winner, hauling Belgium – their one and only win to date – from bottom to top spot.

Eurovision went north to the Norwegian coastal city of Bergen and the UK were represented by Maynard Williams, going by the name of Ryder, with the song Runner In The Night.

It was an unremarkable offering but a spell in the spotlight at least for Maynard, the son of actor Bill Maynard who had taken part in the UK's first national final in 1957.

Maynard carved out a career as an actor and singer and appeared in Starlight Express.

The composer, Brian Wade, went on to work with Swedish Eurovision acts The Herreys and Carola.

Hostess Ase Klevelund welcomed everyone with a rendition of the Eurovision anthem Te Deum, which didn't augur too well, and a low-key contest had little to commend it.

The Swedes treated their neighbours to a bizarre display and Dora from Portugal clumped around in some unsightly boots.

The endearing Sandra Kim – of Belgian and Italian parentage – united the French and Flemish sections in her home country to win by a mile, but in truth there was little in the way of competition.

UK OK? A dodgy two years for the UK began with Ryder's Runner In The Night which stumbled to seventh but picked up ten points from the F-Plan of Finland and France.

Belgium's young Sandra Kim stole the show with J'Aime La Vie, Belgium's only Eurovision success to date and it won in resounding style with five twelves and nine tens from a total of 19 juries..

The UK provided one of the welter of tens, the top twelve points reserved for

Germany's Ingrid Peters.
EUROVISION JURY TOP 5

1	J'Aime La Vie (Sandra Kim)	BEL
2	Ueber Die Bruecke Geh'n (Ingrid Peters)	GER
3	Pas Pour Moi (Daniella Simons)	SWI
4	L'Amour De Ma Vie (Sherisse Laurence)	LUX
5	You Can Count On Me (Luv Bug)	IRE

1987

Brussels, Belgium
9 May
Return: Greece and Italy
United Kingdom entry: Only The Light by Rikki
UK position: 13
Format: A bumper 22 countries turned out in what is now the capital of Europe
Winning song: HOLD ME NOW by Johnny Logan (Ireland)
Nul Points: Turkey
UK maximum: Ireland
Stat: Johnny Logan became the first performer to win Eurovision twice, having also done so in 1980 and so securing Ireland's third victory

A nadir for the United Kingdom arrived in Belgium courtesy of Rikki's weird and not so wonderful Only The Light.

It was unlucky thirteenth for tartan terror Richard Peebles, a minicab driver from Glasgow, who had written hits for Middle Of The Road in the 1970s and who had also worked with Sixties smashers Marmalade.

His Eurovision song, which was about close encounters, did not chart and this has only happened on three occasions.

Fortunately there were plenty of diversions elsewhere on the card to lift the Brussels event.

The female commere was Viktor Lazio, who had appeared in the film Casablanca, and Wind were back for Germany with the feelgood Lass Die Sonne In Dein Herz. However, once more the group had to settle for second place.

Luxembourg were represented by Belgium's Euro punk rock icon Roger Jouret, also known as Plastic Bertrand, but two songs from this contest, more than any other, have lived on in the hearts of fans.

Italy's Gente Di Mare was beautifully delivered by pop rock composer Umberto Tozzi, who had been responsible for the late Laura Branigan's glorious Gloria back in 1983.

But the clear winner was Ireland's Johnny Logan with the history-making

Hold Me Now.

UK OK? Rikki's Only The Light amassed a mere 47 points and slumped to thirteenth place which was certainly unlucky for the Scots singer.

After a zero from the first jury, Norway, Rikki then picked up ten from Israel but that was as good as it got and it certainly numbers as one of the UK's least auspicious entries.

UK's twelve went to Johnny Logan's Hold Me Now – his second winner for Ireland – which finished comfortably ahead of Germany's reggae-style Lass Die Sonne In Dein Herz, the only other song ever in contention.

EUROVISION JURY TOP 5

1	Hold Me Now (Johnny Logan)	IRE
2	Gente Di Mare (Umberto Tozzi & Raf)	ITA
3	Lass Die Sonne In Dein Herz (Wind)	GER
4	Ja Sam Za Ples (Novi Fosili)	YUG
5	Rechtop In De Wind (Marcha)	NET

CLINK CLINK FIZZ!

ALTHOUGH a lot of the bubbles have now disappeared, the Fizz isn't quite flat. And the group's lone surviving original member is hoping that the party can go on for a little while longer yet.

Bobby G now leads the authentic Bucks Fizz in gigs all over the world, accompanied by his wife Heidi and two recent newcomers to the champagne set, Tammy Choat and Paul Fordham.

Bobby – full name Robert Gubby – remains as laid back about the group's future today as he was at the outset in the early 1980s, when the manufactured blond four-piece embarked upon a meticulously-planned all-out offensive on an unsuspecting Eurovision Song Contest.

The G could just as easily stand for Green – Bobby's customary stage colour alongside Mike Nolan (singing the blues), Cheryl Baker (lady in red) and Jay Aston (mellow yellow). A colourful quartet now firmly established in Eurovision folklore!

Bobby recalled: "It was a recognised format for Eurovision in those days, two girls and two guys. But the rock 'n 'roll style of song was different to what they had been putting forward.

"Bucks Fizz was a manufactured group and was effectively controlled by Nichola Martin, who worked for a record company and was very much the ideas person, and Andy Hill who wrote the song Making Your Mind Up which was put forward for Eurovision.

"They came up with every possible hooky thing you could think of to get us noticed. A Eurovision song usually does well with a gimmick and we had loads.

"The song style was different, we had the jive moves and the colourful costumes. And of course the guys whipped the skirts off the girls, and that pretty much sealed our victory in Dublin.

"Our actual performance on the night was pretty ropey as the vocals and harmonies suffered from bad tuning. But visually we came across pretty well.

"Making Your Mind Up actually began life as a jingle, 45 seconds worth of airplay asking people to make up their mind. It was designed to help sell products and the impact had to be instant.

"The whole Eurovision preparation was extremely calculated. The people behind us knew what they were doing and reckoned that to win the contest we had to grab the attention of viewer and the jury voters from the off.

"Mike, Cheryl, Jay and I didn't have any sort of say in the running or the direction of the group and to be fair it was a good job that we didn't."

The current Bucks Fizz line-up, the only existing original member being Bobby G.
www.bucksfizz.co.uk

Bobby was a late addition to the line-up and was only drafted in when Stephen Fischer (who went on to become one half of Bardo, the UK entry in Harrogate the following year) could not extricate himself from prevailing stage commitments.

No such problem for Bobby, who left the production of Jesus Christ Superstar to take a job with Bucks Fizz.

He said: "I decided to join the new group and have a go at the Song For Europe, where eight acts competed for the right to represent the UK in Dublin.

"I was pretty laid back up about the whole thing then. I figured that if we didn't win the British heat, I would go back to doing what I'd been doing before. I honestly didn't reckon on winning the heat, let alone the Eurovision after that!

"All the group members worked well together as colleagues in the workplace and we formed a good bond but on a social level it was different.

"As far as I was concerned, I was 27 at the time and already married with an eight-year-old child. I was already into the house and business scene whereas the others were at a different stage of their lives and careers.

"On the big night in Dublin I can remember I wasn't particularly nervous. It was almost as if I was outside the whole experience, looking down on it.

"I wasn't really that bothered if we didn't win it. It was a new experience for me but I would have been quite happy to move on from it if we hadn't been successful.

"I've always been pretty easy going. For me, having children is a truly life-changing event. I have a little girl with Heidi and nothing else matters in life compared to what you want for your children.

"I didn't envisage for one minute how winning the Eurovision would change my life. I have no regrets at all about doing Eurovision, it was the most fantastic thing and I'd do it all again.

"As a band we went on to experience a few lows along the way but they made the many highs seem so much better."

The low point for Bucks Fizz manifested itself in a coach crash in 1984 in which all the group members were injured, Mike Nolan most seriously.

Bobby added: "The crash did change everything. We'd chalked up a number of hits since Making Your Mind Up and suddenly everything went on hold.

"Had it not been for the crash, I think the success would have continued for a while. But the crash opened up a few cracks which would have appeared eventually any way. It just brought the process forward.

"To get back on top we needed to pull together and hang in there and this put a considerable strain on all the band members.

"Mike suffered a brain haemorrhage in the crash. It left him very poorly but eventually he came back to work. This situation, as far as the band was concerned, benefited Mike more than the rest of the group.

"Jay was the first to leave and she was replaced by Shelley Preston. Then Shelley left, followed by Cheryl and Heidi, now my wife, joined the line-up in 1992.

"Mike then packed up, resulting in further changes, and at a later stage, Mike, Cheryl and Shelley – with former Dollar singer David van Day at one point – performed under a different name.

"But the Bucks Fizz has always stayed with my group as I'm the only original member to have stayed put.

"I have bits and pieces contact with Mike and Cheryl and probably have more to do with Jay than the others.

"Some of them have gone in for this Living TV concept of finding old pop stars, getting them back into shape and teaching them to sing again. That is something I would never do.

"I haven't put any weight on since the 1980s and work as a singing coach. These reality shows are not for me, I always make sure that I steer well clear!"

Making Your Mind Up was a number one smash all over Europe but follow-up Top 20 hits later that year, Piece Of The Action and One Of Those Nights, in Bobby's view, were living off the back of the Eurovision success.

It was the Christmas hit Land Of Make Believe – probably the quintessential Fizz track for more mainstream fans – that took the group back to the top of the tree.

Bidding for the coveted Christmas number one slot in the wonderfully-varied world of popular music that was 1981, it was gunned down by the Human League's evocative Don't You Want Me.

It did reach the top of the charts in January 1982, the band's third and final number one – My Camera Never Lies – coming a few months later.

At this stage, the group members were given a little more licence within the Bucks Fizz empire – they were allowed to write for the group but, while being made to feel much more part of the team, they were still not in control.

Now Those Days Are Gone reached number eight in June 1982 but the group was to celebrate only one further top ten hit – the appropriately-titled New Beginning (Mamba Seyra) – all of four years later.

The band's final chart impact – at number 50 – came with Heart Of Stone in November 1988.

Nowadays, Bobby's Bucks Fizz continues to do a lot of promotional work around Making Your Mind Up on television stations around Europe, usually in the month of May!

A working band, most of their work is Eurovision related and a lot of bids have to be turned down.

The Fizz stages about 15 shows a year with the Brotherhood Of Man and regularly bump into Johnny Logan, Making Your Mind Up following Johnny's Irish winner What's Another Year? into the Eurovision archive.

Eurovision still remains very close to Bobby's heart although mostly he has to make do with watching a recording after the event because of band commitments.

He said: "I watch it religiously every year. I like to keep up with it and know what's going on. I have a tremendous affection for it.

"It's just wonderful being associated with the event and of course it's fashionable for critics to knock it. Who cares what they say, it doesn't have to be credible. When was Eurovision ever credible?!

"I do feel sorry for anyone who has represented the United Kingdom during the last five years or so. They are truly on a hiding to nothing and the contest has always been a little political over the years.

"But since Europe has expanded its borders, and Eurovision has done likewise, we have been squeezed out of the picture. We're not flavour of the month any more and haven't been for the last decade.

"I think we can win Eurovision again but someone will have to come up with something really spectacular.

"I liked the Scooch tribute to Bucks Fizz, of course, but while I think they had the right idea visually, the song and routine didn't work for me. I didn't think it was right.

"I like the idea of a newcomer – a singer or group serving their apprenticeship in the trade – to represent the United Kingdom in the contest. After all, Bucks Fizz was a manufactured group.

"However, my personal view is that I wouldn't let anyone operate on me just because they had won a competition as a doctor.

"I think you do need performers who have a bit of grounding in the business but these days, with the emphasis on entertainment, having a good song isn't really enough.

"In spite of recent disappointments, I would hope that Eurovision is here to stay and that the United Kingdom continues to take part.

"The organisers have to make sure it remains inclusive. The Eurovision has successfully brought countries together on a level that no other event can really match and they have to ensure this continues. We need more of this type of thing, not less.

"Although I've followed Eurovision avidly over the years, I'm always hard pressed to recall memorable winners. For me, the best Eurovision songs tend to be ones that didn't win. Two that immediately spring to mind are Volare and Congratulations.

"I also liked Have You Ever Been In Love, which was a national final song performed by Gem in 1981 and a year later became a hit for Leo Sayer.

"I thought we were a contender for the title in Dublin but I don't remember any songs that I thought posed a real threat, none that I can recall today anyway."

In the first decade of the 21st century, Bobby – in his mid-fifties – is still jiving away and ripping off skirts as good as all the young pretenders.

He said: "I was quite fit when we won the contest and obviously the routines take more out of me these days.

"But I'm still dancing away and throwing the girls around. The band keeps me fit and keeps me young and now of course there is no pressure from within, there is no desire to win or succeed. My family helps me keep everything in perspective."

And still Mr Green? Bobby added: "I happily accepted the green outfit and I've stuck with it all the way through. I've always been easy going as far as anything like that was concerned!

"One year we were asked to do a Christmas Top of the Pops in fancy dress. One of us had to go as Carmen Miranda and, as no-one else fancied it, it ended up being me."

Cheers Bobby, good memories and fans of the one and only Bucks Fizz will certainly drink to that!

YUGOSLAVIA, WE CAN'T HEAR YOU!

1988
Dublin, Ireland
30 April
Withdrawals: Cyprus
United Kingdom entry: Go by Scott Fitzgerald
UK position: 02
Format: A Space Age presentation in Dublin with a black stage and lots of changing neon lighting and lasers
Winning song: NE PARTEZ PAS SANS MOI by Celine Dion (Switzerland)
Nul Points: Austria
UK maximum: Norway
Maximum to UK: Belgium, Italy and Turkey
Stat: No points for Scott Fitzgerald from the final voting country, Yugoslavia, gave victory to an artiste you may well have heard of!
This was the year of Celine Dion, Lara Fabian, the Hothouse Flowers.... and Scott Fitzgerald.

Love or hate the song Go, it was tied up in one of the contest's most eventful finals, losing out to eventual winners Switzerland (an untimely intervention from Yugoslavia right at the death) by a 0.73 per cent winning margin, the closest on record, the ties not withstanding.

Fitzgerald, real name William McPhail from Glasgow, appeared in a powder blue suit and on stage with him was Guys 'N' Dolls singer Julie Forsyth, the daughter of the veteran entertainer Bruce Forsyth.

He delivered the UK's first slow-tempo song since 1966, when compatriot Kenneth McKellar disappeared without trace.

The song charted in the UK only at 58 – he had more success ten years previously with a duet alongside Yvonne Keeley, If I Had Words, and it was this version that was later to feature in the smash hit film Babe.

But Fitzgerald, who later turned to ambient music, ran 19-year-old French-Canadian hopeful Celine Dion mighty close although he was finally forced to concede Switzerland's first success since their victory in the inaugural contest back in 1956.

Dion's look was not all that flattering but there was no doubting her power and presence when she took the stage. Like Abba before, her Eurovision experience did not deny her superstardom.

A little known Irish band by the name of Hothouse Flowers made it big after appearing as the interval act in Dublin and, to cap it all, Turkey gave votes to Greece for the very first time – it was certainly an eventful year!

UK OK? The UK bounced back into title contention with Scott Fitzgerald's Go thwarted at the death by the superstar in the making, Canadian songstress Celine Dion singing for Switzerland.

Belgium, Italy and Turkey smiled on Scott with maximum points and Austria, Denmark Finland, Germany, Israel and Spain also ensured it was well supported.

The UK maximum went to fifth-placed Norway and Celine had to be content with ten points from a kingdom that now holds her very dear!

EUROVISION JURY TOP 5

1	Ne Partez Pas Sans Moi (Celine Dion)	SWI
2	Stad I Ljus (Tommy Korberg)	SWE
3	Lied Fur Einen Freund (Maxi & Chris Garden)	GER
4	Croire (Laura Fabian)	LUX
5	Ka' Du Se Hva' Jeg Sa' (Hot Eyes)	DEN

1989

Lausanne, Switzerland
6 May
Return: Cyprus
United Kingdom entry: Why Do I Always Get It Wrong? by Live Report
UK position: 02
Format: The longest single act was the cabaret – Guy Tell, a crossbow expert off William's old block, took almost ten minutes to set up his trick shock – and then missed his target by inches!
Winning song: ROCK ME by Riva (Yugoslavia)
Nul Points: Iceland
UK maximum: Yugoslavia
Maximum to UK: France, Germany, Luxembourg, Norway and Portugal
Stat: Yugoslavia's one and only victory

It was Cliff Richard who sang about the Young Ones – and for this contest the spirit of Sandra Kim lived on.

Eurovision youth was the new black and both France and Israel (with Nathalie

Paque and Gili respectively, both aged 12) aimed for the cute vote, much to the annoyance of the EBU who were to introduce the minimum age rule the following year.

The UK did not go down this road, sending in a four-piece group Live Report, who started off life as Midnight Blue.

The group was led by Ray Caruana, who five years later featured in the Maltese heats and finished runner-up with Scarlet Song.

More recently, he has made his name as the leading light in a Sammy Davis Junior tribute band.

Caruana and his colleagues also finished second in Lausanne, with the UK invariably the bridesmaids and only occasionally the bride.

This in spite of the fact that the song got it right in terms of 'douze points', recording more maximum awards than their rivals.

On this occasion, the bride emerged from Yugoslavia, the last song up, the Slavs claiming a shock victory with the lively Rock Me sung by Riva.

The song got 12 points from the UK jury but commentator Terry Wogan was far from impressed, suggesting that the winning song sounded the death knell for the contest. Then again, maybe not!

This was the year when Eurovision came home, and host venue Lausanne delivered its contest announcements in French.

Both Austria and Germany submitted songs by the same composers, one of whom was Dieter Bohlen who around this time was wowing the punters at summer discos all around Europe courtesy of Modern Talking's Brother Louie!

The piece de resistance in Lausanne was the interval act starring Guy Tell, a relative of William Tell.

His elaborate stunt to pierce an apple atop his head via a complex crossbow set up took an eternity to set up – and finally, after all the shenanigans, the blessed arrow then missed the apple!

UK OK? There were mixed feelings about the UK entry but it held up very well to notch another runner-up spot, seven points behind the winners Yugoslavia who took an early lead and then never lost it.

Live Report didn't get it wrong and scored well in the middle section of the voting, starting badly and finishing poorly.

The UK helped Riva on their way to victory by awarding it twelve points, Denmark and Switzerland the next in favour.

EUROVISION JURY TOP 5

1	Rock Me (Riva)	YUG
2	Vi Maler Byen Rod (Birthe Kjaer)	DEN
3	Nacida Para Amar (Nina)	SPA
4	En Dag (Tommy Nilsson)	SWE
5	Nur Ein Lied (Thomas Forstner)	AUS

1990

Zagreb, Yugoslavia

5 May

United Kingdom entry: Give A Little Love Back To The World by Emma

UK position: 06

Format: Confusion at the start when the conductor couldn't hear the backing tape for the Spanish song – Azucar Moreno finally walked off and returned for a fresh start

Winning song: INSIEME 1992 by Toto Cotugno (Italy)

Bottom Marker: Finland and Norway

UK maximum: Iceland

Maximum to UK: Belgium

Stat: Yugoslavia, we can't hear you – the home jury could not be contacted for several minutes, even though the jury was based only some 30km from the contest hall in Zagreb!

The Berlin Wall came down in November 1989 – and in May 1990, Eurovision was dominated by the hopeful sound of conciliation.

From top to bottom, Italy, Ireland, Yugoslavia, Germany, Austria, Switzerland, Norway and Finland sent in joyful offerings, enough to darken the heart of every rampant Eurosceptic.

The United Kingdom was not immune, serving up a schmaltzy little number from 15-year-old Bridgend lass Emma Booth entitled Give A Little Love Back To The World.

The Welsh youngster struggled on the big stage and relied greatly on the vocal presence of Miriam Stockley who was supporting her.

The anthem was composed by Paul Curtis, who had enjoyed great popularity for ten years from the mid-Seventies on, and the UK finished up in sixth place which, everything considered, wasn't too bad.

Emma is still singing and has been strutting her stuff on cruise ships in the Caribbean.

The togetherness theme did not extend to the organisation of the contest with plenty of problems before the big night and a disaster at the outset of the live transmission.

Spain's Azucar Moreno, singing Bandido, were first act up, but suffered a false start when the singers were unable to hear their backing tape cue.

They walked off stage but returned to deliver a strong performance, finishing one place above the UK in the final countdown.

The French entry was notable, black artiste Joelle Ursull, from the Antilles, finishing second with the distinctive White And Black Blues, a Serge Gainsbourg composition.

This tied with Ireland's Somewhere In Europe, sung by Liam Reilly – a song which contained so many name checks it was seemingly doomed to failure. But this one bucked the trend and the inclusive theme was obviously striking a chord.

No more so than when Toto Cotugno emerged victorious with Insieme 1992's mantra 'Unite Unite Europe'.

It was enough to make his black hair paint run onto his white suit, a memorable twist on those white and black blues!

UK OK? Emma gave a little love back to the world but Europe wasn't that enamoured, only Belgium giving the entry 12 points towards a final place of sixth.

Instead, Europe embraced a uniting theme from Italy's Toto Cotugno although the UK and Norway stood apart in awarding Toto a zero.

The UK's maximum instead went to Stjornin of Iceland, with the next votes going to Ireland and Austria – singing about Somewhere In Europe and Keine Mauern Mehr (No More Walls) respectively.

EUROVISION JURY TOP 5

1	Insieme: 1992 (Toto Cotugno)	ITA
2	White And Black Blues (Joelle Ursul)	FRA
3	Bandido (Azucar Moreno)	SPA
4	Ik Wil Alles Met Je Delen (Maywood)	NET
5	Eitt Lag Enn (Stjornin)	ICE

1991

Rome, Italy
4 May
Withdrawals: Netherlands
Return: Malta
United Kingdom entry: A Message To Your Heart by Samantha Janus
UK position: 10
Format: A late change of venue, from San Remo to Rome, blighted preparations for the contest – the presenters appeared unrehearsed and there were a number of technical glitches
Winning song: FANGAD AV EN STORMWIND by Carola (Sweden)
Nul Points: Austria
UK maximum: Sweden
Stat: A tie at the top and Sweden's Carola won on countback 'ten point' scores

Samantha Janus, now better known as a television star in the popular British television soap Eastenders, was the United Kingdom representative in Rome.

Her song, A Message To Your Heart, will not be remembered as the UK's finest hour.

Her performance was weak and her dress sense questionable, given that her song was raising awareness of the plight of hungry children across the world. Janus, who was born in Brighton, had an interesting background and had battled a number of demons at a young age.

The gifted Manchester United and Northern Ireland footballer George Best was her uncle and for a while her home address was given as the luxury cruise ship the QE2. Lately, her focus has been very much on acting rather than on singing, which is no bad thing.

This year produced the second winning tie in the contest's history but this time round there was a mechanism for sorting out a clear winner.

Sweden outscored France on 'ten point awards', with nothing to separate the two countries on points and maximums, so victory went to the Swedes and Carola's Fangad Av En Stormwind.

Carola's offering was well presented and energetic and she looked good on stage, benefiting from the wind machine which became her Eurovision trademark.

But it was hard lines on France's Amina Annabi, an Algerian national, whose original approach would have taken the contest in a fascinating new direction. But it was not to be.

Germany continued the unity theme from the previous year by submitting a group Atlantis 2000 – the men from Munich and a girl from Berlin, a heady Bavarian and Prussian mix!

UK OK? The year of actress Samantha Janus and her Message To Your Heart although it never really got the pulse racing.

Samantha picked up no maximums along the way, the biggest score, that of ten points, coming from Malta.

The UK backed the eventual winner from Sweden with twelve points but gave just six to France's Amina who claimed joint top spot before the dreaded countback. Unlucky on France, I say!

EUROVISION JURY TOP 5

1	C'Est Le Dernier Qui A Parle Qui A Raison (Amina)	FRA
2	Fangad Av En Stormwind (Carola)	SWE
3	Canzone Per Te (Sandra Simo)	SWI
4	Kaan (Duo Datz)	ISR
5	Lusitana Paixao (Dulce)	POR

1992

Malmo, Sweden

9 May

Return: Netherlands

United Kingdom entry: One Step Out Of Time by Michael Ball

UK position: 02

Format: Germany, Italy and Switzerland all experienced challenges around their submitted entries

Winning song: WHY ME? by Linda Martin (Ireland)

Bottom Marker: Finland

UK maximum: Iceland

Maximum to UK: Austria, Belgium, Denmark and Germany

Stat: Not one song got votes from all the juries and no-one got the dreaded 'nul points' either

Dismayed by the lack of success since the Bucks Fizz victory of 1981, the United Kingdom reverted back to choosing an established star to represent them at Eurovision.

And it was Michael Ball, esteemed actor and singer from Bromsgrove, who chose to take up the baton. Ball had already enjoyed considerable stage success, notably with the song Love Changes Everything from the musical Aspects Of Love.

The public selected the song for Ball to sing and his confident and powerful rendition of One Step Out Of Time marked him out as one of the favourites in Malmo.

Like many before him though, Ball had to settle for second place and a return to more familiar territory as a housewife's favourite. He wasn't too enamoured by the whole experience, going on record to say that he'd rather stick pins in his eyes than ever again take on Eurovision.

The set was done out as a Viking ship and it was the Irish who advanced as the pillagers, Linda Martin sailing out front to record the Emerald Isle's fourth victory with Why Me?

And so a hat-trick for Johnny Logan, a victory with someone else's song (1980), a victory with his own song (1987) and a victory writing a song for someone else (1992)!

This was to be farewell to Yugoslavia and hello to a new era in Eurovision which would eventually introduce a clear sea change for the whole contest.

Malmo was the last contest without pre-qualification and from this point on, as far as the establishment was concerned, things were never going to be the same again.

UK OK? The UK went back to the established artist's drawing board and Michael Ball certainly delivered with One Step Out Of Time.

Michael collected four twelves from Austria, Belgium, Denmark and Germany but lost out to Ireland's Linda Martin who did not receive as many maximums but scored more solidly at the top of the board.

Ireland gave seven points to Michael the UK eight points to Linda. Top marks from the UK actually went to Iceland (an alphabetical slip maybe as it was Iceland's only twelve of the night). Little did we know it, but the period of Irish domination was upon us!

EUROVISION JURY TOP 5

1	Why Me? (Linda Martin)	IRE
2	Little Child (Mary Spiteri)	MAL
3	Rapsodia (Mia Martini)	ITA
4	Olou Tou Kosmou I Elpida (Cleopatra)	GRE
5	Ze Rak Sport (Dafna)	ISR

1993

Millstreet, Ireland
15 May
New entrants: Bosnia and Herzegovina, Croatia and Slovenia
Withdrawals: Yugoslavia
United Kingdom entry: Better The Devil You Know by Sonia
UK position: 02
Format: The first contest to feature countries from deepest eastern Europe
Winning song: IN YOUR EYES by Niamh Kavanagh (Ireland)
Bottom Marker: Belgium
UK maximum: Ireland
Maximum to UK: Austria, Belgium, Iceland and Israel
Stat: A relegation system was mooted, to allow more countries to enter from the eastern bloc nations. Eurovision was a changing!

Chirpy Sonia Evans, from Skelmersdale, put heart and soul into her Eurovision effort for the United Kingdom in what was unkindly described in some quarters as a 'cowshed' in rural southern Ireland.

Michael Ball finished second to Ireland in Malmo and the sequence was repeated in Millstreet, the unlikely venue for the Grand Prix, when Sonia trailed home to Niamh Kavanagh.

Sonia was promoted by Eurovision fans in the bid to represent her country and she didn't let anyone down.

An extra in the Liverpudlian soap opera Brookside, Sonia's musical career was given a considerable lift by the Eighties pop maestros Stock, Aitken and Waterman.

Her Eurovision song, Better The Devil You Know, was a collaboration between Dean Collinson and Red and was tailor-made for the likeable Merseyside artist.

This year was characterised by the arrival of three Balkans nations, drawn from the former Yugoslavia.

Slovenia, Bosnia and Herzegovina and Croatia made their contest debuts following a musical joust in the Slovenian capital of Ljubljana.

The Bosnian band had fled Sarajevo under gunfire to reach Millstreet, leaving their conductor trapped on the tarmac at the airport.

Noel Kelehan, the veteran Irish conductor, stepped in to assist the Bosnian cause!

And of course there was plenty of discussion about the venue itself, quite a departure from Dublin.

A financial venture persuaded Irish broadcaster RTE to take the contest to Millstreet, comfortably the smallest place to ever host the Eurovision.

The venue was a riding school provided by a local inhabitant and much work was required on the building and the infrastructure so that it could comfortably accommodate 25 participating countries.

The performers were actually based in the nearby city of Cork and travelled to Millstreet for their rehearsals and media commitments.

Ireland won on home turf and Eurovision was turning greener by the minute – it would be back to Dublin though next year!

UK OK? Sonia's Better The Devil You Know was a bouncy affair but again it couldn't get past second place, the way once again blocked by Ireland, this time in the form of Niamh Kavanagh.

Austria, Belgium, Iceland and Israel demonstrated their support for our Sonia but in the end Niamh won by a comfortable margin.

On this occasion, the UK awarded Ireland the twelve with Switzerland and debutants Croatia granted ten and eight respectively. Ireland picked up votes from every country.

EUROVISION JURY TOP 5

1	In Your Eyes (Niamh Kavanagh)	IRE
2	Vrede (Ruth Jacott)	NET
3	Mama Corsica (Patrick Fiori)	FRA
4	Alle Mine Tankar (Silje Vige)	NOR
5	Eloise (Arvingarna)	SWE

1994

Dublin, Ireland

30 April

New entrants: Estonia, Hungary, Lithuania, Poland, Romania, Russia and Slovakia

Withdrawals: Italy

Relegated: Belgium, Denmark, Israel, Luxembourg, Slovenia and Turkey

United Kingdom entry: Lonely Symphony by Frances Ruffelle

UK position: 10

Format: The most successful act to emerge from this particular contest was the interval act – the phenomenon that is Riverdance was born!

Winning song: ROCK 'N' ROLL KIDS by Paul Harrington and Charlie McGettigan (Ireland)

Nul Points: Lithuania

UK maximum: Poland

Stat: Ireland's third successive victory, a parlous state of affairs for Ireland's national broadcaster RTE who braced themselves for another major expense the following year

Musical theatre actress Frances Ruffelle was the surprise choice for the United Kingdom at The Point theatre in Dublin. She sung eight songs at the national selection and the slow-build anthemic Lonely Symphony was put forward.

It did not score well with the juries, finishing a lowly tenth, but remains one of the more popular UK offerings of recent times. Having said that, it achieved little success when released as a single and the accompanying solo album Fragile lived up to its title and was scrapped.

Ruffelle was established as an actress and also as a recording artist and was best known for her roles in Les Miserables and Starlight Express.

The whole scene belonged to Ireland, who recorded a third win on the spin thanks to a shock victory for Paul Harrington and Charlie McGettigan and the simple presentation, not a gimmick in sight, of Rock 'N' Roll Kids.

However, this song proved to be only Irish winner that failed to chart in the UK. Rock 'N' Roll Kids was a clear winner, the first non-orchestrated winner, featured the oldest winning performers; Harrington and McGettigan were the first winning male duo.

But even then they were still upstaged by the most memorable interval act of them all! Riverdance was introduced to the world for seven minutes at half-time – a traditional Celtic music and dance interval act inadvertently set rolling a phenomenon that swept the world and made Michael Flatley a multi-millionaire.

UK OK? Frances Ruffelle's contest offering did not do as well as expected and finished in tenth position with Ireland winning their third Eurovision in a row, an unprecedented achievement.

There were no maximums for Lonely Symphony, the highest marks coming from Portugal and Switzerland who awarded eight apiece.

The UK's twelve went to the popular debutant from Poland with ten going to Ireland, whose laid-back duo struck a chord with viewers – as did a certain combination from Denmark six years later!

EUROVISION JURY TOP 5

1	Rock 'N' Roll Kids (Paul Harrington & Charlie McGettigan)	IRE
2	To Nie Ja (Edyta Gorniak)	POL
3	Vechni Stranik (Youddiph)	RUS
4	Wir Geben 'Ne Party (Mekado)	GER
5	Kinek Mondjam El Vetkeimet (Friderika Bayer)	HUN

1995

Dublin, Ireland
13 May
Withdrawals: Luxembourg
Relegated: Estonia, Finland, Lithuania, Netherlands, Romania, Slovakia and Switzerland
Return: Belgium, Denmark, Israel, Slovenia and Turkey
United Kingdom entry: Love City Groove by Love City Groove
UK position: 10
Format: The number of entries was restricted to 23
Winning song: NOCTURNE by Secret Garden (Norway)
Bottom Marker: Germany
UK maximum: Israel
Maximum to UK: Austria and France
Stat: In a sense this was another Irish victory, with Irish violinist Fionnuala Sherry teaming up with Norwegian composer Rolf Lovland after meeting in Dublin the previous year

A further switch in the Eurovision selection process saw pop maestro Jonathan King charged with returning success to the United Kingdom.

Gone were the big name stars and an appointed song, once more it was down to open selection among aspiring performers.

Love City Groove, a pop/rap group, was the runaway winner in the national selection.

A bold selection, it did not however find Eurovision favour although was rewarded with 12 points from France where rap was very much the thing for the young viewer.

The song did well in the UK chart, reaching seven, but the group struggled in Dublin with their live performance.

Post Eurovision, the group could not find a suitable follow-up and it was not long before they split.

Stephen Rudden tried for Eurovision again in 1998 but could only finish fourth in the national selection with When We're Alone (We Dream).

Paul Hardy and Yinka Charles (MC Reason) are still performing but Jay Williams got suited and booted to join a Swiss global banking group.

The Point Theatre in Dublin was the contest venue for the second year running and although Ireland did not win this one, the green was still shining through as Norway's Secret Garden lifted the Eurovision crown.

Secret Garden were Norwegian composer Rolf Lovland (composer of the much-covered song You Raise Me Up - and his partner Fionnula Sherry, an Irish violinist who he met the previous year when she was performing for the house orchestra.

The song was both unusual and controversial, in that it contained just 24 words spread over seven lines!

Ireland's entrant, Eddie Friel, finished way down the order in 14th place, but there were notable performances from Spain's Anabel Conde and Denmark's Aud Wilken.

With Norway winning and Denmark coming in fifth, Scandinavia had three countries in the top five.

Splitting these was Sweden with Jan Johansen's Se Pa Mej, the pre-contest favourite, not quite able to go all the way.

UK OK? Love City Groove, with Love City Groove, was a bold choice for the contest and the entry actually held up reasonably well in tenth position – not bad for a little slice of Euro rapping!

The group picked up maximums from Austria and France, to Sir Terry Wogan's consternation, but little from elsewhere.

The UK top mark went to Israel and only four went the way of winners Norway, whose success was not without controversy.

EUROVISION JURY TOP 5

1	Nocturne (Secret Garden)	NOR
2	Se Pa Mej (Jan Johansen)	SWE
3	Vuelve Conmigo (Anabel Conde)	SPA
4	Il Me Donne Rendezvous (Nathalie Santamaria)	FRA
5	Fra Mols Til Skagen (Aud Wilken)	DEN

1996

Oslo, Norway

18 May

Relegated: Denmark, Germany, Hungary, Israel and Russia

Return: Estonia, Finland, Netherlands, Slovakia and Switzerland

United Kingdom entry: Just A Little Bit by Gina G

UK position: 08

Format: Audio pre-qualification was used to decide who would make it to the final, the only year this has ever been done. It was not a success!

Winning song: THE VOICE by Eimear Quinn (Ireland)

Bottom Marker: Finland

UK maximum: Cyprus

Maximum to UK: Belgium and Portugal

Stat: Three wins out of four for the Irish – and by this time they'd had enough of a good thing! The big commercial hit though belonged to Gina G.

It only finished eighth in the contest itself, but the United Kingdom entry Just A Little Bit, performed by the alluring Gina G, was the Eurovision song of the year. Gina Mary Gardiner, born in the Australian city of Brisbane, emerged through the dance and pop/house scene Down Under where she made her name as a singer songwriter.

A disc jockey in Melbourne, she performed with the Australian group Bass Culture before basing herself in the UK in 1993 to pursue a solo career.

She snapped up the Eurovision ticket with the catchy Euro pop number Just A Little Bit, Katrina Leskanich's favourite no less.

The Oslo disappointment aside, it hit the number one slot in the UK singles chart and achieved success all over the world, including place 12 on the US billboard chart – the highest-ever placing for a Eurovision song.

Gina G actually knocked George Michael off the top of the UK chart en route to celebrating the biggest Eurovision commercial success since 1976.

Her singing career dipped from that point on and, alongside Sonia, she attempted to resurrect it by appearing in the series Reborn In The USA.

Another tilt at Eurovision came in 2005 with the song Flashback when she found herself up against Javine and Katie Price (aka model Jordan) in the fight for a place in Kiev, won by Javine. She is now based in Los Angeles in the United States, where she devotes a lot of time to her two children.

And Ireland won for the fourth time in five years – and the seventh time overall – with Eimear Quinn's The Voice, pleasant but conservative.

To say that the Oslo audience was underwhelmed hardly began to sum up the prevailing mood, forcing the EBU to push the button on televoting.

UK OK? Gina G's Ooh Ah Just A Little Bit was a Eurovision flop, finishing seventh on the night at the Oslo Spektrum and later dropping one place further to eighth after the righting of a voting irregularity.

Lumbered with a dreaded early slot, there were maximums from Belgium and Portugal and an eight from France – however, the song's commercial success contrasted greatly with conservative nature of the Irish winner and questions were once again asked of the song contest.

The UK saw nothing of value in Eimear Quinn's song, granting it not a single point – the twelve actually went to Constantinos from Cyprus.

EUROVISION JURY TOP 5

1	I Evighet (Elisabeth Andreassen)	NOR
2	Sveta Ljubav (Maja Blagdan)	CRO
3	Kaelakee Haal (Ivo Linna & Maarja-Liis Ilus)	EST
4	Mon Couer L'Aime (Kathy Leander)	SWI
5	Diwanit Bugale (Dan Ar Braz Et L'Heritage Des Celtes)	FRA

1997

Dublin, Ireland

3 May

Withdrawals: Israel

Relegated: Belgium, Finland and Slovakia

Return: Denmark, Germany, Hungary, Italy and Russia

Format: Songs could be performed without any live music if required – the beginning of the end for the orchestra; the recent record at Eurovision determined which countries would be earmarked for the chop

Winning song: LOVE SHINE A LIGHT by Katrina and the Waves (United Kingdom)

Nul Points: Norway and Portugal

UK maximum: Ireland

Maximum to UK: Austria, Croatia, Denmark, France, Hungary, Ireland, Netherlands, Russia, Sweden and Switzerland

Stat: The introduction of televoting with Austria, Germany, Sweden, Switzerland and the United Kingdom the first to pick up the baton. The United Kingdom won by a country mile.

In came partial televoting – and in came Katrina and the Waves, who returned a barnstorming victory for the United Kingdom.

Five countries decided to put the Eurovision fates in the hands of the great general public and ironically it was Ireland –on this occasion playing second fiddle to the UK – who scored the highest points from the nations who were televoting.

And Iceland, who polled just 18 points for Paul Oscar's daring Minn Hinsti Dans, saw 16 of those 18 points come from the televoter!

Katrina and the Waves packed in the votes from both jury and televoter, collecting the most maximum twelves ever.

Love Shine A Light is the favourite UK entrant among the devotees and the song swept away both those lucky enough to be at The Point that evening and also the millions watching on the box.

Eurovision success did not revive the band's fortunes and Katrina soon went her own way.

In 2005, she had another go at reaching the contest stage through Sweden's melodifestivalen selection but was unsuccessful.

Later that year, she co-hosted the prestigious Congratulations 50-year Eurovision celebration event in Copenhagen together with Renars Kaupers, the lead singer of Latvian band Brainstorm.

Italy returned to Eurovision for the first time since 1993, for one year only, and they have not been back since.

And Russia's dishevelled yet iconic Alla Pugachova became a crowd favourite, although the song did not quite match her billing.

So it was farewell to The Point, the old faithful, as RTE gratefully waved the Eurovision bandwagon across the Irish sea.

This was the end of the line for Ireland's domination – it was time to share the thing around a little.

UK OK? Televoting ushered in a brave new world for Eurovision and Love Shine A Light from Katrina And The Waves proved an emphatic winner for the UK in Dublin.

Votes were garnered from every jury and televote and the song racked up 227 points from a bumper field with no less than ten maximums rolling in from all quarters of the continent.

Ireland were a distant second and picked up the maximum from the UK televoters. Of the four televoting nations eligible to vote for the UK song, only Germany did not give Katrina the twelve.

EUROVISION JURY TOP 5

1	Fiumi Di Parole (Jalisse)	ITA
2	Dinle (Sebnem Parker & Group Etnic)	TUR
3	Zbudi Se (Tanja Ribic)	SLO
4	Ale Jestem (Anna-Maria Jopek)	POL
5	Minn Hinsti Dans (Paul Oscar)	ICE

KATRINA AND A PARTING OF THE WAVES

CHANCES are that Love Shine A Light will remain the fifth and final Eurovision Song Contest winner for the United Kingdom.

Should that be the case, at least it can be said that the UK will have gone out on a pretty big high.

Prior to the final voting system introduced in 2004 – which now allows all nations a vote in the final, irrespective of whether or not they actually taking part – Katrina And The Waves notched up a massive record-breaking 227 points from 20 juries and four televoting nations.

That represented 79 per cent of the total of the 288 points available, a percentage only matched by Nicole in 1982 (79 per cent, 161 from 204) and bettered by Brotherhood Of Man in 1976 (80 per cent, 164 from 204) and Anne-Marie David in 1973 (81 per cent, 129 from 160).

A pretty big high, which owed a lot to a feelgood factor in the UK, a cheap Irish green shirt, a cheeky salute and, not least, a barnstorming performance by Katrina and The Waves in Dublin.

A very fond memory for American singer and musician Katrina Leskanich, who found herself up against the novelty that was Eurovision.

Most Americans look to 'do Europe' in their lifetimes and Katrina certainly took that concept to a unique level.

She said: "In the late 1990s, Katrina And The Waves were running out of steam. We remained successful in Germany, but that was about it.

"We had been together for 20 years and had enjoyed considerable success in the 1980s. We charted in the States in 1989 but from then on it was a struggle to get a foothold and we were playing musical chairs with record labels in a bid to get back on the scene.

"Jonathan King, who at that time was looking to promote UK songs in Eurovision, approached us and asked us if we had a suitable song for the contest.

"At that time we had written a song to celebrate the anniversary of The Samaritans called Love Shine A Light which we thought would be perfect for Eurovision.

"So we submitted it, thinking it would be lined up for a 16-year-old emerging talent to take forward.

"But Warner Records came back to us saying that they liked the song and offered us an album deal providing we performed the song ourselves at the national final.

Katrina Leskanich, now parted from The Waves
www.katrinasweb.com

"We won the final but nothing could really prepare us for the Eurovision experience by the time we arrived in Dublin.

"We felt pretty good in the week's build up to the competition. Rehearsals went well although as we got to hear a few more of the songs our confidence and belief did take a bit of a knock.

"The press conferences were something else. Eurovision has a fanatical following and the conferences can also be accessed by fans.

"So you could face a weighty question from a serious journalist followed by one along the lines of 'what's your favourite colour?' Next question please!

"And then there are the blogs, which really say it how it is. They can be cruel and some of the comments can be difficult to take. Life on Planet Eurovision is very strange!

"On the night itself we felt good. As the contest unfolded, we were up second from last and I got the sense that by the time we arrived on stage the audience were waiting to hear a winner.

"The performance went smoothly and I think we delivered what I would call an old school win for the United Kingdom.

"We won because the song had a good beat, it had an international flavour and a truly heart-warming message.

"And it was sung by someone who could actually sing. I mean, the band had done around 2,500 shows prior to Eurovision while other acts in Dublin had only a handful of appearances behind them. For some, it was actually their first time on television!

"The Point in Dublin is an intimate venue. It was packed with Irish, as you would expect, and my cheap green shirt went down well.

"The song itself is a tricky one to perform. It has a huge chorus so we really had to nail that and an awkward beat with a complicated chord progression which is very difficult to get right.

"But it all came good and as we went off stage we were convinced that we would win the contest.

"I don't do choreography. What you got was a strong song and a strong performance and not a gimmick in sight.

"We knew there was a very fine line between a performance being passionate, on the one hand, or hammy on the other. We had 2 minutes 58 seconds to get it right, and we got it spot on.

"I did salute quite a bit and I really don't know where that came from. I suppose it felt like a military conquest, but I've not saluted anyone before or since!

"When were sitting in the Green Room one of our entourage, Miriam Stockley, spent the whole time plying us with champagne.

"By the time it got round to the final votes coming on, our victory assured, we were all 300 sheets to the wind!

"The funniest thing was that the whole time we were over in Dublin, no-one had actually told us that if we won the contest we would be expected to reprise the song at the end of the show.

"So, when we were told this is what we were required to do, it came as a big surprise!

"The walk back to the stage was wonderfully chaotic. I can remember Ronan Keating pulling me forcefully by the arm and I was shouting into the camera 'daddy, don't get too excited' as my father had recently been in poor health.

"After the presentations and the arm-waving it was time for the reprise and the wonderful chaos continued.

"I missed the click of the backing track and all of a sudden there was the sound of a 24-piece orchestra and tambourines being rattled in my ear!

"But we got through it and I came off the stage with goose bumps, knowing we had a delivered a song and performance that had been no disgrace to the competition.

"I got to meet the Irish President and got a message of congratulation from Tony Blair, who only two days earlier had been elected as Prime Minister. It was a wonderful time."

The new PM also managed to detract from the band's triumph on their return to London the day after the contest.

Katrina recalled: "We thought we'd fly back to a good press reception, having landed the first UK win in the Eurovision for 16 years.

"But all there was at the airport was one photographer as all the rest were following Tony Blair on an overseas trip that he was making.

"And there was a heckler who started bad mouthing Terry Wogan, because while Terry was much loved for the way he presented Eurovision there were also some who didn't take too kindly to the way he went about it.

"The song spent 12 weeks on the UK charts, reaching number 3, and we performed an unprecedented four successive weeks on Top Of The Pops.

"Love Shine A Light did well in Europe and we arrived in Germany, where we'd always had a good fan base, to promote the single.

"But we spent three days sitting around in beer gardens eating wurst because the German journalists took a collective decision to boycott the interviews.

"They felt we shouldn't have done Eurovision because it would compromise the rock base that had served us well on tours. I thought it was extremely childish.

"And there was also stuff about that it wasn't right that an American represented the UK?

"Hold on a minute, what about Celine Dion for Switzerland and Gina G for the UK just the year before, to name but two?

"Incidentally, Ooh Ah Just A Little Bit remains my favourite Eurovision song. The hook is irresistible and I couldn't resist working it into the new version of Love Shine A Light which I presented at the national selection in 2008.

"In contrast, the red carpet was rolled out for us in eastern Europe wherever we went, be it Croatia, Bosnia and Herzegovina, Estonia, Poland.

"We were forever tucking into various plates of unknown meat. Probably pork, but I don't want to think too much about that."

It seemed like Love Shine A Light years from the formation of Katrina And The Waves in the English university city of Cambridge back in 1981.

Walking On Sunshine, the group's smash hit from 1985, remains the ultimate in feelgood tracks and a summer anthem to this very day.

Katrina added: "If you haven't yet heard the country version of the song by Dolly Parton then, please, dig it out. It's something else!"

Que Te Quiero and Sun Street quickly followed and the band received a Grammy nomination for Best New Artist.

Eurovision revived the band in 1997 but, just two years after the Dublin success, Katrina was forced to come to terms with the parting of The Waves.

She said: "The band wrote me a letter saying that they wanted to part company from me and so began a protracted court case which lasted three years.

"There were problems, because the band recruited another singer, Linda Hayes, but continued to associate themselves with my name. It was an opportunity for me to go my own way so I set out to pursue a career as a solo artist.

"It was difficult for all of us. For my part, every time the Eurovision thing came around, I was asked about the split.

"I had to smile and try to deflect the inevitable suggestions that Eurovision had broken up Katrina And The Waves. The fact of the matter is that it did.

"But I enjoyed branching out into radio and for a while I had my own show on Radio 2 which went out between midnight and 3am.

"I spent one-and-a-half years in musical theatre, taking the part of Ellie Greenwich as the lead role in Leader Of The Pack which was great as I have always loved the Shangri-Las.

"I've also released a solo record in Scandinavia and have relished the change and the chance to explore new horizons.

"And I've also kept close with Eurovision but limit interviews to once every two years so as not to get stale talking about it all the time.

"I took part in Sweden's Melodifestivalen in 2005 and later that year was lucky enough to co-present the 50th anniversary Eurovision celebration Congratulations, with Renars Kaupers."

Katrina admitted that while she still enjoys following Eurovision, she doesn't really immerse herself in the event until the night of the final.

She said: "I enjoy watching the final but the political voting in recent years has spoilt it. The countries in the eastern blocs keep voting for each other but I suppose you could say the same of the UK and Ireland over the years.

"I hate the cheesy songs and also the dreary ballads. For a time, there was a tendency for countries to try and emulate the success of Abba's Waterloo.

"More recently, the trend was put on a visual spectacular to the sound of a kettle drum, a heavy back beat and a touch of Middle Eastern Riverdance thrown in for good measure.

"When I first saw the Serbian entry in 2007 I thought it broke the mould as they put in a good song and a strong act in which the women and the lead singer were the gimmicks.

"The evolution of the contest has been of great interest to me. It keeps getting bigger and bigger, and with it the stakes are getting higher and higher.

"It certainly represents a vehicle through which you can promote an album and, not least, the artist, as we can testify.

"I'm often asked whether winning Eurovision was the proudest moment of my life. I can't honestly say that it was right at the very top.

"What I can say is there are lots of things that I have done in my personal and professional life that I am immensely proud of and winning Eurovision, and to do it in the manner that we did, is certainly one of them."

BIENVENUE A BIRMINGHAM!

1998

Birmingham, England
9 May
New entrants: FYR Macedonia
Withdrawals: Italy
Relegated: Austria, Bosnia and Herzegovina, Denmark, Iceland and Russia
Return: Belgium, Finland, Israel, Romania and Slovakia
United Kingdom entry: Where Are You? by Imaani
UK position: 02
Format: A successful contest on the back of the phenomenon that was televoting!
Winning song: DIVA by Dana International (Israel)
Nul Points: Switzerland
UK maximum: Malta
Maximum to UK: Croatia, Israel, Romania and Turkey
Stat: Plenty of quirks (Ulrika and Terry) and controversy (Dana International and Guildo Horn) to keep Europe entertained

Eurovision came to 'Brum' and proved to be one of the most memorable of all contests. Imaani Saleem, aka Melanie Crosdale from Nottingham, gave the competition a good run for their money with Where Are You? but little was heard of her following her second spot to Israel's Dana International.

EMI failed to follow up the interest in the artist and a few years on she took the lead vocals for Tru Faith and Dub Conspiracy in a cover of the Adina Howard song Freak Like Me – charting at 12 in September 2000 and doing better than the original.

The winning song Diva had made all the headlines in the run-up to the contest and the Israeli transsexual (aka Yaron Cohen), captivating the audience through sheer presence, did not betray the hype. Although it wasn't a great vocal on the night, the singer's personality shone through to carry the day.

But going into the last round of votes, it looked that the crown would be going to Malta for the very first time. Chiara's simple and understated offering, against a candlelit backdrop, was everything that the Israeli song wasn't.

All it needed to win was a modicum of support from FYR Macedonia but the debutants ignored Chiara completely, prompting Dana International to rush backstage for her Jean-Paul Gaultier costume of feathers.

Amid the excitement there was also irony – as the winning song was performed with no live music, the impressive interval act was actually the last time live music has been heard on the Eurovision stage. The orchestra is dead, long live the backing track?

UK OK? Imaani provided a strong second place for the host country and a tight finish saw the title going to Israel ahead of Malta.

Four maximums came the UK's way and votes were collected from all participating countries for the second year running.

The UK maximum went to Malta's Chiara, who went from potential winner to third on the very last vote submission, and only five points went to winners Israel.

EUROVISION JURY TOP 5

1	Diva (Dana International)	ISR
2	Neka Ni Me Svane (Danijela)	CRO
3	Hemel En Aarde (Edsilia Rombley)	NET
4	Guildo Hat Euch Lieb (Guildo Horn)	GER
5	Is Always Over Now? (Dawn)	IRE

1999

Jerusalem, Israel
Date: 29 May
Withdrawal: Romania
Relegated: Finland, FYR Macedonia, Greece, Hungary, Slovakia and Switzerland
Return: Austria, Bosnia and Herzegovina, Denmark, Iceland and Lithuania
United Kingdom entry: Say It Again by Precious
UK position: 12
Format: The venue was too small to accommodate the orchestra and nations had a free choice of language
Winning song: TAKE ME TO YOUR HEAVEN by Charlotte Nilsson (Sweden)
Bottom Marker: Spain
UK maximum: Sweden
Stat: Shades of Abba, 25 years on!

The Reise Nach Jerusalem, in the words of the German entry from Ralph Siegel and Bernd Meinunger, was effectively the beginning of the end for UK consistency at the top of the Eurovision charts.

The representation this year was from female band Precious, who enjoyed moderate chart success with Say It Again.

Co-founder of the group was Jenny Frost, who later went on to bigger and better things with Atomic Kitten.

The girls were effectively set up as a rival to The Spice Girls but they never got to play in the same league.

In Jerusalem, nations had a free choice in terms of language and the Swedes capitalised, Charlotte Nilsson's Take Me To Your Heaven chiming with the silver jubilee of Abba's victory in Brighton to win the Grand Prix.

Iceland's Selma stormed to second place with the equally catchy All Out Of Luck – considering she performed from position thirteen on the night, All Out Of Luck indeed she was!

Latvia was forced to withdraw from the contest for financial reasons and the fancied Cypriot entry, Tha'ne Erotas, proved a flop.

And the French displayed a rather scary singer called Nayah, who, it transpired, was the member of a bizarre religious cult – Nayah's song was the only one on the night actually sung in French.

Beforehand, there was much discussion as to whether the contest would actually be held in Jersualem.

In the event, amid very tight security, it was but the tiny venue limited the number of media and fans present.

With no room for the orchestra, and the re-introduction of the free language choice rule, Eurovision legend Johnny Logan likened the contest to a karaoke competition.

What with Dana International's security scare tumble during the presentation to Charlotte Nilsson, which required the intervention of Mossad, and the Hallelujah international chorus at the conclusion, this contest was certainly out of the ordinary.

UK OK? The good run for the UK began to peter out in Jerusalem with the girl group Precious finishing in the bottom half of the table.

There were no maximum votes on this occasion for the song Say It Again, the biggest return coming from Malta who gave eight points.

The UK televoters awarded the top mark to the winning song from Sweden, the ten points staying up north and going the way of Iceland's Selma.

EUROVISION JURY TOP 5

1	Take Me To Your Heaven (Charlotte Nilsson)	SWE
2	Marija Magdalena (Doris Dragovic)	CRO
3	All Out Of Luck (Selma)	ICE
4	Tha'ne Erotas (Marlain Angelidou)	CYP
5	Reise Nach Jerusalem (Surpriz)	GER

2000

Stockholm, Sweden
Date: 13 May
New entrants: Latvia
Relegated: Bosnia and Herzegovina, Lithuania, Poland, Portugal and Slovenia
Return: Finland, FYR Macedonia, Romania, Russia and Switzerland
United Kingdom entry: Don't Play That Song Again by Nicki French
UK position: 16
Format: The circular Globen Theatre was able to house 16,000 spectators – and Eurovision moved into the new Millennium without the orchestra. The Big Four – France, Germany, Spain and the UK – were allowed automatic entry into the final
Winning song: FLY ON THE WINGS OF LOVE by The Olsen Brothers (Denmark)
Bottom Marker: Belgium
UK maximum: Denmark
Stat: A long shot victory for the Danes – their first success since 1963

Welcome to the land of the Melodifestivalen and the capital Stockholm; a victory for Scandinavia; a great year for the Baltics and a contest which hinted at the Eastern Promise to come.

Nicki French was the chosen UK artist with her Steps-like up-tempo Don't Play That Song Again. One of the contest favourites, it remains a popular tune for Eurovision devotees across the continent.

French remains one of Eurovision's greatest advocates and threw heart and soul into her Stockholm experience. But sadly her enthusiasm was not matched by that of the voters and, criticised for her dress sense, she finished way down in 16th, then the lowest finish for a UK entry.

It fared little better in the charts, scraping in at 34 – the popular club singer, born in Carlisle and raised in Tenterden, deserved rather better.

The winner came from Denmark and, as French's star faded in the hours leading up to the contest, that of the Olsen Brothers was clearly on the rise.

Fly On The Wings Of Love barely registered on the radar during practice but, as the rehearsals got underway, it steadily grew on observers and the fans in the hall. A polished performance on the night gave the Danes only their second Eurovision victory – and the success was all the sweeter against a Swedish backdrop!

Equally significant though was the emergence of the competitiveness of Latvia and Estonia, especially the former – Brainstorm's My Star clearly established itself as one of the Eurovision greats.

UK OK? Nicki French's Euro offering was one you either loved or hated – unfortunately the Eurovision voters didn't want Nicki to Play That Song Again and it slumped to 16th place, the poorest UK finish to date.

Unsurprisingly, there were no maximums for Nicki in Stockholm, six points apiece from Turkey and Malta being as good as it got.

Again the UK voters backed the eventual winner, the surprise package from Denmark, with Ireland getting the ten.

EUROVISION JURY TOP 5

1	Fly On The Wings Of Love (The Olsen Brothers)	DEN
2	My Star (Brainstorm)	LAT
3	Once In A Lifetime (Ines)	EST
4	Solo (Alsou)	RUS
5	My Heart Goes Boom (Charmed)	NOR

2001

Venue: Copenhagen, Denmark

12 May

Relegated: Austria, Belgium, Cyprus, Finland, FYR Macedonia, Romania and Switzerland

Return: Bosnia and Herzegovina, Greece, Lithuania, Poland, Portugal and Slovenia

United Kingdom entry: No Dream Impossible by Lindsay Dracass

UK position: 15

Format: 38,000 packed into the Parken Stadium – the biggest contest audience ever for Eurovision

Winning song: EVERYBODY by Tanel Padar & Dave Benton with 2XL (Estonia)

Bottom Marker: Iceland and Norway

UK maximum: Estonia

Stat: Ireland ended up relegated and the UK only just made the cut, their automatic final qualification aside!

Lindsay Dracass brought something of the street to Copenhagen with No Dream Impossible.

This is a song that you again either loved or hated – for me it was more like than dislike and it was a brave attempt at a challenging song from the sociable Sheffield lass who didn't quite pull it off.

Critics argued that the Eurovision was beyond her performance experience but she gave it a very good shot.

The year before venturing out to Copenhagen, a 15-year-old Lindsay had actually turned out as a backing singer at Glastonbury. So she had seen a crowd before!

103

And the esteemed musician Paul Carrack has obviously seen enough in her to offer a place on tour with his band.

And it was quite a crowd in Copenhagen – the contest was staged in the city's Parken Stadium which was packed with 38,000 spectators housed under a temporary roof, still the largest-ever audience for the event.

The organisers were immensely proud of this achievement, Estonia building on their good run in Stockholm to register victory, yet another surprise, through the joint efforts of Tanel Padar and Dave Benton.

Purists criticised the winner as having little to do with a song contest, but this was to be the thin end of a very thick wedge in light of what was going to be unleashed on an unsuspecting public in the years to come!

Interestingly, in the Eurovision Jury list below, the winner failed to feature in the Top 5 poll – only one of two years that this has occurred.

Leading on that front were a Greek band Antique, based in Sweden. The hosts did well, as did the French thanks to the superlative talent of Natasha St-Pier.

Ireland suffered the humiliation of relegation, five years on from their record-breaking seventh victory.

And Terry Wogan upset the Danish nation by dubbing the two hosts, who spoke in rhyming couplets, as Doctor Death and the Tooth Fairy. How's your Danish, Tel?

UK OK? Sheffield youngster Lindsay Dracass represented the UK in Copenhagen and improved the UK position by one place on the previous year, so no discernible improvement for the testing No Dream Impossible.

No maximums for Lindsay, the biggest slice coming from Ireland with four points – elsewhere there were three lots of three points and three lots of two points, nowhere enough to make any sort of impact.

The UK maximum went to Estonia – so backing the winner for the third year running – and the ten went to hosts Denmark.

EUROVISION JURY TOP 5

1	Die For You (Antique)	GRE
2	Energy (Nusa Derenda)	SLO
3	Never Ever Let You Go (Rollo And King)	DEN
4	Je N'Ai Que Mon Ame (Natasha St-Pier)	FRA
5	Wer Liebe Lebt (Michelle)	GER

2002

Tallinn, Estonia

Date: 25 May

Withdrawals: Portugal

Relegated: Iceland, Ireland, Netherlands, Norway and Poland

Return: Austria, Belgium, Cyprus, Finland, FYR Macedonia, Romania and Switzerland

United Kingdom entry: Come Back by Jessica Garlick

UK position: 03

Format: Sweden and Finland stepped in to help Estonia stage the contest

Winning song: I WANNA by Marie N (Latvia)

Bottom Marker: Denmark

UK maximum: Malta

Maximum to UK: Austria

Stat: Latvia, reprieved by Portugal's withdrawal, traded on the gimmick to win in neighbouring Estonia

A refreshing stop-off in Tallinn, where the unusual qualities of the host city and a stirring UK performance made for a memorable contest.

Welsh lass Jessica Garlick stepped up with the strong ballad Come Back which heralded a top three finish – the best since 1998 and never to be repeated since!

Garlick was selected following her Pop Idol reality television adventure, where she had trailed the eventual top three of Will Young, Gareth Gates and Darius Danesh. And she played it straight, in direct contrast to the top two songs delivered by Latvia and Malta.

But her career never took off and she received a little stick for branding the Austrian entry in 2003, from Alf Poier, a joke. Fair enough, some might say!

Estonia revelled in their role as Eurovision host and much was made of the nation's singing heritage. The theme of the contest was a fairy tale and the fact that emergency funding from the home authorities saw the show through, against a backdrop of severe difficulties, was indeed the stuff of fairy tales.

Spain also hit the reality beat with their entrant Rosa, successful in the country's Triunfo competition, belting out a song about Europe living a celebration.

Slovenia featured Sestre, three transvestite air hostesses, and unsurprisingly this met with a fair amount of controversy.

The battle for the Eurovision crown turned out to be a straight fight between Malta's Ira Losco and Latvia's Marie N. An overloaded gimmick from the Latvians, a triumph for choreography, saw Marie N pile on the outfit changes during the course of I Wanna. Marie won out and Eurovision stayed in the Baltics!

UK OK? A much better picture for the UK in Tallinn thanks to the talented and well-presented Jessica Garlick whose early offering of Come Back was strong enough to finish in third place.

Austria liked it enough to award it the full 12 points and there was a ten from Malta, in amongst some consistent chunky scoring elsewhere.

The UK voters ignored the change-dressing talents of Marie N and preferred to give their top votes to Malta and France respectively.

EUROVISION JURY TOP 5

1	Il Faut Du Temps (Sandrine Francois)	FRA
2	I Wanna (Marie N)	LAT
3	Seventh Wonder (Ira Losco)	MAL
4	Runaway (Sahlene)	EST
5	Light A Candle (Sarit Hadad)	ISR

2003

Riga, Latvia

Date: 24 May

New entrants: Ukraine

Relegated: Denmark, Finland, FYR Macedonia, Lithuania and Switzerland

Return: Iceland, Ireland, Netherlands, Norway, Poland and Portugal

United Kingdom entry: Cry Baby by Jemini

UK position: 26 LAST!

Format: The largest contest to date, boasting 26 nations – a good year to come last and say you finished 26th!

Winning song: EVERYWAY THAT I CAN by Sertab Erener (Turkey)

Nul Points: United Kingdom!

UK maximum: Ireland

Stat: A first victory for Turkey – and the Belgians finished second with a song in a make-believe language! The bottom three had been the top three in 2002!

A short hop from Tallinn south to Riga, and the Latvian capital took its turn to wear the Eurovision hat.

This also proved to be a memorable contest, but for all the wrong reasons as far as the United Kingdom was concerned.

The war in Iraq inflamed the conspiracy theories around an outcome which saw the UK get the big round 'nul points' for the one and only time in its history.

Now I like a conspiracy theory as much as anyone but the denouement was clear from the moment Jemini – Gemma Abbey and Chris Cromby – walked onto the stage.

The song Cry Baby was uninspiring, the singing was dreadful and the performance was crass.

It really had nothing going for it and frankly I would have questioned the credibility of any nation that actually gave it even a single point.

The Liverpool duo died on stage the moment Abbey plunged into the song resoundingly off key.

Jemini were dropped by their record label – they later featured in the Tim Moore book 'Nul Points', Gemma working in a car showroom and Chris (who still sings a bit) plying his trade in a clothes shop.

It was the first year for Ukraine and their mundane offering was obviously just a warm up act for some very big fish to follow.

The jeers rang out for the Russian girls t.A.t.U, who ignored their rehearsal schedule, threatened to behave indecently and flounced around with the worst of them. They won few friends. Good song though.

Austria's Alf Poier appeared with two ladies and four stuffed animals for a healthy dose of eccentricity which won the novelty vote.

Malta's Lynn Chircop was so distressed with her poor finish that she took it out on her management team in a bust up on the plane home.

And it was interesting to note that the top three of 2002 – Latvia, Malta and the UK – were the bottom three of 2003. Where did that leave the political voting?

The very popular winner, long overdue, was Turkey with Sertab's catchy Everyway That I Can and there was a second place for Belgium with a song built around a nonsense language. You couldn't make it up?!

UK OK? Not okay, enough said! The UK affiliation with the invasion of Iraq may have had something to do with it but so too the respective dubious Eurovision star qualities of the hapless Jemini.

The one and only 'nul points' embarrassment co-incided with the one and only time that the Green Room, above the stage, was unveiled to the full glare of those packed into the auditorium.

This was also the largest-ever number of nations appearing in the final prior to the Istanbul shakedown – so to finish 26th in the Eurovision Song Contest is a record that the UK could hold forever!!

EUROVISION JURY TOP 5

1	Everyway That I Can (Sertab Erener)	TUR
2	Ne Verj, Ne Bojsia, Ne Prosi (t.A.t.U)	RUS
3	Open Your Heart (Birgitta)	ICE
4	I'm Not Afraid To Move On (Jostein Hasselgard)	NOR
5	Give Me Your Love (Fame)	SWE

2004

Istanbul, Turkey

15 May

New entrants: Albania, Serbia & Montenegro

Non-qualified: Estonia, Israel, Latvia, Portugal and Slovenia

Return: FYR Macedonia

United Kingdom entry: Hold On To Our Love by James Fox

UK position: 16

Format: With so many countries now wanting to take part, the semi-final was introduced. It featured the worst performing songs in Riga, with the top ten scoring nations qualifiying for the Saturday night final

Winning song: WILD DANCES by Ruslana (Ukraine)

Bottom Marker (final): Norway

UK maximum: Greece

Stat: No points for Eurovision pathfinders Switzerland – in the semis!

Istanbul was the wondrous venue in 2004, the year which saw two contests for the very first time – a semi-final eliminator on the Thursday followed by Saturday's grand final.

James Richard Mullett (aka James Fox) once more flew the flag for Wales with his song Hold On To Our Love.

The song did not fare too well but Fox – who appeared in Fame Academy – has notched some notable entries on his CV. He has sung for the Armed Forces, and has appeared at the House of Commons and the Welsh Assembly.

As well as a supporting role in Jesus Christ Superstar, he has enjoyed a good career in musical theatre and has made a number of television appearances.

His Eurovision song made it into the Top 20 and in 2008 he penned a tribute to his beloved Cardiff City FC reaching the FA Cup Final.

While Fox did not trouble the scorers at the top of the Eurovision table, neither did the rest of the automatic finalists. In fact the top seven were all songs that had come through from the semi-finals.

Ukraine won on only their second appearance, the dynamic and attractive Ruslana blowing away all the opposition with her wild dances.

They were given a good run for their money by Serbia & Montenegro, whose offering Lane Moje definitely struck a chord with the voters.

Greece's Sakis Rouvas wowed the continent with Shake It and Lena Phillipson got physical with her microphone stand singing for Sweden. It Hurts was the song and, yes, it probably did.

UK OK? It was left to Welsh singing hopeful James Fox to lift the UK out of their nadir and he achieved it, although not too convincingly, with 29 points and 16th position in Istanbul.

There were no maximums for James – that may have been a step too far! – although Ireland delivered a friendly eight points.

Ukraine, Serbia & Montenegro and Greece fought out an intriguing battle at the top with the UK reserving their top mark for Sakis Rouvas, the ten straying not too far in the direction of England-based Lisa Andreas who was singing for Cyprus.

EUROVISION JURY TOP 5

1	Wild Dances (Ruslana)	UKR
2	Lane Moje (Zeljko Joksimovic)	SEM
3	Stronger Every Minute (Lisa Andreas)	CYP
4	It Hurts (Lena Philipsson)	SWE
5	Shake It (Sakis Rouvas)	GRE

2005

Kiev, Ukraine
21 May
New entrants: Moldova
Non-qualified: Austria, Belgium, Iceland, Ireland, Netherlands and Poland
Return: Denmark, Hungary, Israel, Latvia and Switzerland
United Kingdom entry: Touch My Fire by Javine
UK position: 22
Format: A contest played out against political protest over the Orange Revolution
Winning song: MY NUMBER ONE by Elena Paparizou (Greece)
Bottom Marker (final): Germany
UK maximum: Greece
Stat: Malta's Chiara is second again and The Big Four becomes the Bottom Four!

Kiev played host to the 50th staging of the Eurovision and the capital of Ukraine certainly went to town in its staging and promotion.

Javine, a contestant on Popstars The Rivals, who narrowly missed out on becoming a member of the smash hit girl band Girls Aloud, was the UK representative in a challenging environment.

Full name Javine Dionne Hylton, from London, Javine found herself up against some sturdy competition to even win the ticket out to the Ukraine.

Up against her in the heats was the garish Jordan, aka Katie Price – reality TV star, supermodel, horse rider, authoress, occasional 'singer'.

Not only that, but the 1996 darling Gina G was back to try and resurrect her career. As for her song and performance, Just A Little Bit it was not.

In spite of a wardrobe malfunction on the night, Javine won through with Touch My Fire.

Blighted by a throat infection in Kiev, she did not give of her best and the song almost apologetically drifted down to the lower reaches of the scoreboard.

It charted at 18 in the UK but will not go down as one of the memorable home entries. All in all it was pretty bland.

Since Eurovision, Javine has reverted back to reality TV and her life has not been without incident.

The Greek winner from Elena Paparizou was popular in the hall and with the voters across Europe but lacked the distinctive edge that is normally associated with any Eurovision winner, be that for good or bad!

Again, many felt Malta – in the unfortunate shape of bridesmaid Chiara – brought the true quality to the competition but post-contest awards for her song from the cognoscenti were scant consolation.

UK OK? A slump in fortunes for the UK and Javine, who had seen off the scary challenge of Jordan, aka Katie Price, in the national final.

She could muster only a handful points, boosted by the inevitable eight from Ireland and a sprinkling of good wishes from Cyprus, Malta and Turkey.

Greece held off a strong challenge from Malta at the top of the tree and the UK vote went to form, with the two top marks going to the top two respectively.

EUROVISION JURY TOP 5

1	My Number One (Elena Paparizou)	GRE
2	Angel (Chiara)	MAL
3	Talking To You (Jakob Sveistrup)	DEN
4	Let Me Try (Luminata Angel & Sistem)	ROM
5	The Silence That Remains (Shiri Maymon)	ISR

2006

Athens, Greece
20 May
New entrants: Armenia
Withdrawals: Serbia and Montenegro
Non-qualified: Albania, Cyprus and Hungary
Return: Finland, Ireland and Lithuania
United Kingdom entry: Teenage Life by Daz Sampson
UK position: 19
Format: Eurovision visits the birthplace of the Olympic Games
Winning song: HARD ROCK HALLELUJAH by Lordi (Finland)
Bottom Marker (final): Malta
UK maximum: Finland
Stat: Finland's very professional novelty act sweeps the board with a monster 292 points! A first win for Finland!

Eurovision's first visit to Greece brought with it some memorable songs and a firecracker of a winner.

Daz Sampson was the commercial dance artist surprisingly chosen by BBC TV viewers to take his cutting edge sound to the foothills of the Acropolis.

Sampson is a Stockport lad, a dance music producer and vocalist who had achieved notable chart success with the band Uniting Nations.

The provocative nature of the performance could well have lost Sampson and his crew votes, providing of course there were votes to be lost in the first place.

The song went down well in the UK charts, peaking at number 8 – the best finish for a UK Eurovision entry since Precious in 1999.

The scary display from the Monsters of Rock, Finnish entry Lordi, did not work against them. Scary they may have been, but this band knew their stuff and they ticked all the boxes in terms of quality, originality and popular appeal.

But, in truth, they were never expected to win Eurovision – do well as a novelty act, yes; but win the thing, no. But win it they did and they won very big, drawing huge votes from every quarter of the continent. Class will out.

While Finland cannot be classed as eastern Europe per se, they are handily positioned to take votes from the Scandinavian, former Soviet and Baltic blocs.

It resulted in Finland's first-ever win and a good number on the world rock music circuit for the band.

There were some good songs this year, but spare a thought for Lithuania's LT United who surely had come up with the novelty song to beat all novelty songs?

We Are The Winners, Of Eurovision ….. not quite. If only they'd invested in some grotesque masks, a stack of pyrotechnics and an air of mystery!

UK OK? Up to the heady heights of 19th for Daz Sampson and his troupe of lovelies but it was clearly getting increasingly different for the UK and other Western European nations to register on the new Eurovision map.

No maximums again for the UK but eight points from….yes, you guessed right… good old Ireland!

Finland won with a massive 292 points, a resounding endorsement for the sheer quality of their act with Russia and Bosnia and Herzegovina their closest rivals. It was novelty time for the UK, with twelve going to the monsters of rock and ten to 'Eurovision winners' Lithuania!

EUROVISION JURY TOP 5

1	Hard Rock Hallelujah (Lordi)	FIN
2	Invincible (Carola)	SWE
3	Tornero (Mihai Traistariu)	ROM
4	No No Never (Texas Lightning)	GER
5	Lejla (Hari Mata Hari)	BOS

2007

Helsinki, Finland
12 May
New entrants: Belarus, Bulgaria, Georgia and Serbia
Non-qualified: Croatia, Denmark, Israel, Malta, Norway and Switzerland
Return: Hungary and Slovenia
United Kingdom entry: Flying The Flag by Scooch
UK position: 22
Format: The semi-final produced ten qualifiers from the east of Europe and the neighbour voting row reached its peak
Winning song: MOLITVA by Marija Serifovic (Serbia)
Bottom Marker (final): Ireland
UK maximum: Turkey
Maximum to UK: Malta
Stat: No matter what was said about the voting, the three strongest songs were those that occupied the top three positions

And so to the UK's golden jubilee Eurovision celebration, where bubblegum pop was carelessly discarded down Helsinki way.

Love it or loathe it, Scooch's Flying The Flag will not be forgotten in a hurry – the bright blue airline uniform, the Union Jack backdrop, the flag-bedecked cabin trolleys, the bottle of Bucks Fizz and the overdose of choreography remains an all-too-vivid memory.

It was a case of too many Steps too far – the UK had entered a song which would have been roundly pilloried had any other nation deigned to submit it as their entry.

Fun it may have been, credible it wasn't – if the UK can't take the contest seriously, why should we expect others to take us seriously. What is the point of going on?

An ironic 12 points came from Malta, otherwise Scooch were relying on some neighbourly voting to keep them off the bottom.

The east European drift in recent years alarmingly tilted full pelt into this contest.

The EBU, while declaring 'crisis, what crisis?' sensibly took steps to iron out what has now become a large geographical malfunction.

Serbia though was a deserving winner, Marija Serifovic and her backing singers delivering a passionate rendition of a simple and beautiful song.

Molitva was however completely ignored by the UK televoters, who presently tend to favour the Greeks and the Turks.

The Russians were once again made to hang on for their first victory while Scooch's quest for the novelty honours were blasted out of the water by Ukraine, who are beginning to make a sizeable impression on the Eurovision stage.

Danzing Lasha Tumbai from Verka Serduchka was overblown silliness from start to finish but the impact factor, so important in Eurovision, was instant and impressive. Danzing!

UK OK? Equal second bottom with the French in Helsinki, what was Eurovision coming to? The seaside humour from Scooch was rather lost on Europe although Malta weighed in with a pointed 12 points, clearly still riled by their semi-final failure.

The only other points for Scooch came from Ireland, although the now traditional eight points on this occasion dropped down to seven.

East Europe dominated from start to finish with Serbia coming home first but strongly challenged by Ukraine and Russia. The UK voters ignored the trend, awarding Serbia zero, and awarding 12 points to Turkey and ten to Greece.

EUROVISION JURY TOP 5

1	Molitva (Marija Serifovic)	SER
2	Danzing Lasha Tumbai (Verka Serduchka)	UKR
3	Song Number One (Serebro)	RUS
4	Shake It Up Shekerim (Kenan Dogulu)	TUR
5	Work Your Magic (Koldun)	BLA

HEAVY ON THE EAR

I set off for Helsinki with a light heart and a heavy ear.

Eurovision has always had the knack of filling me with joyful anticipation but an infection in my left ear, which set in just two days before the great event, had frustratingly reduced my surround sound from stereo to mono.

You might argue this was no bad thing as far as the Eurovision was concerned and, that if I was really lucky, the infection would swiftly sweep its way across to the right ear too.

But I didn't see it that way at all, let alone half hear it. I have always been very fond of Eurovision and could not believe my misfortune. Why had my volume been turned down on the eve of planet earth's greatest musical cheese festival?

A half-hearted syringing and all manner of gurning attempts to clear the aural fuzz proved unsuccessful but I was nevertheless in good voice as a taped collection of contest winners sped me down the motorway from Northampton to London.

Nel Blu Di Pinto Di Blu (although not a Eurovision winner) whisked me past Newport Pagnell service station, Merci Cherie greeted the passage into Hertfordshire and, as I located my Heathrow hotel, the cassette player was belting out the dubious Ding Dinge Dong.

This being the case, I made sure I shut the window quite quickly after negotiating the entrance barrier.

Partial deafness not withstanding, I was in relaxed mood as I checked in to my airport hotel and made my final preparations for the morning flight to darkest Scandinavia.

On boarding the Finn Air flight, it was clear the airline was well into the Eurovision vibe. Johnny Logan's Hold Me Now was being piped through the cabin as I took my seat, in itself a welcome distraction from the impending horrors of the safety demonstration and take-off.

A smooth flight negotiated, the tiresome experience of baggage reclaim was then enlivened by a group of pushy Greeks clearly confident of Sarbel's chances of notching a second win in three years.

Greece and Turkey, once the outsiders of Eurovision, have never had it so good and expect a return to one of the two before too long.

I had never been to Helsinki before but all commentaries on the Finnish capital beforehand had been very encouraging. The three keywords had been 'small', 'clean' and 'healthy'.

The press centre at the Hartwall Areena in Helsinki, the centre of cool

The description 'healthy' stuck with me throughout my visit as I took in the sort of fresh air that you seldom experience in the UK and certainly not in the major cities.

As the airport bus wound its way into the tiny city centre, the scene was festooned with rows of daylight vehicle headlights and roadside flags and there were plenty of Lordi tee-shirts on view.

I left the bus by the railway station, which was about the size of the one in Northampton. Tiny, considering it was serving a north European capital, but the destination boards throwing up a list of unpronounceables certainly made more exciting reading than the one at home.

My hotel was situated handily opposite the Lasipalatsi, a bustling square in the centre which boasted a good-sized screen showing clips of all the action at Eurovision headquarters.

There was just about enough time to shower and change in readiness for the semi-final at the Hartwall Areena, just one stop out of Helsinki Central by rail. The railway link was a considerable blessing as it did away with the usual requirement of chasing buses from the accredited hotels to the venue.

At Eurovision, each country has a delegation comprising artist, entourage, facilitators and media and fans of the contest are also pretty well looked after, with some of them also being accredited.

This enables them to take photos of their favourites during rehearsals and at press conferences, where they join journalists in the quest for information. I don't know of this journalist and fan link being replicated at other sporting and music events and the mix is both frustrating and refreshing in equal measure.

Although there are many who feel this mix is a step too far, there is no denying that Eurovision is inclusive and all followers, working or playing, are pretty well looked after.

Accredited journalists and fans in Helsinki were allowed a free pass on the train to the venue. The short journey saw the train packed with flag-waving fans, with support for Turkey and newcomers Georgia to the fore.

The atmosphere was good-natured, with resident Finns and curious visitors quick to debate the merits of the songs and the chances for the competitors at the upcoming semi-final.

By the doors opposite me stood a tiny chap, distinctively attired in a white chapeau (which covered thin blonde hair), tinted glasses, black leather drainpipe trousers and big buckle shoes.

116

It looked for all the world as if Norway's Eurovision legend famous for 'nul points', Jahn Teigen, was in town. And why wouldn't he be?

Before I managed to get round to making an enquiry, the chap had scuttled out of sight and took the left tunnel towards the arena, while I veered right to the press centre handily situated within walking distance.

First stop was the accreditation centre, where I picked up my necklace press accreditation pass for the event.

And then into the centre itself and, wow, what a revelation! At previous contests, the press areas invariably tended to be a little cramped and hectic but this centre was blessed with Finnish cool.

It represented a huge area, well served with screens and information desks, and littered with comfy bean bags as far as the eye could see.

The workstations were in another large neighbouring room and on the upper level was a sizeable restaurant.

The Finns had done their homework and had got it absolutely right. The whole feel was laid back and so much the better for it.

Slumming down in the nearest bean bag, I found myself among the Swiss support for DJ Bobo, an artist who was highly fancied to do well with his much-promoted Vampires Are Alive.

With 28 songs to get through, it looked like being a long night and thankfully the new format of two semi-finals – introduced the following year in Belgrade – is much more manageable.

The Icelandic contingent across the way warmed up the Swedes as the proceedings got off to a slow start – the Israeli song was not taken seriously, euro pop from Cyprus was not in favour and the jury was out on Belarus.

The Georgian entry was greeted with loud applause and Ukraine's Verka Serduchka (aka Andriy Danylko) found himself in competition with another drag artist, this time DQ (Peter Andersen) who was representing Denmark.

Portugal and Norway both adopted 'comigo/conmigo' in their song title and these easy-going offerings got a few Swiss couples waltzing around the concourse.

Hungary put in a strong performance, the hyped Maltese entry came and went (they wanted it so much), Andorra offered up a breath of fresh air and the Czech Republic sadly had many scuttling for the bars or the loos.

Moldova gave us plenty of raunch, as extensively advertised in the press, and two operatic numbers were offered up for consideration – Latvia and Slovenia.

Iceland delivered a pleasantly understated song and the general view was that Turkey needed to step up to the plate in the final, where they were inevitably headed.

But as it had been the whole fortnight, the good money was flocking across to Serbia and Marija Serifovic did not disappoint.

The Irish song received no applause within the press centre, which didn't augur well, and there was no reaction to UK entrants Scooch either when they were previewed in the run up to the votes being announced.

Talk about a long old night, this certainly looked as if it was going to be a long last few days for the UK and probably for the rest of Western Europe too!

When the results came through, there was a collective sharp intake of breath across the press centre.

Not one western European nation made it through to the final and the likes of Moldova, FYR Macedonia and Georgia surprisingly progressed at the expense of Andorra, Denmark and Switzerland, not forgetting Poland and Portugal.

There were many glazed expressions and much wailing and gnashing of teeth and certainly the delegations of Malta, Switzerland and the Netherlands – amid talk of withdrawal - found the outcome very hard to take.

For me, it was proof that the geographical influence from televoting had become hugely disproportionate. The song was no longer to the fore in the decision-making process and something had to be done about it.

It made me wonder about what we were in for on Saturday night, when the whole of Europe got the chance to vote on the finalists, irrespective of whether the voting nation was in the final or not.

I couldn't stomach the semi-final press conference – the hour was late and I skipped quickly back to the station and into town, where the disquiet among fans was palpable.

The semi-finalists would be hosting a party at a club a short distance from my hotel but it was by invitation only. Just as well, it was time for an 'early' night. It had been a very long day and I wasn't in the mood for dancing.

I spent most of the morning of the day before the contest touring the city centre on a search (which proved to be in vain) for a phone card as the mobile rates were exorbitant.

Then it was on the train to the venue, where I teamed up with a couple of French colleagues who I had known through Eurovision association for several years.

The afternoon brought the first dress rehearsal for those who had made the final, often the best opportunity to scope how the act does on the stage and to assess the all-important impact factor.

The rehearsals are televised so, should a glitch occur in the final transmission on Saturday night, one of the rehearsals will be broadcast instead. Not live, but the show must go on.

Accredited members get good seats for the rehearsals and members of the public can buy tickets for the warm-ups too (naturally at cheaper prices than the tickets for the final) and therefore tap into the Eurovision experience.

The rehearsal is camera heaven for a whole legion of enthusiasts, who bring with them anything from expensive photographic kits or humble mobile phones.

After the dress rehearsal it was over to the press centre for a round of reports, radio interviews back home and a good opportunity to study the form over a beer. Serbia, by this time, had established itself as a strong favourite with Ukraine running it close.

During the evening, great excitement, as tickets were made available for the Eurovision after party, which would take place during the early hours of Sunday morning at a conference hall just down the road from the press centre.

The tickets were available on a 'first come first served' basis and the queues at the information desk were lengthy.

I had a good chat with a Finnish fan clearly enjoying the Lordi legacy and adamant that Finland was not a country of the east but of the north, allied to the other Scandinavian nations.

However, you can see that the edges are blurred, as Finland has both strong Baltic and Russian connections. They should win it more often!

I was then interviewed by a Finnish radio reporter who wanted my view on a lady called Krisse Salminen, a Finnish stand-up comedian and television talk-show hostess who was the master of ceremonies in the Green Room – the stilted part of the contest where the artists are shown relaxing, cheering and speaking nonsense to the prying television camera.

When I first saw Krisse, I thought she was extremely entertaining but, by the end of the event, I felt she had somewhat overplayed her hand and had developed into an irritant.

Media information is routinely displayed in the press centre and it can also be distributed via individual pigeon holes, which, in addition, are receptacles for a wide variety of promotional information from the competing nations.

The mad scramble for such items never ceases to amaze me, also the amount of money which must be spent on what are, for the most part, distinctively average acts.

In this respect, the former Soviet states are the worst offenders and Belarus probably top of the list!

A busy day over, the evening was spent with my French colleagues winding down at a kebab restaurant downtown and we all then attended a Eurovision party night at the Con Hombres bar where the emphasis was clearly on having fun and staying safe.

My left ear was at its fuzziest – providing a new slant on a number of Euro tunes – but thankfully the fuzz had lifted by the time Gina G's classic was belted out.

Flying The Flag got a good reception when it was played and there was airplay too for Bucks Fizz, Nicki French and – biggest surprise of the night – Bardo!

Saturday provided an opportunity to take a good look at Helsinki and while my colleagues had tickets for the show itself, I headed for the press centre after a little light refreshment to watch proceedings from there.

On this occasion, I found myself bean-bagged among the Belarus contingent who enthusiastically supported Koldun, applauded the other former Soviet entries and demonstrated a complete disinterest in anything vaguely west of Minsk.

We almost had a press centre incident when an errant Russian plonked himself in front of a screen, effectively blocking everyone else's view. One of the locals got pretty angry and we came mighty close to steward intervention.

Bulgaria and Moldova showed well, Sweden and France served up a pleasing interlude mid-stream, I hoped that Hungary would do well and Latvia was the popular vote in my text inbox but I felt, as most did, that the title would be between Serbia and the Ukraine.

Ireland came and went, it was a pretty dreadful song and probably the worst entry they have submitted. At least Dustin The Turkey had some novelty value in Belgrade and you have to credit an act that had 'Terry Wogan's wig' as a lyric.

Scooch had some supporters in the hall and there was no denying its fun value but it was never going to be the song to restore UK credibility on the Eurovision map.

An argument against the UK is that recently the nation hasn't been taking the contest seriously and has submitted poor songs.

There is some merit in that argument – more to the point is that the UK has become complacent, in that their place in the final is guaranteed as one of the Big Four.

And I am sure that many voters across Europe are more likely to send votes to nations who have had to fight for their place at the top table.

However, I don't buy into the school of thought that the east has done well because they have put forward better songs.

There have been good songs from both east and west in recent years, but the west has been squeezed out and that is entirely down to the geographical make-up of the competing nations.

Serbia went on to claim its first victory and there was much chest thumping and tickertape to accompany Marija's success.

Greek singer Sarbel relaxes on the bean bags

It was a worthy winner, in spite of considerable criticism from these shores, and the strong songs will always pick up votes from all over the continent.

That said, Helsinki saw Eurovision at a crossroads with the disenfranchised threatening to go their own way but, to their credit, the EBU has listened and has taken initial steps to redress the balance with two semi-finals (Belgrade) and the partial return of jury voting (Moscow).

Flying out of Helsinki late the next morning, I had a brief chat with Icelandic representative Eirikur in the duty free shop. I'd liked his song but the softly-spoken rocker was polite and philosophical about his fate. He did say, however, that he felt he deserved better and amen to that.

THE FINLAND STATION

In this section is a snapshot of the nations that took part in the Eurovision Song Contest in Helsinki in 2007, the United Kingdom's fiftieth participation.

What follows were my personal impressions of the songs and their predicted fortune.

And of course a note as to how they eventually fared, in what turned out to be the most myopic song contest of them all in terms of partisan voting.

I start with the semi-final on Thursday 10 May, featuring no less than 28 nations all bidding for one of ten places on offer in the grand final the following Saturday.

The Finland Station, the rail stop in Helsinki with the Hartwall Areena in the background

1 BULGARIA   Water/Elitsa Todorova and Stoyan Yankoulov

What a bloody racket! A lot of wailing, gnashing of teeth and banging of drums, this song would surely be soon forgotten having had the misfortune to have been drawn first in a very long semi-final. It would not have a prayer. How wrong could you be? It grew on me a little as time wore on and it represents Bulgaria's finest hour at Eurovision.

2 ISRAEL   Push The Button/Teapacks

A lot of hype had surrounded this song as Israel threw in one of their bizarre entries all about pushing the button. It put me in mind of dear old Kojo singing Nuko Pommin (No Bombing) for Finland many moons ago. You have to go nuclear at some point down the Eurovision line. Frenzied activity on the stage but, with little else to commend it, it failed to capitalise on the hype.

3 CYPRUS   Comme Ci Comme Ca/Evridiki

Sung by Evridiki, in the French language at that, I liked the song and it made its way into my list of 2007 favourites. It represented a far from traditional approach from Cyprus and fair play on that score. But like all the other songs in the first ten of the semi, it required a big impact and here it failed. Maybe a Bulgarian crashing drum was required!

4 BELARUS   Work Your Magic/Koldun

Deep intakes of breath from the sizeable Belarusian contingent in the press centre as Dmitri Koldun took to the stage. An early appearance for a song tipped as a possible winner and the striking if somewhat fey Koldun worked his magic on a sound-alike Bond theme. The song irritated the hell out of me though and I really don't know why.

5 ICELAND   Valentine Lost/Eirikur Hauksson

When I first heard this song from the old rocker Eirikur it passed me by but the more I heard it, the more I liked it. I didn't think it was strong enough to trouble the scorers on finals night but its non-qualification was a surprise. I put it down to the early slot and for just being too gentle and unremarkable and its removal from the competition was a shame.

6 GEORGIA   Visionary Dream/Sopho Khalvashi

Plenty of neutrals among the media and fans were getting very excited about Sopho's Visionary Dream, which represented a debut for a nation that like England sports the cross of St George on its national flag. The song itself was strange and the euphoria failed to sweep me up. But geography and novelty got it through to the final.

7 MONTENEGRO   Ajde Kroci/Stevan Faddy

Another debut here from Montenegro, following her declaration of independence from Serbia, but there was never really any good vibe around this entry. A British connection here though too, in that singer Stevan Faddy had Scottish roots. His song never really went anywhere and, all in all, was a turgid affair. I suspected it might sneak through and was glad it didn't.

8 SWITZERLAND   Vampires Are Alive/DJ Bobo

I was sitting among the Swiss media in the press centre and there were very high hopes for DJ Bobo and Vampires Are Alive, which had been slickly promoted and, like Belarus, was tipped to go strong. On the CD, the song sounded really good; this didn't quite translate live and there was little going on around it but nevertheless it was a travesty that it failed to qualify.

9 MOLDOVA   Fight/Natalia Barbu

I hated this song with a vengeance. It didn't have anything to commend it and it needed all of Natalia Barbu's outrageous dress sense and feminine wiles to keep the attention of the rest of Europe outside of wider Transyllvania. She was actually scarier than DJ Bobo's vampires. And somehow it bloody well qualified?

10 NETHERLANDS   On Top Of The World/Edsilia Rombley

Every year I feel sorry for the Netherlands, one of the stalwart nations of the Eurovision. Like the UK, they have by and large presented acceptable songs in recent years but nothing which really grabs you from the off. Even the wonderful Edsilia Rombley could not pull a qualification out of the hat. Great singer, but the song wasn't up to scratch.

11 ALBANIA   Hear My Plea/Frederik Ndoci feat Aida

Hear My Plea was the song from Albania and thankfully the voters did as it failed to make the cut. Really at a loss as to what to say about this apart from bring back Anjeza Shahini and quickly! I hope Albania can bounce back into contention before too long but they won't do it any time soon if they bring along stuff like this.

12 DENMARK   Drama Queen/DQ

DQ, aka Peter Andersen, was tipped to take this schlager song sailing into the semis but promptly joined Switzerland in the 'surprise elimination' box. You couldn't fault DQ's profile during the Eurovision week, even after failing to reach the final. I would have liked to have seen some more glitter and sequins on the Saturday night.

13 CROATIA   Vjerujem U Ljubav/Dragonfly feat Dado Topic

A middling song that pottered along from its middling placing in the semi-final draw and even the Balkan bounce wasn't big enough to ensure there was a serious regional rival to Serbia in the final. For me, one of the most forgettable songs and not Croatia's finest hour – compounded of course by the result on Saturday!

14 POLAND   Time To Party/The Jet Set

I quite liked this entry from the Jet Set and was disappointed that it had narrowly failed to make the cut when the semi-final placings were finally announced. I fancy Poland was also squeezed out by the eastern bloc vote, as it has no natural affinity with the former Soviet nations or with the Balkans and cannot rely on a regional boost.

15 SERBIA Molitva/Marija Serifovic

When I first saw Marija she reminded me of one of the Krankies, a Scots comedy duo from another age; when I first heard her, I wasn't automatically taken. But the song built throughout the week – a bit like Fly On The Wings Of Love in 2000 – and became a firm favourite with the fans. It was Serbia's year and deservedly so.

16 CZECH REPUBLIC   Mala Dama/Kabat

Talk about after the Lord Mayor's Show – the Czech Republic's debut entrant opened promisingly enough from an instrumental standpoint, only for the singer to then open his mouth. Oh no! It was a dreadful introduction for the Czechs and it finished bottom of the pile, again deservedly so and they can only do better.

17 PORTUGAL   Danca   Comigo   (Vem   Ser   Feliz)/ Sabrina

This one had them dancing around the colourful bean bags in the press centre and there were high hopes of a rare strong showing from Portugal, who are very much the poor relations of Eurovision and are still waiting for their first victory. But as soon as the shape of the voting came through, you knew this one was doomed. Squeezed out, like Poland.

18 FYR MACEDONIA Mojot Svet/Karolina Goceva

How in heaven's name did this song qualify? If you want an example of the powers of bloc voting, then Macedonia is it. They really have never presented an outstanding song – Athens was probably their strongest offering – but always qualify. Here it happened again and now the natives really were getting restless.

19 NORWAY   Ven A Bailar Conmigo/Guri Schanke

Not to be confused with Portugal's Comigo, this was a pleasant enough ditty from good old Norway which meandered tunefully along for three minutes. But this was to prove a poor old year for Scandinavia at the Finland Station; indeed, as powerful new voting blocs strengthen in the east, the oldest one in the north looked to be on the way out.

20 MALTA   Vertigo/Olivia Lewis

Plenty of hype, plenty of hope but Olivia Lewis's Vertigo never reached the heights, never reached the final and sent the entire Maltese delegation into a violent spin. The song was okay but nothing more and I wasn't that gutted when Malta's name was not read out. A good spin-off for Scooch in the final – 12 ironic points from Valetta!

21 ANDORRA   Salvem Al Mon/Anonymous

This song woke everyone up - a fresh sound for Eurovision from a tiny country deserving its moment in the sun. A place late in the semi-final order beckoned qualification but, surprise surprise, Andorra too was squeezed out of the reckoning. Anonymous remained exactly that, the final had been deprived of a youthful spark and, all in all, a terrible injustice.

22 HUNGARY   Unsubstantial Blues/Magdi Rusza

Another cracking song from a nation not accustomed to hitting the heights and at least Unsubstantial Blues and that portable bus stop did make it through into the final round. In my mind, this song stood out from much of the rest of the field and Magdi Rusza certainly did her country proud. Hungary's best by a mile!

23 ESTONIA   Partners In Crime/Gerli Padar

Once more, this was a song that was pleasant enough but did not stand out although, like Norway and Portugal before, it did benefit from some audience participation which showed that observers were still awake on what was turning out to be a very long evening. If you compare it to Estonia's recent standards, this was a decent effort.

24 BELGIUM   Love Power/Krazy Mess Groovers

The Krazy Mess Groovers and their zany Love Power was likened to the style of UK chart sensation Mika but it wasn't enough to take them to the top of the charts and into the final. There were plenty worse songs than this but then again some that were infinitely better and this never really had a fighting chance of getting through.

25 SLOVENIA   Cvet Z Juga/Alenka Gotar

So many people hated this and given that here was another potential Balkan shoo-in, I really should have complied with the general consensus. But while I didn't love it, I actually quite liked it and felt it squared up effectively to the other operatic offering from Latvia. So I was pleased it qualified, you can't have enough high-brow!

26 TURKEY   Shake It Up Shekerim/Kenan Dogulu

You can always rely on the Turks to come up with a half decent song and there was never any doubt that this had the potential to go far. While not as impactive on stage as it might have been, Shake It Up Shekerim ticked plenty of boxes and was blessed with a good semi-final draw and there were no problems with this song qualifiying.

27 AUSTRIA   Get Alive, Get A Life/Eric Papilaya

Nearly there, and the penultimate song came from dear old Austria and it as good as sank without trace. It just wasn't the right song at the right time and ticked no boxes, apart from the one that you may just remember it because it was on near the end. But it helps if you have a hook and a presence and this had neither.

28 LATVIA   Questa Notte/Bonaparti.lv

Final song, which can be a blessing in the world of televoting but, with 28 songs in this running of the Eurovision semi-final handicap (as Sir Terry Wogan might say), it can also be a curse. Thankfully, the top hats and tenors went down a storm and Questa Notte – thank goodness for some Italian – cantered through.

My ten personal favourites (in running order):

03 Cyprus, 05 Iceland, 08 Switzerland, 15 Serbia, 17 Portugal, 21 Andorra, 22 Hungary, 25 Slovenia, 26 Turkey and 28 Latvia

My ten tips for the final (in running order):

08 Switzerland, 12 Denmark, 13 Croatia 15 Serbia, 20 Malta, 21 Andorra, 23 Estonia, 24 Belgium, 25 Slovenia, 26 Turkey

And the ten songs that were actually voted through (in running order):

01 Bulgaria, 04 Belarus, 06 Georgia, 09 Moldova, 15 Serbia, 18 FYR Macedonia, 22 Hungary, 25 Slovenia, 26 Turkey and 28 Latvia

And so to the running order for the final which was staged on Saturday 12 May, with 24 nations vying for the Eurovision crown.

1 BOSNIA AND HERZEGOVINA RijekaBezImena/ Marija Sestic

Top of the shop for Bosnia and Herzegovina, opening the final is a traditionally difficult slot. You can win from this position but you have to have a real show-stopper of a song. This one never really registered and was quite a lame offering following the success of Lejla in Athens. I was confident this wouldn't trouble the scorers.

POSITION: 11

2 SPAIN I Love You Mi Vida/D'Nash

Automatic final qualification from Spain but the dreaded number two slot beckoned. The portents were not good, no-one has ever won from this slot. D'Nash were lively enough but Take That they were not. The song was a typical Euro pastiche. It might pick up a few points here and there but it wouldn't reverse Spain's recent dismal ESC fortunes.

POSITION: 20

3 BELARUS Work Your Magic/Koldun

There was plenty of money riding on the Koldun but I never really fancied it. An early draw was also bad news in terms of sustaining an impact, although the singer did a good job in this regard. So near but yet so far.

POSITION: 6

4 IRELAND They Can't Stop The Spring/Dervish

Dear old Ireland were also out front and this with a pretty dire tinkly tinkly song which amounted to one of the weakest contributions ever from the Eurovision royals. I couldn't see this picking up anything and another year of reflecting on past glories beckoned. The song did not go anywhere and had little to commend it.

POSITION: 24

5 FINLAND Leave Me Alone/Hanna Pakarinen

The hosts were also up in the first quarter of the show and in danger of being lost to the televoters. A decent enough rocky number from the sombre Hana Pakarinen, a difficult one this for the Finns because just how could you possibly follow Lordi? It was an okay song, but the best it could hope for was a place somewhere in the middle of the field.

POSITION: 17

6 FYR MACEDONIA   Mojot Svet/Karolina Goceva

The fact that this song made it to the final says everything you need to know about the disproportionate power of voting blocs in the Balkans. To call this ordinary would be kind. I hoped it would sink without trace.

POSITION: 14

7 SLOVENIA   Cvet Z Juga/Alenka Gotar

On the other hand, this song from Slovenia, not too far from Macedonia, was much more worthy. I was pleased that this managed to get through and I hoped its early slot would not prove too much of a disadvantage.

POSITION: 15

8 HUNGARY   Unsubstantial Blues/Magdi Rusza

This song grew and grew on me, a wonderful slow burner from Hungary and I did hope that Magdi would do well, with or without her beloved bus stop. Could have done with a later draw but surely class will out?

POSITION: 9

9 LITHUANIA   Love Or Leave/4 Fun

Like Finland, Lithuania had a hard act to follow from Athens and this shadowy offering did eschew some appeal, although it was limited in terms of the number of votes it actually attracted. The disapora vote ensured some support from the west but the song was also going to be an also-ran in this particular handicap.

POSITION: 21

10 GREECE   Yassou Maria/Sarbel

The Greeks always put in a good shift when it comes to supporting their acts at Eurovision and Sarbel's popular appeal was there for all to see. His up-tempo number was one of the favourites and was sure to get votes from all over the continent. His stage demeanour was confident and impressive and I had this in my top five.

POSITION: 7

11 GEORGIA Visionary Dream/Sopho Khalvashi

I couldn't really see the appeal of this song, which was too screechy for me, but the euphoria attached to Georgia's debut appeared to sweep it through. It could do well with the bloc vote, but again that would be unfair.

POSITION: 12

12 SWEDEN The Worrying Kind/The Ark

When I first heard this song during the previews, I was convinced Sweden was on to another winner but unfortunately the package did not quite come off on stage. I liked the retro feel, which transported me back to the 1970s, the draw was reasonable but technically it was not the slickest operation and it cost the band dearly. Loved Ola's look though!

POSITION: 18

France's Les Fatals Picards caught off guard

13 FRANCE L'Amour A La Francais/Les Fatals Picards

Another wonderfully quirky song, this was one section of the contest not to forsake for either refreshment or a toilet stop. The colourful group represented a breath of fresh air from previous French entries. However, although popular in the hall, the curse of the Big Four struck once again and it found itself near the bottom of the pile, which was dreadfully unfair.

POSITION: 22

14 LATVIA Questa Notte/Bonaparti.lv

Here come the men with top hats, last up in the semi-final draw and handily placed for the final. This song was tremendously popular in the UK, not though across the rest of the continent.

POSITION: 16

15 RUSSIA
Song Number 1/
Serebro

This song represented a serious threat to the favourites Serbia, three good-looking girls who were dressed provocatively and singing a contemporary number. The bass was too overpowering for my liking but it ticked a lot of boxes and grew into a major contender during the week. After all, Russia surely has got to win this thing before too long?

POSITION: 3

Ukraine sensation Verka Serduchka in full effect

16 GERMANY   Frauen Regier'n Die Welt/Roger Cicero

A pleasant and competent departure from the old order by Germany and Roger Cicero deserved rather better, had it not been for the west having their pips well and truly squeezed. The genre may well have been lost on traditional Eurovision voters, but well done Germany for being bold with the selection. And a name check for David Beckham and Bill Clinton too!

POSITION: 19

17 SERBIA   Molitva/Marija Serifovic

A great draw for Serbia, which gave the song every chance of victory and it clearly struck a chord with fans from all over the continent. Fortune favoured this classy ballad which was sung in Serbo-Croat!

POSITION: 1

18 UKRAINE   Danzing Lash Tumbai/Verka Serduchka

But hold on, here's drag artist Verka Serduchka with a song that had the potential to blow much of what had gone before out of the water. With a quarter of the songs to go, this is a good place in the running order to be. Verka certainly succeeded on impact. A big ham favourite in the hall and discos across Helsinki, this manic tinfoil creation could very well win!

POSITION: 2

19 UNITED KINGDOM   Flying The Flag (For You)/Scooch

And which act had the great misfortune to follow the great Serifovic and Serduchka? Dear old Scooch, I'm afraid. While a favourable draw, you wouldn't want to follow the barnstormer of the evening, especially if you have a gimmick or two of your own up your sleeve. But that was Scooch's fate, and the result is history. The bubblegum came unstuck big time.

POSITION: 23

20 ROMANIA   Liubi, Liubi, I Love You/Todomondo

Another silly song in a run of silliness as the contest approached its end and this kitsch offering would, like Scooch before it, also struggle to get off the ground. Romania, while in the east, are struggling to make an impact on the Eurovision as they have few natural allies. They need an outstanding song, this was not it.

POSITION: 13

21 BULGARIA   Water/Elitsa Todorova and Stoyan Yankoulov

For me this was the surprise package of the entire contest. Having survived a poor draw in the semi-final, an impactive performance was blessed with a good place in the final running order and delivered Bulgaria's best Eurovision result.

POSITION: 5

22 TURKEY   Shake It Up Shekerim/Kenan Dogulu

You can never discount Turkey thanks to the good spread of televotes they are guaranteed from all corners of Europe, especially when they have a decent song and a decent draw. With Greece, surely a top five finish beckoned?

POSITION: 4

23 ARMENIA
Anytime You Need/Hayko

I didn't think I would but I quite liked this song, preferring it to Andre's debut the year before in Athens. Although as a ballad it didn't pull up any trees, the performance was pleasingly simple and the backdrop was stunning. The penultimate place in the running order is always a good place to be and it certainly stuck in my mind when it came to casting the old votes.

POSITION: 8

Russ Spencer in philosophical mood

24 MOLDOVA   Fight/
Natalia Barbu

Last, and for me anyway pretty much least, came Moldova which to my mind, like Macedonia, had deprived a nation like Andorra of a place at the top of the table. Blessed with a good draw and extremely good fortune!

POSITION: 10

My ten personal favourites (in running order):
07 Slovenia, 08 Serbia, 11 Hungary, 12 Sweden, 13 France, 15 Russia, 16 Germany, 18 Ukraine, 22 Turkey, 23 Armenia

My top ten tips (in running order):
03 Belarus, 07 Slovenia, 08 Serbia, 10 Greece, 11 Hungary, 12 Sweden, 15 Russia, 18 Ukraine, 22 Turkey, 23 Armenia

The actual top ten (in running order):
03 Belarus, 08 Serbia, 10 Greece, 11 Hungary, 15 Russia, 18 Ukraine, 21 Bulgaria, 22 Turkey, 23 Armenia, 24 Moldova

A SPOT OF TURBULENCE!

WHEN Sir Terry Wogan announced the Making Your Mind Up winner and the act that would represent the United Kingdom in the 2007 Eurovision Song Contest, I confess to feeling a distinct sense of relief.

This lasted for all of a split second as Sir Terry had somehow got it wrong, requiring co-presenter Fearne Cotton to intervene and issue the correct information.

And this in turn was met with a sense of disbelief and borderline despair as Scooch, and not Cyndi, stepped up to fly their very own flag in Helsinki.

Natalie Powers plays on the Lasipalatsi big screen.

Now I'm normally partial to a large chunk of cheese but the blue airline uniforms and the camp routine did not float my boat. Or fly my plane for that matter.

There was no denying that Flying The Flag had more gimmicks than you could throw a bottle of bucks fizz at and that their performance was eye catching and polished.

And that the group certainly threw themselves into the whole Eurovision thing, waving the red, white and blue with gusto.

But the innuendo was cringe worthy and the song tried to tick so many boxes, ignoring the fact that most continental observers would have been none the wiser as to what they were signing up to.

The entry, quite simply, was the sort of offering that Britons would have sneered out of court had one of our hapless European brethren put it forward.

It was a retrograde step, at a time when the United Kingdom was struggling to find its footing on the increasingly precarious Eurovision landscape. It was not our finest hour and another 'nul points' beckoned.

As it transpired, Scooch – Russ Spencer, David Ducasse, Caroline Barnes and Natalie Powers - put heart and soul into their Helsinki experience. The song, while receiving a luke-warm reception at rehearsals, nevertheless attracted a cult following among some of the fans.

And the United Kingdom's golden jubilee entry picked up 19 points on the final night – seven from the trusty Irish and a surprise 'douze points' from Malta who, unhappy that their fancied song had failed to get past the semi-final stage, decided to play the irony card and vote for a 'neighbour'.

At the Eurovision after-party, flight captain Russ Spencer gamely made an appearance while the rest of the crew stayed in quarters.

Catching the eye of the Andorran boy band Anonymous in the vast hangar of an exhibition hall a short hop from the Hartwall Areena contest venue, he shouted: "They all f****** hate us."

I'm not sure that is the case, it is too simplistic an argument. However there are plenty who subscribe to that view and, it has to be said, since the invasion of Iraq in 2003 the United Kingdom's Eurovision hopefuls have all flopped.

Russ was a little more considered during an interview in the aftermath of contest a couple of days later.

Chatting to the BBC alongside David and Natalie, he said: "At least Malta love us. But it quickly became obvious as the voting unfolded that we were only going to be going in one direction so we hit the champagne and got on with enjoying the show.

"We had such a good time in Helsinki. We didn't let the voting nonsense spoil it, it was a great event to be involved in and I'd happily go through it all again.

"I think the United Kingdom goes into Eurovision now hoping that somehow it will be different and that people will go and vote for the song and not for the country. But it isn't going to happen.

"Ukraine, with Verka Serduchka, put in an act which resembled an aluminium-clad tellytubby.

"We could have put in the same act and we'd still have finished second from bottom, I'm convinced of that. We could have put Elton John forward, he wouldn't have won."

Scooch celebrated a UK top five single in the UK with Flying The Flag, which at least struck a chord with the home voters.

And this outcome, an extremely positive one for a contest entrant that finished second bottom, was enough to convince the quartet that project Eurovision – the result apart – had indeed been worthwhile.

The chart position actually equalled the band's previous best finish, back in the year 2000, when More Than I Need To Know reached the same position.

And it was the best placing for a Eurovision song in the UK charts for ten years since Katrina and the Waves peaked at number three.

Fondly described as a bubblegum dance group, Scooch actually formed in October 1998 after attending auditions for an 'all singing, all dancing' pop group in front of the noted song writers and producers Mike Stock and Matt Aitken (minus Pete Waterman) and their future manager, Steve Crosby.

They were signed in 1999 to Accolade, the pop imprint of EMI-Parlophone, and the group set about creating their image and sound.

The group's name actually comes from a term used to ask someone to move up or along a bench or sofa. Scooch! Not a word that had ever formed part of my vocabulary before!

The group won a contest on BBC 1's Saturday morning show Live & Kicking and competed against a boy band to have their single released.

Even though the bands were already formed, this contest was unique as it pre-dated the format of the first music talent reality show to be aired in the United Kingdom – ITV's Pop Stars (year 2000), from which the band Hear'Say was created.

Scooch's debut single – When My Baby – charted within the Top 40 and this prompted a tour supporting the Irish girl band B*Witched, during which they promoted their second and biggest single More Than I Need To Know – which was released globally and hit the top of the charts in Japan.

There followed a support tour for boy band Five, which spawned their third single The Best Is Yet To Come, and the group followed this up by recording their debut album Welcome To The Planet Pop.

Japan was obviously the place to be for Scooch as the album made the Top 20 there and the number one hit More Than I Need To Know actually featured in the video game DDRMAX2: Dance Revolution 7thMix.

Single number four was the flamenco-inspired For Sure – which made number 15 – but the second album proved a disappointment and, in light of this, the band were dropped by their record label and privately split.

In February 2007, Scooch re-formed for their Eurovision bid and won the Making Your Mind Up UK selection in a sing off against a ballad against the French-connected Cyndi, registering 53 per cent of the public vote to book their passage to Helsinki.

Russ Spencer bemoaned the domination of Eastern Europe which prevailed in Finland. He added: "It was a big surprise when Malta failed to qualify for the final and Denmark and Switzerland, favourites in the run up to the competition, also didn't get through.

"We thought that the Danish act, DQ, had a great song. But not one western European nation qualified from the semis, so something wasn't quite right there.

"We wore pink airline suits for the promo of Flying The Flag but we switched to electric blue for the competition because we felt it went better with our spray-on tans!

"And we toyed with the idea of getting a giant colourful flag on the backdrop of our set but that didn't quite work so we settled on an arrangement of colourful dots and no flag. We made quite a few changes to the set and the routine during the rehearsals in Finland.

"It was quite a gay look and of course Eurovision has a massive gay following. We had a great response from the fans while were in Helsinki and a big thank you from us all for that, it was much appreciated.

"Throughout the rehearsals we were so 'on it'. We were delighted to represent United Kingdom at Eurovision and we remain grateful to everyone who voted for us to give us the opportunity.

"We actually missed the maximum 12 points from Malta when it was first announced because we were still at that point celebrating the seven from Ireland! And we didn't see the Serbian winner coming. That was a surprise to us, although David liked the song.

"Helsinki was a lovely city, really clean and spacious and you could really taste the fresh air! The people were really welcoming and they really embraced the Eurovision and that was quite an eye-opener for all of us.

"The United Kingdom would not have embraced the contest the way that the Finns did. It was a big thing for Finland, as they had won the Eurovision for the first time the year before.

"We tend to take a rather negative view of what is after all a fun competition and that wasn't the case in Helsinki."

A rather personalised negative view flew Scooch's way in the shape of Welsh songbird Charlotte Church, who claimed they were not worthy of entering the song contest.

In a video blog, released six weeks before the contest, the singer turned TV presenter referred to Flying The Flag as "absolute s***" and an embarrassment for the United Kingdom.

She added rather forcefully that she felt that Cyndi should have won Making Your Mind Up instead.

Scooch's Natalie quickly hit back, saying: "As a mother of a young child myself, I found her behaviour and language quite unacceptable. What kind of role model was she for a mum-to-be?"

And Russ chipped in: "What a pity the voice of an angel has acquired the mouth of a sewer."

Which rather neatly put Ms Church in her place, but within a matter of days, a Swedish singer by the name of Pandora was also on Scooch's case.

She claimed that the chorus of Flying The Flag was a clear-cut case piece of plagiarism of the chorus to her song No Regrets, which was released in 1999.

With the help of the Swedish Musicians' Union, she later contacted the European Broadcast Union in an attempt to have Scooch's entry disqualified from the competition.

In response, the BBC issued a statement confirming the Scooch song as an original and that the writers had never been aware of Pandora or her songs and there was therefore no duplication of her work.

In April, Scooch signed up with the Warner Bros record label and, as part of the contract, the group recorded several different language versions of Flying The Flag in which the phrases in the song are spoken in French, German, Spanish, Danish and……. Bulgarian!

This ploy also attracted some controversy on many internet forums. Despite claiming the voices in the tracks were their own, many correspondents felt that the voices were not the foursome but native speakers of the languages.

In any event it was a dubious ploy and resulted in no points from France, Germany, Spain, Denmark and even Bulgaria!

After Eurovision, Scooch announced that although they were staying together as a group, they had no plans to produce new material as they were too busy.

Three of the individual members announced that they would be concentration on the theatre – Russ, a television presenter, went on to play The Child Catcher in Chitty Chitty Bang Bang, Caroline continued her role in The Producers and David, a teacher and talent spotter in the north-east of England, took on the lead character in Jack And The Beanstalk.

Natalie, whose hopes of a career in music nosedived when two single releases missed the top 200, returned to family duties.

So there you have it, the rise and fall of Scooch and the rather bumpy ride into Eurovision history.

The flight was certainly an eventful one but Flying The Flag was not the best way for the United Kingdom to celebrate the big 5-0.

Would you like something to suck on for landing sir?

I think not!

HEADS ON THE BLOC

SO we've had 50 years of the United Kingdom in Eurovision. But will the Eurovision Song Contest last for another half century?

And if it does stand the test of the time, will the United Kingdom still be flying the flag for a centenary celebration?

To discuss the whys and wherefores of Eurovision – past, present and future – three of the contest's main players in recent years came to the table to discuss some of the major talking points.

Kevin Bishop was BBC Television's executive producer of the Eurovision Song Contest for many years up until his retirement, alongside that of Sir Terry Wogan, after the Belgrade contest in 2008.

For many of the recent contests, Kevin stood shoulder to shoulder to the United Kingdom's Head of Delegation, Dominic Smith, who stepped down the year previously.

And they were joined in discussion by the man they did most of their recent business with – the European Broadcasting Union's progressive Eurovision Song Contest executive supervisor, Svante Stockselius.

So will Eurovision last the test of time?

Svante: "I honestly must say yes, I think it will still be there in one way or another."

But will it remain a song contest? Many people argue that Eurovision is no longer a song contest.

Svante: "I see no contradictions here. We are producing a television show, not a radio programme. Of course the song is important, but so too is the act and the performance. It is a whole package of entertainment."

Under the Swede's stewardship, the EBU has been actively pursuing world domination through the Eurovision Song Contest format.

But how realistic is the prospect of the event being embraced by the diverse and disparate continents of America, Australasia and Africa?

Svante: "I think it is quite possible that we will see a World Song Contest within the near future and we have already sold contest rights to Asia."

Kevin: "I understand the keenness of the EBU to expand the contest onto a global stage but I think that is a tough ask.

"We've seen how American Idol, for example, is struggling for a foothold and I'm not so sure Eurovision could manage it."

There is no doubting, however, the enduring popularity of the contest on the ever-expanding continent of Europe.

And nowhere is the contest more popular (but please don't shout it from the roof tops, or as Sir Terry Wogan might say 'keep it down to a dull roar') than in the United Kingdom.

Kevin: "We get 11 million viewers and the biggest televote of all the competing nations, so in those terms Eurovision is extremely popular in the UK.

"Much of the show's continuing success has to be down to the fact that Sir Terry Wogan was at the helm of our broadcasts for 28 years.

"The concerns over charging around phone-in programmes have led us to dropping the SMS element of the televote.

"But we are very pleased with the way Eurovision is received in this country. The viewers keep it going."

Dominic: "On a personal note, it is nice now to once more relax and watch the thing again without having the role of Head of Delegation.

"It has helped me remember why I love Eurovision. The contest has a special format which is not matched in quite the same way elsewhere.

"Take the complexity of the staging and the lighting, there is now nothing on television with the same scale and complexity.

"Most people are cynical about it beforehand but when they actually sit down to watch it they inevitably get drawn in and love it.

"There is a real sense of occasion of being at Eurovision; a slightly utopian feeling of nations coming together and through it I've made some good friends all over Europe.

"The fans turn out from all over and they tend to be true protagonists of Europe. They are accredited to turn up at press conferences and among them you tend to get quite a few stattos and nerds.

"Their questions can be quite off the wall, and often not at all helpful, like.... we have done a poll and your song is the 19th best in the contest. I mean ....great, how was I supposed to turn that into a 'positive' for the poor act?!

"There are always lots of British and German fans at Eurovision and the fans do help make the contest what it is – a fun and inclusive event.

"Some countries do send 'proper' journalists to cover the event in depth. But in the UK, we have to fight hard to stir up press interest – most of it comes from listings magazines."

The BBC's Eurovision year is shoe-horned into two frenetic phases around the national selection, staged early in the year, and then two weeks at the contest in May.

Kevin: "As the national broadcaster, we oversee the selection and the presentation of the United Kingdom entry.

"The producer for the show is appointed and a lot of work then goes into getting the CD together, promoting the song and getting word out to the record companies.

"But we have to work on the basis that our Eurovision budget decreases by around five per cent each year."

The Head of Delegation has an all-encompassing job on his or her hands and has to oversee virtually every aspect of the Eurovision experience.

Dominic: "It really gets underway with preparation for the national selection, best known as the Song For Europe, and we then spend about eight concentrated weeks working on the national final and then two weeks at the contest itself.

"If a large band gets the nomination to represent the nation that can be a big organisational test for everyone involved.

"The Head of Delegation is required to attend delegate meetings where the EBU regale us with the regulations they are looking to push through and appraise us of all kinds of policy matters.

"That person is also responsible for organising the hotels in the host city, ensuring that everything was in order with costume demands, looking after the needs of the performers and their entourage and managing the press.

"The role would also involve giving media training to the performers to make sure they knew what to expect from the journalists at the event.

"Also to ensure they were always all singing, all dancing and all sparkling in front of the cameras, selling the Eurovision experience. I have to say this was not always easy as this approach did not always sit readily alongside Sir Terry's take on the song contest!

"Then there were the seemingly reams of paperwork, making sure nothing is overlooked as regards copyright and the like.

"And last but by no means, the Head Of Delegation has to ensure that the fans are appropriately catered for in terms of what they would like to do.

"It was enjoyable but I had done the job long enough and I am happy to have moved on and to have handed the baton over to someone else."

The contest format is forever changing in light of the increasing numbers of European nations falling over themselves to get in on the Eurovision act, with the notable exception of Italy which has never ever been able to play a full part in this form of musical union.

Fundamental changes occurred in the run up to the 2008 event in Serbia, with the introduction of two semi-finals – off limits to only the host nation and the major financial player nations France, Germany, Spain and the United Kingdom (collectively known as 'The Big Four').

Kevin: "We're happy with the new format. It did provide us with a few logistical problems though as both semi-finals have quite a lengthy duration.

"As they are scheduled for a Tuesday and Thursday, it meant they would be up against Eastenders and we couldn't move Eastenders from its normal time. Happily we were able to schedule both semis in full on BBC3, leaving the final showpiece on BBC1."

Dominic: "The new structure seems okay and I'm glad the semis are not both taking place on the same day.

"The organisers have recognised the problems created by neighbour voting in recent years and the concerns that have been raised.

"They have had to make subtle changes to address this and I think they are taking exactly the right approach, given how damaging the reality or perception that neighbourly voting occurs is for the contest.

"On the subject of the voting in Helsinki in 2007, I still can't believe that Scooch got 12 points from Malta.

"I know Malta was unhappy at not making the final and they made big noises about the unfairness of the voting. Their maximum vote for the United Kingdom had to be ironic!"

Eurovision fans have broadly welcomed the move to two semis but an argument persists that a free draw should have been rejected in favour of one that split the nations into west Europe and east Europe groupings.

Svante: "I cannot agree with that. The aim of the Eurovision Song Contest is to unite Europe, not to divide it. We have had enough of iron curtains on this continent."

Voting in the semi-finals is essentially restricted to those nations actually competing, with the automatic finalists allowed to vote on one of the semi-finals by means of a draw allocation.

Why then is voting on the final open to all nations who entered the contest, irrespective of whether or not they made the final or not?

Svante: "In the semi-finals I think it is fair to place restrictions but the final is a showpiece and should be open for all participating countries of that year, whether they qualify for the final or not.

"How could you maintain the interest for the final in the countries that have been eliminated, if their viewers are not allowed to vote?"

A fair point, but does that regulation not still leave the Eurovision Song Contest open to claims of bloc voting, where certain clusters of nations wield a disproportionate voting power that can effectively influence the final places, as has been the case in recent years?

I mean, how great a concern to the future of the Eurovision – and the spirit of fair play – is the bloc voting that clearly takes place between Scandinavian, Baltic, Balkan and the former Soviet nations?

Svante: "I wouldn't call it block voting, I call it neighbour voting. And this is not so surprising.

"An artist might also be a star in a neighbouring country, the song might be in the charts in that country, the language might be the same and the musical traditions might be shared."

Televoting has proved an appealing feature, and not least profitable to the Eurovision coffers. But isn't that largely down to abuse, because of multiple voting?

Svante: "No, televoting is 100 per cent democratic. But we also feel that a balance of mixed voting with professional experts, which we have introduced for the 2009 contest, can balance the televoting in a creative way.

"The juries will have the chance to listen more times to the songs and juries can limit the diaspora factor."

It is difficult to argue against that standpoint but splinter nation states, creating voting blocs, and the advent of televoting have conspired to skew the results of semi-finals and finals at the contest.

The concept was certainly accentuated in Helsinki 2007, where neighbour voting advanced songs from the east of Europe at the expense of those from the west.

Consider the United Kingdom, whose voters cannot vote for their home country.

If, however, the United Kingdom splintered and competed as England, Northern Ireland, Scotland and Wales, then each of these nations, potentially, would have 36 more points from 'home' voters than the United Kingdom before it.

In the same vein, consider the former Yugoslavia.

Instead of the former Yugoslavia, we now have Bosnia and Herzegovina, Croatia, the Former Yugoslav Republic of Macedonia, Montenegro, Serbia and Slovenia.

All these countries can now reasonably expect to benefit from large points totals from their neighbours. And the fate of Yugoslavia before the splintering set in? A big fat zero!

Neighbour voting is inevitable, a fact of life – but could the voting system be moderated in some way to ensure that all the big points are not spread around all the members of a certain voting bloc?

It wouldn't have a dramatic effect on the influence generated by neighbour voting but the introduction of an element of fair play may sit more comfortably with critics clearly disconcerted by the emerging predictability of the scoreboard composition.

Wouldn't it go some way to ensuring that the fun of the voting is not replaced by farce?

Svante: "Firstly, I think this system would be very hard to explain. Secondly this would mean implementing censor-like restrictions to a democratic method of voting."

In fairness, the EBU has tacitly acknowledged they have a problem and have introduced changes to help address it although the argument is that they still have not gone far enough.

Svante: "We are moving back to juries which were used before as back-up if something went wrong with the televoting.

"They have a bigger direct impact once more and we believe that the balance between juries and televoting will now be more vital."

The United Kingdom, while acknowledging the popular unrest around it, has maintained a diplomatic line on the controversy over the voting system.

Kevin: "What I would say about the voting is that every year, when we open the phone lines to the public, the United Kingdom wins our vote! Even though we make it abundantly clear that viewers cannot vote for their own country's song!

"I found it interesting that when Abba won in 1974 with Waterloo, the most memorable Eurovision song of all time, the United Kingdom didn't vote for it!

"And the same thing happened in 2007. While the Serbian winning song in Helsinki picked up points from all over Europe, not just the east, it didn't get any votes from us!

"Yes, there have been justifiable concerns about the way some of the voting has gone in recent years.

"But I think that we have to accept that the voting in the Eurovision Song Contest is going to be, and always has been, as unpredictable as it is parochial."

On the subject of controversy, the United Kingdom's membership of the Big Four nations – the four highest net financial contributors to the Eurovision Song Contest – brings privileges that are far from universally accepted.

When Eurovision got so big that some nations had to be designed out through first relegation and then non-qualification from a semi-final, the United Kingdom – together with France, Germany and Spain – insisted they got a bye into the final.

Their argument is clear – we are keeping this show, in all its weird, wonderful and diverse glory, on the road, so we demand the right to play an integral part in it. And that means a place at the top table on the Saturday night!

Kevin: "All the countries lower down the pecking order in terms of contributions to the European Broadcasting Union's contest budget think our status – and that of the other three countries – is unfair.

"The Eurovision Song Contest strategists think our position should not be set in stone but at our regular meetings we hold a firm line.

"After all, the Big Four contribute 40 per cent of the EBU budget. Without that contribution, there would not be a Eurovision Song Contest for the less-wealthy competing nations to enjoy and be a part of.

"And this all represents a lot of viewers and a lot of television sets. Would these other countries want their fees to go up?"

Dominic: "The automatic inclusion of the Big Four in the final has certainly created problems among other nations who view this as a cosy 'private club' arrangement.

"But there would be no Eurovision Song Contest without the Big Four's money, especially with Europe and the contest spreading ever further afield.

"The greater diversity now on show at Eurovision would not be possible without our money.

"The European Broadcast Union was specifically created to promote new and emerging technology throughout the continent.

"The contest is playing its part in achieving that goal but the contribution of those nations bankrolling this development should not go unrecognised.

"When Estonia won the right to host Eurovision in 2002, the capital city Tallinn enjoyed a massive profile and the country as a whole got an incredible boost from staging the event.

"To hold a Eurovision Song Contest now in the Big Four capitals – London, Paris, Berlin or Madrid – would just not have the same impact.

"With a nation like Estonia having to bear smaller costs than the Big Four countries, the contest brings with it a disproportionate influence and makes it more special. We saw the same thing happen in Riga the following year after Latvia's success."

Svante: "My view is that the privileges enjoyed by the Big Four countries should be negotiable and this procedure might be changed.

"The success of the Eurovision is not dependent on money from the Big Four, I firmly believe that to be the case.

"France, Germany, Spain and the United Kingdom between them contribute around 40 per cent of the participation fees, that is correct, and if these countries decide to drop out then this 40 per cent must be carried by the other participants.

"But with more and more sponsors coming into the Eurovision project, we are hearing more and more voices objecting to this quite undemocratic procedure where four countries effectively buy their way into the final."

All of which begs the question – would the United Kingdom withdraw from the Eurovision project if its status was undermined?

Or why not withdraw, full stop? Has Eurovision ever been relevant to the United Kingdom? If the answer is no, isn't the question then…. why?

Kevin: "The viewers certainly think that Eurovision is relevant but it isn't relevant to today's music industry.

"It had greater relevance in the 1960s when the likes of Cliff Richard, Sandie Shaw and Lulu were on the scene.

"Record companies are not interested these days and, while we applaud the EBU's decision to introduce a winner's tour, we will struggle to accommodate it over here as we just do not have a suitable vehicle with which to promote the Eurovision winner in the UK.

"We have not considered withdrawal at present. The viewing figures have been very good over a number of years and while that continues we will always go in. If they fell away significantly, then we would re-consider our participation."

Dominic: "The contest isn't relevant to the music industry or the record companies – the industry does not currently need Eurovision.

"But as an entertainment package, I think the Eurovision is relevant today. I think you need to compare Eurovision with ballroom dancing. The BBC's Strictly Come Dancing show is incredibly popular and demonstrates that there is an audience out there for middle of the road entertainment.

"Withdrawal from Eurovision has not been considered at any stage but, realistically, nothing can last forever.

"I don't think anyone ever thought that Top of the Pops would come off the screen. But it did come to an end because it wasn't deemed to be succeeding.

"The Eurovision is a success for the BBC in terms of its viewing figures. It does well, with 11 million viewers, and a fair amount of this I think can be attributed to the presence of Sir Terry Wogan.

"It will be interesting to see how Eurovision fares in the UK now that Sir Terry has stepped down from the helm."

Ah, Sir Terry … now most observers would suggest that he doesn't take Eurovision at all seriously. Some would say we should take it much more seriously, as most of our continental competitors appear to do.

Dominic: "In Helsinki, the Serbian girl was the best singer in the competition and she was surrounded by 'serious' voices.

"And it's true that many nations, especially those from the east of Europe, treat Eurovision very seriously indeed.

"Marija Serifovic ticked a lot of boxes and secured a good victory but most of the music entered by the new eastern European nations has a more conservative taste in terms of musical choice and the music is not contemporary.

"The UK's viewing figures for Eurovision are actually on the increase whereas elsewhere in Europe they are falling.

"Whatever your view on how seriously we take Eurovision, or how seriously we should take it, we must be doing something right.

"My personal view is that people in the UK tune in for the spectacle and partly because the contest re-enforces the negativity directed at Europe and it can feed anti-European Union prejudices.

"It gives rise to the voice of cynicism, in particular the voting. And it's true, the audience figure peaks when the voting is underway!"

And what of the view of an outsider looking in – does the United Kingdom treat Eurovision seriously and afford the competition due respect. If not, is this an issue?

Svante: "With the rich tradition of great music writers and artists that has always been the trademark of the United Kingdom, I would have hoped see to have seen some better entries submitted in recent years.

"It would really be a shame if the United Kingdom did not participate in the Eurovision. But you cannot now expect to turn up and expect people to vote for you.

"In order to be successful, you also need to be serious about it. You might think that the Lordi act from Finland, which won in Athens, was for fun.

"But I can assure you it was far from it. Behind those masks and costumes, these guys were really serious about their work and were very professional to work with."

The recent run of failure for the United Kingdom on the Eurovision stage has once again resurrected the old chestnut of wheeling an established artist out to sing for Queen and country.

The BBC flirted with the notion in the early 1990s but it was swiftly put on the back burner – and won't be returning any time soon.

Kevin: "At the beginning of the 1990s we returned to the idea that it would be a good thing to put forward established artists for Eurovision, but we could not sustain this as it was causing the BBC a helluva lot of money.

"There just isn't a big pot of cash to spend on Eurovision these days. We also have to consider the position of taking an established artist out of their comfort zone and asking them to spend a week rehearsing and promoting themselves in the host city.

"I couldn't envisage too many artists, especially those who had already made their name in the world of music, falling over themselves to spend a week or so in Serbia for example."

Dominic: "I agree with that entirely. You also have to ask yourself the question as to why signed and known acts would want to enter into a competition against other signed and known acts.

"Okay, in the past we had ITV's Record of the Year competition in which A-List acts competed but the stakes there were completely different. They'd all had number ones, had nothing to lose and plenty of albums to sell.

"By vying for a winner's trophy in Eurovision, a big artist risks total humiliation in front of 150 million viewers. People often ask why we can't get Robbie or Kylie to represent the UK. But why would they want to do it?"

Svante: "I understand the argument but it is a shame. I think the United Kingdom's most significant influence on Eurovision since its first participation in 1957 has been some excellent songs and artists."

And with reality television shows coming out of our ears – and with the emphasis on emerging artist rather than established – why has reality not been seriously considered at an earlier stage in the search for a Eurovision winner and a future star?

Kevin: "We have had representatives who have come from the Pop Idol reality stable and it is true to say that a reality show around the selection has been discussed in the past by the BBC.

"But before the Andrew Lloyd-Webber collaboration, the concept was dismissed because too many resources would have been needed to have been committed and there would also have been the danger of potential overkill.

"Eurovision is cheap television for the BBC and there was a clear desire to keep it that way."

Dominic: "The BBC doesn't really want to invest in the Eurovision to the extent that other countries choose to.

"Sweden has considerable success with its melody festival (melodifestivalen) but we have to be realistic here – the record companies are reluctant to get involved and for established artists, like Katrina and Javine, going through the selection process in recent years was a risky business.

"In addition, there are at least three extremely successful TV music brands in the UK. And why interfere with a successful brand?"

So with emerging acts battling it out for Eurovision glory in the future, and the glorious spotlight overshadowed by those towering neighbour voting blocs, can the United Kingdom realistically ever win the Eurovision again?

Kevin: "Yes. But only if we are able to put forward a really good song. The war in Iraq was not helpful when we scored nul points in Latvia in 2003.

"But that can't be the whole story for that failure. I'm pretty sure we must have been at war with someone when Katrina and the Waves won in 1997?!"

Dominic: "Yes, I'm sure we can. But nowadays I think our entry has to be 50 per cent better than anyone else to get through all the hoops.

"There has been an argument at recent contests that western European countries should stop moaning and look at the quality of the songs they are submitting to the contest.

"The continuation of that argument is that the songs from eastern European countries are better. I don't know if that is true.

"What I do think is true is those middle-ranking songs from the east appearing to prosper at the expense of middle-ranking songs from the west.

"And what I find particularly irksome at Eurovision is the way some nations just throw money at the promotion of their songs.

"In some cases you find an oligarch is funding the promotion of songs and acts to such a ridiculous extent that the whole thing becomes nothing more than an empty public relations exercise."

Svante: "The answer to your question is yes, of course they can. Some say the Big Four will never win again but I cannot accept that view. With the right song, the right artist and the right performance, the United Kingdom can win again."

And what about the dear old jury, now seen in a respectful new light? And what about the orchestra, whose absence since the advent of the new Millennium is much lamented by devotees?

Svante: "From 2009, juries will contribute half the votes towards the Eurovision result but I cannot ever see us returning to a jury system ahead of televoting.

"And yes, I know a lot of people miss the orchestra. But Eurovision has to move with the times and I don't think the orchestra will return to Eurovision, I am quite convinced about this."

Kevin: "The contest in Birmingham in 1998 was actually the last one to feature the orchestra. I'm a showman, so yes I do miss it. I always felt it added to the entertainment provided on the evening.

"To this day I don't know why on earth Malta didn't use the orchestra for their song in Birmingham? It was such a close run thing in the end, I think the orchestra would have helped Chiara win with the strong song they had that year.

"In retrospect, I'm so pleased with the interval act we put on in Birmingham which was a true musical extravaganza.

"In Jerusalem, where the contest was staged the following year, the venue was so small that there was no room for the orchestra. And then in Stockholm in the year 2000, where Svante helped staged the contest, they just didn't go for it and it hasn't been back since.

Dominic: "I was sad to see the orchestra go. It used to give each song a distinctive sound and make them sparkle. Now with backing tracks they all tend to sound the same.

"The Eurovision organisers have a desperate need to make the contest relevant and modern. That plus the considerable cost, time and expertise required meant that the orchestra had to go.

"As for the jury system, I think returning to that format is back-pedalling. It is easy to forget the controversy you had with juries which resulted in the clamour for a public vote. It seems you can't win.

"I mean, who would you have on the jury? Joe Public? Open to debate. Music experts? I would hope so. Television bigwigs? No!

"I think the televote is popular and should stay in place. You can't turn your back on democracy."

In terms of their favourite Eurovision experiences, during their respective spells at the United Kingdom helm, both Beeb men had special memories.

Kevin: "I would have to say there have been many memorable moments, notably the superb victory by Katrina and the Waves in Dublin in 1997.

"I also enjoyed Stockholm in 2000, not so much for the UK result – Nicki French's song didn't do at all well – but mainly for the great party we had over there.

"Nicki certainly put heart and soul into the whole Eurovision experience and it went with a swing.

"And of course I have to say Birmingham in 1998, from a different perspective, as we had to organise the whole thing.

"We had all of the major cities to choose from in terms of hosting the event but Birmingham had a certain appeal.

"We wanted somewhere that would have all the delegation hotels close to the contest venue and the canal-side location in Birmingham fitted the bill.

"We were very pleased with the organisation of the whole event and could even afford to sit back and relax!

"Helsinki in 2007 also sticks in the memory for the winning song from Serbia, which I just didn't rate! Yet one top music executive knew he was on to a good thing, backed the song and won a cool ten grand! I wish I'd listened to him!

"But the city that has left the biggest impression on me has to be the Estonian capital of Tallinn – simply lovely!"

Dominic: "In terms of organisation, my favourite years were Birmingham, Tallinn and, best of all, Athens a few years ago where everything went swimmingly.

"The year before in Kiev, Javine represented the United Kingdom and the culture shock produced by the Ukrainian capital made a big impression on the whole delegation and one that was not entirely favourable. However, I found it a truly fascinating place."

And finally… what about Scooch's song Flying The Flag, which had the honour of becoming the United Kingdom's fiftieth offering to the Eurovision table.

The marmite of United Kingdom entries, you either loved it or hated it. Should they have scored more? Should they have scored nothing? Breath of fresh air? Or just an embarrassment?

Kevin: "Flying The Flag was a great Euro song. I did not think it would win the UK final and I was amazed that it did.

"It was a fun, jokey offering and we were happy to run with it. The group members certainly played a full part in promoting the song and the contest helped raise their profile.

"As I think everyone knows, the national final presenters Sir Terry Wogan and Fearne Cotton actually announced different winners.

"Fearne got it right with Scooch but, in making a joint announcement, Sir Terry proclaimed that singer Cyndi had won at exactly the same time.

"We probably didn't help ourselves by deciding that the presenters should themselves be kept in the dark right to the end and then getting them to make a simultaneous proclamation.

"Terry actually said later that a member of the audience had told him that Cyndi had won through so he made the announcement on that basis! Why he went on the word of an audience member I do not know?!

"Many may not have been happy with Scooch's selection but I should point out that even respected musical gurus can get it wrong as far as Eurovision is concerned.

"Back in the late 1990s, Jonathan King served as a music executive to our Eurovision selection process in an attempt to get the UK back to winning ways.

"Jonathan did a great job in helping freshen up our outlook to the contest and played a significant part in enabling Gina G to score a big chart success with her Eurovision hit.

"But the following year, in 1997, he briefed us as to what we should put forward for the contest.

"He ran through all the bid songs and concluded by saying that, whatever we did, we shouldn't go for Katrina and the Waves.

"But he was over-ruled, as most of the selection panel enjoyed the video and felt that this strong anthem could do really well.

"The rest, of course, is Eurovision history! And it just goes to show that even some of the best musical minds can occasionally get it wrong."

Dominic: "I wasn't really surprised when Scooch won the national final. They actually won it by a mile on the back of an eye-catching and entertaining routine.

"Rightly or wrongly it summed up, in three minutes, what BBC viewers think works at Eurovision. And they selected a song which was nostalgic, colourful and a bit silly.

"I thought they might be higher at the actual contest but I don't think the Europeans really ever connected with the very British seaside humour feel of the entry.

"They were more at home backing a rather butch chanteuse from Serbia who delivered a powerful and emotional ballad which was, I suppose, a positive and inclusive development.

"The band took the disappointment of the final result pretty well. They re-formed on a whim for Eurovision and did okay with the single release.

"Two weeks in the top ten is a real achievement, even in today's fractured market. The individual band members have gone back to doing their own projects and all are doing okay.

"Scooch were also signed on a whim by Warner Brothers. It was down to the Warner Brothers boss's daughter, who had watched the UK selection and liked the dance routine. So dad signed them up!"

Breath of fresh air or source of embarrassment, some would argue that the Scooch entry was basically a cry for help on behalf of those marginalised by Eurovision's ever expanding border.

So what did the EBU's Eurovision chief make of the camp airline cabin crew's package of entertainment?

Svante: "Eurovision always provides plenty of variety but of course it is not my job to judge the songs.

"However, if you want my opinion about Scooch, then I have to admit that I wasn't too impressed."

Much more from that flight path and it remains to be seen for how much longer the United Kingdom will be flying that flag.

160

A KICK IN THE BALTICS!

I once read, probably in the Anorak Times, that someone had devised a formula which could be applied to any Eurovision Song Contest final line-up and which would predict the contest winner from a certain position in the running order.

This before anyone had even played a note or opened their mouth. What's more, the report added, the formula had never been known to fail.

What the report omitted was any hint as to how the formula was applied. So presumably those with the knowledge are now sitting on the formula while very wealthy and watching the contest from some far-flung exotic shore.

It is an apocryphal tale, no doubt, but one which serves the Eurovision legend well. Not so much of an urban myth, but a global one.

However, in truth you can have a pretty good stab at predicting the winner of any Eurovision Song Contest. But you do have to study the form.

Prior to the 2008 contest in Belgrade, the BBC predicted correctly that Russia would emerge to claim its first victory.

With Sir Terry Wogan in full flow, this would purely be achieved through 'political voting'. It was a factor certainly, but not the whole story.

Let's face it, if the former Soviet nations were so keen on remaining servile to Russia, then surely the Russians would have won the contest many years ago? And how would those upstarts from the Ukraine have been allowed to pip Russia to the victory post?

I agree with the European Broadcasting Union chief Svante Stockselius, who prefers to call it 'neighbour voting' rather than 'political voting'.

There is of course an element of the latter present as well. I give you Armenia and Azerbeijan in 2008, Greece and Turkey for too many years.

But neighbouring countries which share a language and culture will form a natural bond.

Someone living in Country A may have friends and relatives in Country B. They may have been born in Country B. They will know of celebrities in Country B and there may be many people from Country B living in Country A.

This familiarity is bound to result in traded votes when it comes to points make prizes time at the end of a contest.

Sweden and Denmark, Estonia and Latvia, Greece and Cyprus all readily spring to mind but don't forget the United Kingdom and Ireland.

Before the West starts howling wolf at how unfair all this political voting is, remember this particular fire has always been burning and it started in western Europe.

So let's have a go at predicting a Eurovision winner. From my standpoint, there are five key elements to consider but how much weight you give to each of these components is debatable.

A Eurovision winner will ideally need to have an element of all of the following in the package it presents to a Eurovision audience:-

- A STRONG SONG
- A SLICK PERFORMANCE
- NOVELTY VALUE (GIMMICK)
- REGIONAL SUPPORT
- A FAVOURABLE DRAW

Like it or not, the Eurovision is no longer just a song contest. In the throwaway world that we live in, impact is all.

The impact factor has always been important in Eurovision, where you have just three minutes to make an impression that has to be long and lasting.

But in this televisual age, where an audience now demands to be entertained, impact value has assumed increasing importance.

Sir Terry Wogan, and many of his compatriots, got very upset at the failure of the UK's Andy Abraham in Belgrade.

Andy finished last but most would agree that his song and performance on the night was of a high standard, certainly compared to some of the other songs that immediately followed.

But while Andy ticked boxes one and two in the list above, he didn't have the full set.

Four and five were beyond his control – the UK, as a western nation, were never going to be able to rely on regional support and significantly it is this box which currently holds the most influence.

Where you appear in the running order on the night has always been important and when Andy was drawn at two – the early death slot from where no-one has ever won – his already slim chance of a good finish was all but obliterated.

Where he could have helped himself was in box three – the impactive novelty value, otherwise known as the gimmick.

A strong song and performance should be enough to win the Eurovision but you cannot rely on it.

Let's have a look at the UK winners over the years – Sandie Shaw was a class act in 1967 but she also stood out because she used a hand-held microphone and performed without shoes.

Lulu, two years later, also delivered a strong song and performance but could not be separated from three other joint winners.

Brotherhood of Man, in 1976, captured the mood from the off with a simple, twee but pleasing song. Remember the dance routine? They were on first in The Hague and made an immediate impact and from that point on the competition did not get a look in.

Bucks Fizz in 1981? We were in gimmick heaven! The song itself was a novelty, and though the presentation on the night was poor, all anyone ever remembers is the skirts coming off the girls!

Katrina and the Waves, in 1997, delivered a striking song, a brilliant performance and not a gimmick in sight. They were blessed with a great draw as the penultimate song, and stormed to victory.

As Katrina herself said, she sensed the Dublin audience had not heard a winner by the time she and the group had taken the stage. After they had left it, the result was never in doubt.

Back to Belgrade, Andy's song had no impact. As Andy took the stage, second song up, a German observer sitting near to me in the press centre opined that now was a good time to go to the bar for a drink. It was a harsh assessment but, in the scheme of all things Eurovision, fair.

There is no reason why a gimmick should be introduced into a routine for the sake of it.

But in the long haul that is Eurovision, a hook can be pretty useful and Andy's contribution faded away in the face of a barrage of Azerbaijani angels, Bosnian washing lines, Russian ice skaters, Ukrainian head flicks and Croatian old boy scratchers.

Since the turn of the century, let's have a quick look at the acts that have won the Eurovision:-

2000   Olsen Brothers (Denmark) Fly On The Wings Of Love
A great example of simplicity and stage presence, it worked without a gimmick.

2001   Dave Benton and Tanel Padar (Estonia) Everybody
Again a male double act which offered up something a little bit different and at this time the Baltic nations were a novelty

2002   Marie N (Latvia) Marie N
Clothes changes galore and an eye-catching performance from Marie N but nevertheless a victory for the gimmick

2003   Sertab Erener (Turkey) Everyway That You Can
Great song and performance, we had whirling dervishes and fabric wraps to remember the song by

2004   Ruslana (Ukraine) Wild Dances
A vibrant song and a great show from The Warrior Princess with a lot of hair being thrown around

2005   Elena Paparizou (Greece) My Number One
This one bucked the trend, ticking most of the boxes but no discernible hook to remember it by

2006   Lordi (Finland) Hard Rock Hallelujah
A rocking success with a song which had everything with all the performers in monster mode

2007   Marija Serifovic (Serbia) Molitva
A gentle ballad sung in Serbo-Croat but an eye-catching delivery from the backing singers and the geeky Marija as the gimmick

2008   Dima Bilan (Russia) Believe
An r'n'b entry to the Eurovision is something of a novelty but an ice skater on stage was definitely a first for the contest!

In conclusion, six of the nine winners since the turn of the century have succeeded off the back of some form of novelty value.

You can win without a gimmick, but the song and performance have to be spot on to capture the mood and to never let it go!

So when the contest comes around, consider the five factors when predicting a winner.

The value of any song and a performance is obviously in the ear and eye of the beholder but, whatever, you will get a sense of what is likely to do well if a nation ticks all or most of the boxes.

Song

The baseline is a strong song. This is quite obviously the starting point and without it you are doomed from the off.

Performance

The song has to be supported by a good performance so it helps if the performers are accomplished in their particular field.

Draw

It certainly helps if you have a favourable draw and, as a general rule, the further down the running order you are on finals night the better.

The draw is important as this falls into the 'impact' category. As a rule, 24 or 25 nations take part in the Eurovision final, so have a look at the draw and see where they line-up.

Whoever is first on actually has a reasonable chance of success but only if the song and performance is worth writing home about. Winners from opening the contest are Netherlands 1975, the United Kingdom 1976 and Sweden 1984.

Second up is where no-one wants to be. No-one has ever won from position two and this is the song that is in danger of really getting lost.

Andy Abraham knows that full well and Gina G in 1996, the contest favourite and one of Eurovision's biggest commercial successes, could only finish eighth from this position.

However, Jessica Garlick finished equal third from here in 2002 – which is a tribute to both the song and the performer.

There have been four winners from position three, the last being Rock 'N' Roll Kids for Ireland in 1994.

Turkey won from position four in 2003, the only time this has been achieved, but victories are then few and far between until you reach position eight – about a third of the way through – which has produced five winners including Israel in 1998.

Positions nine to 13 are not great, the only recent winner from this area being Ukraine (position 10) in 2004.

Position 14 is one of the most profitable with five winners, the last being Denmark in 2000.

There have been no winners to date from positions 16 and 21, but positions 17 to 20 are really the places most acts would want to be.

These four slots produced 14 of the winners between 1972 and 2007 and six of them from position 17 – both Finland and Serbia won from here in successive years - which is certainly the prize draw to have.

Two songs have won from position 24 – the UK in 1997 and Russia in 2008, although these were the penultimate songs from the respective contests.

There have been six winners from acts performing last, the most recent being Yugoslavia 1989.

Gimmick

Does the song have a gimmick with which to remember it by? Many songs do not require one but don't underestimate the novelty factor.

Support

Finally, and nowadays most importantly, can it rely on support from its regional neighbours. In the old days it was mainly the Scandinavian nations that benefited from this aspect, but these days it is hugely beneficial to many countries in the east of Europe.

Those nations from the various voting blocs will be able to rely on support from those that form part of the same bloc and, of the five tick boxes, this now holds greater sway than the actual song or performance and, in my view, needs to be addressed.

If a turkey, for example, had represented FYR Macedonia or Belarus, it almost certainly would have fared a lot better than poor old Dustin did for Ireland in 2008.

Looking at the 2007 contest in Helsinki, where the east/west debate really came to the fore, let's study the finalists against the above criteria.

In each of the categories – song, performance, gimmick, draw and support – I listed what I considered the ten strongest songs for each category.

How attractive a song, performance or gimmick is boils down to a matter of opinion. The draw is fixed, the potential for neighbour or diaspora support is debatable. Anyway, here goes....

Song
Finland, Slovenia, Serbia, Hungary, Sweden, France, Russia, Latvia, Ukraine, Turkey

Performance
Spain, Belarus, Serbia, Greece, France, Russia, Latvia, Ukraine, Bulgaria, Moldova

Gimmick
Belarus, Slovenia, Serbia, Hungary, Sweden, Germany, Latvia, Ukraine, United Kingdom, Bulgaria

Geography
Belarus, Slovenia, Serbia, Greece, Georgia, Russia, Ukraine, Turkey, Armenia, Latvia

Draw
Bosnia and Herzegovina, France, Serbia, Ukraine, United Kingdom, Romania, Bulgaria, Turkey, Armenia, Moldova

*****	Prediction	Actual
Serbia	1	1
Ukraine	2	2
****		
Latvia	3	16
***		
Turkey	4	4
Russia	5	3
France	6	22
Slovenia	7	15
Belarus	8	6
**		
Moldova	9	10
Armenia	10	8
Bulgaria	11	5
United Kingdom	12	23
Sweden	13	18
Hungary	14	9
Greece	15	7
*		
Romania	16	13
Germany	17	19

Georgia	18	12
Finland	19	17
Spain	20	20
Bosnia / Herzegovina	21	11
0		
Lithuania	22	21
FYR Macedonia	23	14
Ireland	24	24

On my calculations, Serbia and the Ukraine ticked every box and on the night finished winners and runners-up.

I had Latvia third (16) and predicted strong showings from Belarus (6), Slovenia (15), France (22), Russia (3) and Turkey (4).

Bulgaria proved to be the surprise package as far as I was concerned, the impact and the draw serving them well!

The surprise leaps were in the east, with Georgia, Bosnia and Herzegovina and FYR Macedonia doing rather better than expected.

The 'Macedonia Question' was partially addressed by the EBU at Belgrade in 2008 but for my money there is still a way to go.

So what more can be done?

In the early days of Eurovision, the only traditional voting bloc was Scandinavia and while Denmark, Sweden and Norway all tended to support each other the trading never resulted in domination from the frozen north.

But the fragmentation of eastern Europe in the early 1990s has completely changed the face of Eurovision.

The contest has a problem now in that several pronounced voting blocs have emerged in the east – the Baltics, the Balkans and the former Soviet republics.

The sheer weight of these blocs has tilted vote spans so far to the east that any prospect of a western nation ever winning Eurovision again is extremely remote, if not zero.

Televoting has re-enforced the strength of these blocs and it is doubtful whether the partial re-introduction of juries into the mix will markedly alter the picture.

Given the make-up of Europe now, and the number of nations looking to take part in Eurovision, I believe the EBU has to further shake up the voting process to make it more inclusive.

In light of the obvious favouritism between neighbours as outlined above, voters have to be encouraged to look beyond their own regions.

This after all is pan-European competition and that aspect should be at the forefront of any future evolution and moderation process.

My own view is that the Big Four should be relieved of their status and that all competing nations, the hosts apart, be drawn into two semi-finals which have a geographical balance.

All the semi-final nations should then be split into five regional groups of five nations each – roughly Scandinavia, the Baltics, the Balkans, the former Soviet Republics and the rest of Europe.

A mix of televoting and jury submissions, as outlined for Moscow, should then apply.

But these votes should then be moderated to ensure that every nation spreads its ten votes equally across the five groups.

A nation should split its ten votes, in whatever denomination it wants to, to two competitors in each of the five groups.

And why not make a rule that the maximum award, be it 12 points or whatever, goes to a country in another voting group. So much the better!

The top twelve nations from each semi-final would then go through to the final where the same process would apply.

This would keep the contest inclusive and almost certainly a good battle to the finish between the strongest songs from all corners of Europe.

In Helsinki, the 24 nations in the final could have been split into the following regional groups:-

SCANDINAVIA AND BALTICS
Finland, Germany, Latvia, Lithuania and Sweden

BALKANS
Bosnia and Herzegovina, Serbia, Slovenia and FYR Macedonia

FORMER SOVIET REPUBLICS
Armenia, Belarus, Georgia, Ukraine and Russia

WESTERN EUROPE
France, Hungary, Ireland, Spain and the United Kingdom

EASTERN EUROPE
Bulgaria, Greece, Moldova, Romania and Turkey

Crucially, whatever the outcome of the contest, the process would be regarded as having been fair with integrity built in.

Italy, Luxembourg and Monaco are seemingly gone forever and Austria isn't interested in the Eurovision any more. Plenty of other nations have serious misgivings.

In spite of timely interventions from the EBU, the process remains flawed and the Western nations do feel as if they are being proverbially kicked in the Baltics.

If these nations are to return, and if the Eurovision is to remain a viable product in the years ahead, the kicking has got to stop.

IMAANI, IMAANI, AH AH IMAANI.....

United Kingdom Eurovision super fan David Allan reckons that only one UK song has been deserving of victory in the contest during the 50-year participation.

And, surprisingly, it's not one of the five songs that have actually achieved the feat – David's winner actually finished second on home soil in 1998.

He said: "In my opinion, Imaani's entry was possibly the only UK song I thought should have won Eurovision.

"It is certainly one of my favourites. And I have also always had a secret love for Belle and the Devotions and Kathy Kirby, whose song I Belong was just wondrous.

"My least favourite UK song is Scott Fitzgerald's Go and to think that it nearly won up against Celine Dion! I truly think it is abysmal.

"No Dream Impossible comes close in my most-hated list, but I think that is tinged slightly by the involvement of the rebarbative Lindsay Dracass.

"Of my favourite Eurovision songs of all time, Apres Toi from Vicky Leandros is right up there. Other winners I am partial to are Net Als Toen, Viva Cantando and La La La.

"I think La La La is great and often play it, together with the Joan Manuel Serrat I Teresa versions. I know I probably stand alone in Europe on this!

"For the record, I've only ever predicted the winner twice – Johnny Logan in 1980 and Maria Serifovic in 2007.

"Of all the wins in Eurovision, Linda Martin's for Ireland in 1992 surprised me the most as I loathed this song from first hearing and I thought the performance on the night was atrocious.

"She looked like she worked in a bad hairdressing salon, shrieking her head off while wearing an unattractive lampshade made of sludge-coloured felt. Appalling, appalling, appalling.

"Fangad Av En Stormwind also annoys me, but some of that may be to do with Carola who really annoys me - similarly Hallelujah and Gali Atari.

"Along with those winners already mentioned, I have a few songs which are on my constant play list. I seem to have an attraction for the underdog and whatever I like can almost be guaranteed to do badly, if not fail totally and get no points.

"Of the favourite contests, I've always enjoyed watching the Naples contest of 1965. I think Renata Mauro did a great job presenting and the overall look of the contest is really good, in spite of the strange and difficult-to-see scoreboard, although that in itself was an attempt at something different.

"Of the later contests, Millstreet 1993 and Oslo 1996 stand out and, this century, Riga 2003 was the one I enjoyed the most.

"I enjoyed the fun Josiane Shen brought to Luxembourg 1966 and I also liked Lolita Morena and Jacques Deschenaux in Lausanne 1989, Fionnuala Sweeney in Mill Street 1993 and Carrie Crowley in Dublin 1997.

"Of the more recent contests, I don't think any of the presenters have been much up to the job, although I thought mad Meltem Cumbul in Istanbul 2004 did well.

"I've never either been a great admirer of the great Katie Boyle, or Miss Catherine Boyle as she was originally known.

"She never seemed to understand the rules properly and often confused the jury spokesperson. I blame her totally for the 1963 voting fiasco.

"Ignoring Ms Cinquetti and Mr Cutugno in Rome 1991, who I actually thought were quite fun in a deranged sort of way, the worst presenter ever is Gerry Ryan who was at Dublin in 1994. In fact I have to watch the voting with the sound turned down as the man annoys me so much!"

David kicks off our list of Eurovision fan favourites as part of a worldwide UK Invitation Jury vote. In each case, the selections relate to the following categories:-

1) Favourite UK entry
2) Least favourite UK entry
3) Favourite Eurovision winner
4) Favourite Eurovision song
5) Favourite Eurovision year

The selections of 75 Eurovision fans follow with nation tags as appropriate – the results of all the selections received are tabulated in the following chapters, Flying The Flag and We Only Watched The Voting.

David's selections are as follows:-

1) 1998 Where Are You (Imaani)
2) 1988 Go (Scott Fitzgerald)
3) 1972 Apres Toi (Vicky Leandros) LUX
4) 1976 Ne Mogu Skriti Svoju Bol (Ambassadori) YUG
5) 1965 NAPLES

Phil Ronald-Price's favourite UK entry is Sandie Shaw – simply because it represented the popularity of Eurovision in the country.

He said: "I was only 19 at the time, but it was a great moment as I had watched ESC since it began in 1957 (UK participation).

"I didn't like the Live Report song because I think that the UK can produce far better songs than this, and this song, to me, was the worst sort of song we could enter.

"Sandra Kim's win for Belgium was a great moment for me as she symbolised a youthful, exciting winner who really demonstrated what ESC is all about.

"She sung in French and, as I speak the language, this song was made even more attractive – but I liked it whatever!

"I like the countries to sing their song in their own language – it is much more authentic and romantic.

"In 1964, I just loved Gigliola's song as it was such a romantic song, sung with such feeling; for me, at the age of 16, it is the one I remember most.

"1963 was the year I really took a great interest in Eurovision, especially because I had heard several ESC songs on the radio and wanted to know more and it still seemed an amazing technical feat to have all the countries linked together in one show.

"We still had black-and-white television then, so it was really something! So 1963 is certainly my favourite year, not so much for the songs but for the era and the technology.

"I've loved music since I was a baby (literally) and the ESC is just one area of music where I am always interested to hear the latest entries and to see how it changes as time goes on. Now, at 60, I still love it!"

1) 1967 Puppet On A String (Sandie Shaw)
2) 1989 Why Do I Always Get It Wrong? (Live Report)
3) 1986 J'Aime La Vie (Sandra Kim) BEL
4) 1964 Non Ho L'Eta (Gigliola Cinquetti) ITA
5) 1963 LONDON

Terry Clark is an Abba fan but he didn't really think a great deal of their Eurovision winner in 1974.

He said: "Everyone says Abba for their favourite Eurovision winner but the UK didn't even give it a single point! It did turn a massive corner musically but the performance was not that polished really. It doesn't sound like it, but I am actually an Abba fan!

"I was on the UK jury in 1988 so Celine Dion's win was special for me and it is my personal favourite.

"My favourite Eurovision was in Gothenburg – I thought that Lill Lindfors was the most relaxed and natural presenter the show has ever had. Norway won for the first time and there were some very good entries as well so it always stands out for me.

1) 1968 Congratulations (Cliff Richard)
2) 1994 Lonely Symphony (Frances Ruffelle)
3) 1988 Ne Partez Pas Sans Moi (Celine Dion) SWI
4) 2005 Angel (Chiara) MAL
5) 1985 GOTHENBURG

Brian Gilbert has been a fan of Eurovision since 1967, when his favourite UK female singer of that time – Sandie Shaw - was chosen to enter, and won.

He said: "I've been hooked ever since although I was only allowed up to see her sing the first time so I didn't know she'd won until the next day. To this day, I don't understand how the BBC thought Kenneth McKellar, an old man in a kilt, would win!! And I also disliked the James Fox entry - pure boredom.

"My favourite winner is Vicky Leandros – her song, Apres Toi, was sheer class and for me the 1970s was the best decade of the contest.

"My favourite song though was from Norway - Anne Karine Strom's Mata Hari. The gold lurex dress and the Deirdre Barlow glasses swung it for me, but I still don't get why it did so badly.

"For favourite contest, I am a little torn. I think 1975 for the songs, but 1985 for the whole package. The first contest where the audience really started to get involved was in Gothenburg in 1985 and that was down to the presenter Lill Lindfors.

"I still wish that we'd been able to put the two 1956 UK songs in. I've often wondered what Shirley Abicair, with Little Ship, would have sounded like."

1) 1970 Knock Knock Who's There? (Mary Hopkin)
2) 1966 A Man Without Love (Kenneth McKellar)
3) 1972 Apres Toi (Vicky Leandros) LUX
4) 1976 Mata Hari (Anne-Karine Strom) NOR
5) 1985 GOTHENBURG

Alasdair Rendall's favourite UK entry was Lonely Symphony by Frances Ruffelle, a chord struck by many.

He said: "I loved that song and I think she is hugely under-rated. An entry I didn't like at all was Touch My Fire which was derivative, contrived and ethno-lite that deserved the low placing it got in Kiev. And having had the misfortune to interview Javine, it's clear she had no interest in the contest whatsoever!

"It was hard to pick my favourite year but I'd say the 'golden age' were the periods 1988-1993 and 1998-2001. But overall I'd go for 1990, just decent songs, nothing over the top. 1998 and 2006 are also special ones though, as I was in the audience for both of them.

1) 1994 Lonely Symphony (Frances Ruffelle)
2) 2005 Touch My Fire (Javine)
3) 1979 Hallelujah (Gali Atari with Milk and Honey) ISR
4) 1990 Bandido (Azucar Moreno) SPA
5) 1990 ZAGREB

Sarah Beer also tapped into the anti-Javine vibe. She said: "I didn't like her at all, a dreadful woman.

"My favourite songs are both winners – Waterloo, somewhat predictably, and Johnny Logan's Hold Me Now. I loved that song – I was 15 at the time it won Eurovision and I played this record all the time!

"And a special mention too for those two Russian minxes t.A.t.U, another song I really liked."

1) 1996 Just A Little Bit (Gina G)
2) 2005 Touch My Fire (Javine)
3) 1974 Waterloo (Abba) SWE
4) 1987 Hold Me Know (Johnny Logan) IRE
5) 1981 DUBLIN

Gareth Letton is in no doubt about his favourite UK entry – Olivia Newton-John's Long Live Love, by a country mile!

But he didn't have a good word to say about Ryder's Runner In The Night in 1986. He said: "The 1980s were dark days for Eurovision, and not the classics that many fans seem to think.

"This was just awful. The 'tonight Matthew I'm going to be Cliff Richard' didn't do it for me!

"Frida Boccara's Un Jour Un Enfant was class on a stick. Nothing in the following 40 years has even come close. A very passionate performance del Teatro Real, en color! Goosebumps ahoy!

"In the 1980s there were only two highlights and Portugal's Silencio E Tanta Gente was one of them.

"My favourite year was really hard to judge. I tend to judge any contest on the 'skip' factor. The only contests where I do not skip forward on any songs are 1966 and 1992.

"But one thing is for certain, no post-1999 contest even comes close to the Top Ten!"

1)	1974 Long Live Love (Olivia Newton-John)
2)	1986 Runner In The Night (Ryder)
3)	1969 Un Jour Un Enfant (Frida Boccara) FRA
4)	1984 Silencio E Tanta Gente (Maria Guinot) POR
5)	1966 LUXEMBOURG

Birmingham in 1998 was a special year for Ace Frehmen – it was the first and only Eurovision that he has attended.

He said: "Of the recent entries, I certainly hated Latvia's entry from 2007. I could happily have shot the singers one by one as they came on to the stage.

"The year before, Athens had been a step forward. But Latvia and Slovenia from 2007, the operatic songs, were two giant leaps backwards.

"My favourite Eurovision entry is the only Finnish winner from Lordi. My favourite UK entry is more difficult as the ones I like best from the national selection do not get through. But we got it right in 1997, so it's Katrina and the Waves for the best UK entry and winner.

"I thought that in Helsinki the stage was far too small. Dummies were used in the Swiss entry, which was a bad mistake.

I was expecting to see some Goth-type performers but there were none, another mistake. That is why Swiss failed to qualify.

"As for Austria, they came on last and sang 'Get A Life'. What was the singer wearing? The costume would have put a lot of voters off and it was so embarrassing. I loved the song, but the presentation stank.

"Ireland needed to change their kind of tunes and act as it was getting repetitive. Dervish's appearance wasn't good though and as always a lot depends on presentation. Those two entries got it all wrong.

"As for us, I don't trust the UK voters to select a strong song and I don't think the recent UK entries have been varied enough.

"What would be my least favourite UK entry? I can list a heck of a lot but James Fox had nothing to offer the rest of Europe other than his good looks."

1)   1997 Love Shine A Light (Katrina and the Waves)
2)   2004 Hold On To Your Love (James Fox)
3)   2006 Hard Rock Hallelujah (Lordi) FIN
4)   2006 Hard Rock Hallelujah (Lordi) FIN
5)   1998 BIRMINGHAM

Roelof van der Merwe, from South Africa, lists Jack In The Box by Clodagh Rogers, Co Co's Bad Old Days and the Katrina and the Waves winner Love Shine A Light among his top UK favourites.

And the least favourite? He said: "Absolutely no question – Love City Groove! I hate hate hate hate hate it!

"My favourite Eurovision winner is a little more difficult. I do like Love Shine A Light but equally Charlotte Nilsson's Take Me To Your Heaven – I predicted that song to win the moment I first heard it.

"Germany's Ein Bisschen Frieden was also very special. 1981 was my favourite Eurovision year as this was the first year I could see the contest.

"South Africa did not have television until 1976 and it was not broadcast, but in 1981 my friend from the UK recorded it on video and posted to me, so 1981 was the first year I could see it.

179

"It also had so many great songs and hardly any that I hate. The other side of the coin was 1992 when I liked only one song, from Sweden, and it did so badly.

1) 1971 Jack In The Box (Clodagh Rogers)
2) 1995 Love City Groove (Love City Groove)
3) 1982 Ein Bisschen Frieden (Nicole) GER
4) 1988 Lied Fuer Einen Freund (Chris Garden and Maxi) GER
5) 1981 DUBLIN

Deo Grech, from Malta, had Imaani as top of his UK pops, with Frances Ruffelle in second place and Sandie Shaw a close third.

And he too did not care much for Love City Groove. He said: "This song was awful to the eyes and ears!

"My favourite winner has to be Abba and Waterloo, as they changed the face of Eurovision that day and re-wrote the history books too! Chiara's Angel is my favourite Eurovision song of all time, but obviously I'm a little biased as I'm Maltese too!

"But it's so hard to pick one favourite Eurovision song from all those which took part, with so many different genres and music styles. My favourite Eurovision year was 2006 – it was a great experience to be in Athens for the contest."

1) 1998 Where Are You? (Imaani)
2) 1995 Love City Groove (Love City Groove)
3) 1974 Waterloo (Abba) SWE
4) 2005 Angel (Chiara) MAL
5) 2006 ATHENS

Morten Thomassen – Norway

1) 1984 Love Games (Belle and the Devotions)
2) 2004 Hold On To Your Love (James Fox)
3) 1968 La La La (Massiel) SPA
4) 1964 Des Que Le Printemps Revient (Hugues Aufrey) LUX
5) 1976 THE HAGUE

Joan Street – UK

1) 1964 I Love The Little Things (Matt Monro)
2) 1987 Only The Light (Rikki)
3) 1970 All Kinds Of Everything (Dana) IRE
4) 2000 My Star (Brainstorm) LAT
5) 1985 GOTHENBURG

Marcus Keppel-Palmer – UK

1) 1982 One Step Further (Bardo)
2) 1994 Lonely Symphony (Frances Ruffelle)
3) 1971 Un Banc, Un Arbre, Une Rue (Severine) MON
4) 1987 Gente di Mare (Umberto Tozzi and Raf) ITA
5) 1991 ROME

Gary Shackle – UK

1) 1998 Where Are You? (Imaani)
2) 1975 Let Me Be The One (Shadows)
3) 1998 Diva (Dana International) ISR
4) 2004 Wild Dances (Ruslana) UKR
5) 2005 KIEV

Michel Pallares – France

1) 1967 Puppet On A String (Sandie Shaw)
2) 2003 Cry Baby (Jemini)
3) 1974 Waterloo (Abba) SWE
4) 1978 Parlez-vous Francais? (Baccara) LUX
5) 1978 PARIS

Max Mannola – Finland

1) 2000 Don't Play That Song Again (Nicki French)
2) 1993 Better The Devil You Know (Sonia)
3) 1963 Dansevise (Grethe and Jorgen Ingmann) DEN
4) 1975 Seninle Bir Dakika (Semiha Yanki) TUR
5) 1971 DUBLIN

Gary Speirs – UK

1) 1977 Rock Bottom (Lyndsey de Paul and Mike Moran)
2) 2007 Flying The Flag (Scooch)
3) 1979 Hallelujah (Gali Atari with Milk and Honey) ISR
4) 2006 Tornero (Mihai Traistariu) ROM
5) 1985 GOTHENBURG

Sanio Silva – Spain

1) 2001 No Dream Impossible (Lindsay)
2) 2006 Teenage Life (Daz Sampson)
3) 2007 Molitva (Marija Serifovic) SER
4) 2007 Mojot Svet (Karolina) MAC
5) 1994 DUBLIN

Cyril Second – France

1) 1996 Just A Little Bit (Gina G)
2) 2003 Cry Baby (Jemini)
3) 1994 Rock N Roll Kids (Paul Harrington and Charlie McGettigan) IRE
4) 2004 It Hurts (Lena Phillipson) SWE
5) 1996 OSLO

Alain Musitelli – France

1) 1967 Puppet On A String (Sandie Shaw)
2) 2007 Flying The Flag (Scooch)
3) 1964 Non Ho L' Eta(Gigliola Cinquetti) ITA
4) 1972 Apres Toi (Vicky Leandros) LUX
5) 1989 LAUSSANE

Christian Dufresnes – France

1) 1996 Just A Little Bit (Gina G)
2) 1988 Go (Scott Fitzgerald)
3) 1988 Ne Partez Pas Sans Moi (Celine Dion) SWI
4) 1994 To Nie Ja (Edyta Gorniak) POL
5) 1998 BIRMINGHAM

Patrick Racine - France

1) 1996 Just A Little Bit (Gina G)
2) 1987 Only The Light (Rikki)
3) 1998 Diva (Dana International) ISR
4) 1990 White And Black Blues (Joelle Ursul) FRA
5) 2004 ISTANBUL

Laurent Nietge – France

1) 1997 Love Shine A Light (Katrina and the Waves)
2) 2007 Flying The Flag (Scooch)
3) 2005 My Number One (Elena Paparizou) GRE
4) 1991 Le Dernier Qui A Parle Qui A Raison (Amina) FRA
5) 2003 RIGA

Phillipe Bonnecarrere – France

1) 1998 Where Are You (Imaani)
2) 2007 Flying The Flag (Scooch)
3) 1993 In Your Eyes (Niamh Kavanagh) IRE
4) 1997 Ale Jestem (Anna-Maria Jopek) POL
5) 1993 MILLSTREET

Martyn Clarke – UK

1) 1967 Puppet on a String (Sandie Shaw)
2) 2007 Flying The Flag (Scooch)
3) 1972 Apres Toi (Vicky Leandros) LUX
4) 1972 Apres Toi (Vicky Leandros) LUX
5) 2007 HELSINKI

Steen Vinlov – Sweden

1) 1985 Love Is (Vicky)
2) 2003 Cry Baby (Jemini)
3) 1965 Poupee De Cire, Poupee De Son (France Gall) LUX
4) 1965 Poupée De Cire, Poupee De Son (France Gall) LUX
5) 1985 GOTHENBURG

Juan Anibal - Colombia

1) 1976 Save Your Kisses For Me (Brotherhood of Man)
2) 1981 Making Your Mind Up (Bucks Fizz)
3) 1997 Love Shine A Light (Katrina and the Waves)
4) 1998 Diva (Dana International) ISR
5) 2005 KIEV

Olivier Morice – France

1) 1982 One Step Further (Bardo)
2) 2003 Cry Baby (Jemini)
3) 1974 Waterloo (Abba) SWE
4) 1980 Amsterdam (Maggie MacNeal) NET
5) 1981 DUBLIN

Alain Fontan – France

1) 1996 Just A Little Bit (Gina G)
2) 1995 Love City Groove (Love City Groove)
3) 1966 Merci Cherie (Udo Juergens) AUS
4) 1972 Nur Die Liebe Laesst Uns Leben (Mary Roos) GER
5) 1965 NAPLES

Alex Rouffignac – France

1) 1994 Lonely Symphony (Frances Ruffelle)
2) 1993 Better The Devil You Know (Sonia)
3) 1964 Non Ho L'Eta (Gigliola Cinquetti) ITA
4) 1975 Ein Lied Kann Eine Bruecke Sein (Joy Fleming) GER
5) 1985 GOTHENBURG

Gordon Lewis – UK

1) 1994 Lonely Symphony (Frances Ruffelle)
2) 1966 A Man Without Love (Kenneth McKellar)
3) 1964 Non Ho L'Eta (Gigliola Cinquetta) ITA
4) 1997 Fiumi Di Parole (Jalisse) ITA
5) 2000 STOCKHOLM

Richard Crane – UK

1) 1995 Love City Groove (Love City Groove)
2) 1997 Love Shine A Light (Katrina and the Waves)
3) 2006 Hard Rock Hallelujah (Lordi) FIN
4) 1984 I Treni Di Tozeur (Alice & Franco Battiato) ITA
5) 1998 BIRMINGHAM

Klaus Woryna – Germany

1) 1988 Go (Scott Fitzgerald)
2) 1995 Love City Groove (Love City Groove)
3) 1985 La Det Swinge (Bobbysocks) NOR
4) 1995 Nocturne (Secret Garden) NOR
5) 1985 GOTHENBURG

Karen Fricker – Ireland

1) 1997 Love Shine A Light (Katrina and The Waves)
2) 2005 Touch My Fire (Javine)
3) 1998 Diva (Dana International) ISR
4) 2005 Talking To You (Jakob Sveistrup) DEN
5) 1998 BIRMINGHAM

Toni Sant – Malta

1) 1976 Save All Your Kisses For Me (Brotherhood Of Man)
2) 2007 Flying The Flag (Scooch)
3) 2006 Hard Rock Hallelujah (Lordi) FIN
4) 2007 Visionary Dream (Sopho) GEO
5) 2006 ATHENS

Rene Kern – Austria

1) 1964 I Love The Little Things (Matt Monro)
2) 2007 Flying The Flag (Scooch)
3) 1988 Ne Partez Pas Sans Moi (Celine Dion) SWI
4) 2007 Cvet Z Juga (Alenka Gotar) SLO
5) 1974 BRIGHTON

Peter Ramon Baumann – Switzerland

1) 1997 Love Shine A Light (Katrina and the Waves)
2) 2003 Cry Baby (Jemini)
3) 2000 Fly On The Wings Of Love (Olsen Brothers) DEN
4) 2005 My Number One (Helena Paparizou) GRE
5) 1999 JERUSALEM

Matteo Aldrovandi – Italy

1) 1994 Lonely Symphony (Frances Ruffelle)
2) 1995 Love City Groove (Love City Groove)
3) 2003 Everyway That I Can (Sertab Erener) TUR
4) 1997 Dinle (Sebnem Parker and Group Etnic) TUR
5) 1997 DUBLIN

Antonio Sergio Texeira – Portugal

1) 1994 Lonely Symphony (Frances Ruffelle)
2) 1995 Love City Groove (Love City Groove)
3) 1969 Un Jour, Un Enfant (Frida Boccara) FRA
4) 1993 Vrede (Ruth Jacott) NET
5) 1996 OSLO

Mikael Olofsson – Sweden

1) 1982 One Step Further (Bardo)
2) 2003 Cry Baby (Jemini)
3) 1990 Insieme 1992 (Toto Cotugno) ITA
4) 1984 Ik Hou Van Jou (Maribelle) NET
5) 2000 STOCKHOLM

Pedro Sa – Portugal

1) 1997 Love Shine A Light (Katrina and the Waves)
2) 1966 A Man Without Love (Kenneth McKellar)
3) 1965 Poupee De Cire, Poupee De Son (France Gall) LUX
4) 1982 A Little Peace (Nicole) GER
5) 1968 LONDON

186

Patrik Rosell – Sweden

1) 1965 I Belong (Kathy Kirby)
2) 1966 A Man Without Love (Kenneth McKellar)
3) 1965 Poupee De Cire, Poupee De Son (France Gall) LUX
4) 1998 Neka Ni Me Svane (Danijela) CRO
5) 2000 STOCKHOLM

Vlad Yakovlev – Russia

1) 1988 Go (Scott Fitzgerald)
2) 2007 Flying The Flag (Scooch)
3) 2004 Wild Dances (Ruslana) UKR
4) 2006 Congratulations (Silvia Night) ICE
5) 2000 STOCKHOLM

Peter Goessnitzer – Austria

1) 1981 Making Your Mind Up (Bucks Fizz)
2) 2005 Touch My Fire (Javine)
3) 2004 Wild Dances (Ruslana) UKR
4) 2004 Wild Dances (Ruslana) UKR
5) 2000 STOCKHOLM

Chris Erhard - Austria

1) 1976 Save Your Kisses For Me (Brotherhood Of Man)
2) 1977 Rock Bottom (Lyndsey De Paul & Mike Moran)
3) 1972 Apres Toi (Vicky Leandros) LUX
4) 1972 Apres Toi (Vicky Leandros) LUX
5) 1983 MUNICH

Roland Putz – Austria

1) 1997 Love Shine A Light (Katrina And The Waves)
2) 1989 Why Do I Always Get It Wrong (Live Report)
3) 1982 A Little Peace (Nicole) GER
4) 2001 Je N'Ai Que Mon Ame (Natasha St Pier) FRA
5) 1981 DUBLIN

Wolfgang Merkens – Austria

1) 1972 Beg, Steal Or Borrow (New Seekers)
2) 1986 Runner In The Night (Ryder)
3) 1979 Hallelujah (Gali Atari with Milk And Honey) ISR
4) 1967 Il Doit Faire Beau La-Bas (Noelle Cordier) FRA
5) 1968 LONDON

Robert Weixelbaum - Austria

1) 1967 Puppet On A String (Sandie Shaw)
2) 2007 Flying The Flag (Scooch)
3) 2004 Wild Dances (Ruslana) UKR
4) 2002 Light A Candle (Sarit Hadad) ISR
5) 2004 ISTANBUL

Markus Duernberger - Austria

1) 1981 Making Your Mind Up (Bucks Fizz)
2) 1989 Why Do I Always Get It Wrong (Live Report)
3) 1973 Tu Te Reconnaitras (Anne-Marie David) LUX
4) 1980 Quedate Esta Noche (Trigo Limpio) SPA
5) 1980 THE HAGUE

Richard Nakowitsch – Austria

1) 1994 Lonely Symphony (Frances Ruffelle)
2) 2007 Flying The Flag (Scooch)
3) 2003 Every Way That I Can (Sertab Erener) TUR
4) 1984 100% D'Amour (Sophie Carle) LUX
5) 1993 MILLSTREET

Norbert Reiner – Austria

1) 1967 Puppet On A String (Sandie Shaw)
2) 2007 Flying The Flag (Scooch)
3) 1969 Vivo Cantando (Salome) SPA
4) 1994 Kinek Mondjam El Vetkeimet (Friderika Bayer) HUN
5) 1998 BIRMINGHAM

Christian Weis – Austria

1) 1976 Save Your Kisses For Me (Brotherhood Of Man)
2) 2005 Touch My Fire (Javine)
3) 1994 Rock 'N' Roll Kids (Paul Harrington and Charlie McGettigan) IRE
4) 2006 No No Never (Texas Lightning) GER
5) 1985 GOTHENBURG

Gerald Gruenauer – Austria

1) 1997 Love Shine A Light (Katrina And The Waves)
2) 2007 Flying The Flag (Scooch)
3) 1998 Diva (Dana International) ISR
4) 1997 Zbudi Se (Tanja Ribic) SLO
5) 1997 DUBLIN

Roman Leschitz – Austria

1) 1996 Just A Little Bit (Gina G)
2) 2007 Flying The Flag (Scooch)
3) 2006 Hard Rock Hallelujah (Lordi) FIN
4) 2006 Hard Rock Hallelujah (Lordi) FIN
5) 2006 ATHENS

Marco Schreuder – Austria

1) 1967 Puppet On A String (Sandie Shaw)
2) 1957 All (Patricia Bredin)
3) 1964 Non Ho L'Eta (Gigliola Cinquetti) ITA
4) 1964 Non Ho L'Eta (Gigliola Cinquetti) ITA
5) 1966 LUXEMBOURG

Martin Huber – Austria

1) 1970 Knock Knock (Who's There) (Mary Hopkin)
2) 1975 Let Me Be The One (The Shadows)
3) 1971 Un Banc, Un Arbre, Une Rue (Severine) MON
4) 1983 Ruecksicht (Hoffmann and Hoffmann) GER
5) 1984 LUXEMBOURG

Andreas Artner – Austria

1) 1981 Making Your Mind Up (Bucks Fizz)
2) 2007 Flying The Flag (Scooch)
3) 1988 Ne Partez Pas Sans Moi (Celine Dion) SWI
4) 1974 Waterloo (Abba) SWE
5) 1981 DUBLIN

Andreas Horvath – Austria

1) 1994 Lonely Symphony (Frances Ruffelle)
2) 1979 Mary Ann (Black Lace)
3) 1988 Ne Partez Pas Sans Moi (Celine Dion) SWI
4) 2007 Work Your Magic (Koldun) BLA
5) 1989 LAUSSANE

Bernd Reisner – Austria

1) 1997 Love Shine A Light (Katrina And The Waves)
2) 1995 Love City Groove (Love City Groove)
3) 1990 Insieme 1992 (Toto Cotugno) ITA
4) 1990 Insieme 1992 (Toto Cotugno) ITA
5) 1990 ZAGREB

Hannes Schweiger – Austria

1) 1997 Love Shine A Light (Katrina And The Waves)
2) 1987 Only The Light (Rikki)
3) 1998 Diva (Dana International) ISR
4) 2001 Energy (Nusa Derenda) SLO
5) 2005 KIEV

Sascha Franz – Austria

1) 1998 Where Are You? (Imaani)
2) 2001 No Dream Impossible (Lindsay Dracass)
3) 1994 Rock 'N' Roll Kids (Paul Harrington and Charlie McGettigan)
    IRE
4) 1994 Rock 'N' Roll Kids (Paul Harrington and Charlie McGettigan)
    IRE
5) 2006 ATHENS

Stefan Ball – Austria

1) 1973 Power To All Our Friends (Cliff Richard)
2) 2007 Flying The Flag (Scooch)
3) 1980 Hold Me Now (Johnny Logan) IRE
4) 1988 Stad I Ljus (Tommy Korberg) SWE
5) 1973 LUXEMBOURG

Kristian Jensen – Denmark

1) 1976 Save Your Kisses For Me (Brotherhood Of Man)
2) 1990 Give A Little Love Back To The World (Emma)
3) 1987 Hold Me Now (Johnny Logan) IRE
4) 1987 Hold Me Now (Johnny Logan) IRE
5) 1995 DUBLIN

Martin Backhaus – Germany

1) 2001 No Dream Impossible (Lindsay Dracass)
2) 2003 Cry Baby (Jemini)
3) 1993 In Your Eyes (Niamh Kavnagh) IRE
4) 2001 Energy (Nusa Derenda) SLO
5) 1998 BIRMINGHAM

Jacob Laursen – Denmark

1) 1988 Go (Scott Fitzgerald)
2) 2003 Cry Baby (Jemini)
3) 2003 Every Way That I Can (Sertab Erener) TUR
4) 1991 C'est Le Dernier Qui A Parle (Amina) FRA
5) 2000 STOCKHOLM

Stefan Adamski – Germany

1) 1997 Love Shine A Light (Katrina and The Waves)
2) 1999 Say It Again (Precious)
3) 2000 Fly On The Wings Of Love (Olsen Brothers) DEN
4) 1993 Iemand Als Jij (Barbara) BEL
5) 2000 STOCKHOLM

Alessandro Banti – Italy

1) 1989 Why Do I Always Get It Wrong (Live Report)
2) 2003 Cry Baby (Jemini)
3) 1988 Ne Partez Pas Sans Moi (Celine Dion) SWI
4) 1988 Ne Partez Pas Sans Moi (Celine Dion) SWI
5) 1990 ZAGREB

Rod Skilbeck – Australia

1) 1981 Making Your Mind Up (Bucks Fizz)
2) 2005 Touch My Fire (Javine)
3) 1974 Waterloo (Abba) SWE
4) 2000 My Star (Brainstorm) LAT
5) 2004 ISTANBUL

Biff Williams – UK

1) 1997 Love Shine A Light (Katrina and the Waves)
2) 1984 Love Games (Belle and the Devotions)
3) 1988 Ne Partez Pas Sans Moi (Celine Dion) SWI
4) 1988 Ne Partez Pas Sans Moi (Celine Dion) SWI
5) 1975 STOCKHOLM

Dominic Smith – UK

1) 1998 Where Are You? (Imaani)
2) 1993 Better The Devil You Know (Sonia)
3) 1977 L'Oiseau Et L'Enfant (Marie Myriam) FRA
4) 1998 Hemel En Aarde (Edsilia Rombley) NET
5) 1999 JERUSALEM

Jess Cully – UK

1) 1997 Love Shine A Light (Katrina and the Waves)
2) 2003 Cry Baby (Jemini)
3) 2003 Every Way That I Can (Sertab Erener) TUR
4) 1996 Mon Coeur L'Aime (Kathy Leander) SWI
5) 2001 COPENHAGEN

John Jago – UK

1) 2001 No Dream Impossible (Lindsey Dracass)
2) 1995 Love City Groove (Love City Groove)
3) 1998 Diva (Dana International) ISR
4) 1993 Hombres (Eva Santamaria) SPA
5) 1990 ZAGREB

Miguel Montero – Spain

1) 1997 Love Shine A Light (Katrina and the Waves)
2) 1999 Say It Again (Precious)
3) 1972 Apres Toi (Vicky Leandros) LUX
4) 1998 Neka Ni Me Svane (Danijela) CRO
5) 2003 RIGA

Michael Potter – UK

1) 2007 Flying The Flag (Scooch)
2) 1966 A Man Without Love (Kenneth McKellar)
3) 2005 My Number One (Helena Paparizou) GRE
4) 2005 Angel (Chiara) MAL
5) 2005 KIEV

Pawel Wolski – Poland

1) 1997 Love Shine A Light (Katrina and the Waves)
2) 1993 Better The Devil You Know (Sonia)
3) 1973 Tu Te Reconnaitras (Anne-Marie David) LUX
4) 1991 Le Dernier Qui A Parle (Amina) FRA
5) 1995 DUBLIN

I am grateful to Eurovision fans from all corners of the world that took part and became members of the UK Invitation jury.

Most respondents were from the United Kingdom, Austria and France but there was also good representation from Germany and Sweden.

Other nations to be represented included South Africa, Malta, Norway, Finland, Spain, Colombia, Ireland, Switzerland, Italy, Portugal, Russia, Denmark, Australia, Poland, Greece, FYR Macedonia and Lithuania.

WE ONLY WATCHED THE VOTING!

In the United Kingdom, your average television viewer does not watch the actual Eurovision Song Contest – apparently, they only watch the voting!

Balderdash! Come out and be proud, that's what I say. There is nothing to be afraid of!....

In this section, we examine a few Eurovision polls from a largely United Kingdom perspective.

To that end, a number of the polls feature votes cast from a panel of 100 Eurovision fans – half drawn from the United Kingdom, the rest from all around the world.

I am assured that these UK fans on this Invitation Jury do actually have knowledge of songs from the shows and not just the voting!

Some of the meanderings from jury members on all things Eurovision appear earlier in the book.

But we asked all those who kindly took part in the survey to make the following choices:-

   a)   Favourite UK entry
   b)   Least favourite UK entry
   c)   Favourite Eurovision winner
   d)   Favourite Eurovision song
   e)   Favourite Eurovision year

Grateful thanks to everyone who took the trouble to take part - but in particular I would like to reserve a special mention for Peter Goessnitzer, of OGAE Austria, and Christian Dufresnes, of OGAE France, who really rallied their respective memberships to the cause.

Invitation Jury Vote – Favourite Eurovision Song

The Top 100

This is the vote that really matters across the continent and the leading two Eurovision songs of all time are predictable choices.

Tying for the top honour are the iconic Swedish folk-rockers Abba, with the song synonymous with the contest, a thumping signature tune for all those who believe success can follow a win in the contest.

Ola from glam band The Ark, in Helsinki, representing Sweden,
who do Eurovision better than anyone else

Alongside is a lady who did not do too badly for herself after representing Switzerland in the late 1980s – the one and only Celine Dion.

So far, so predictable – Dana International weighs in at three and I'm delighted the classy Apres Toi from Vicky Leandros made the top five.

Mr Eurovision, Ireland's Johnny Logan, had to feature and he does so at five – although personally I preferred What's Another Year? to Hold Me Now. I was more impressionable in 1980!

195

There is a great result at six, the highest placing for a song that didn't actually win the contest.

I'm delighted for the lovely Danijela, who got the Birmingham contest off to a flying start in 1998 with the stirring Neka Ni Me Svane. For me it is one of the great Eurovision songs.

A tremendous outcome too for Gigliola Cinquetti who comes in at nine with Ho Non L'Eta – considering this won in 1964, it is testament to its enduring quality. This was a winner that literally got many hooked on the contest.

Ireland and Switzerland each have three songs in the Top 20 and there are placings too for non-winners from France and Poland – the ground-breaking Amina and a stunning debut from Edyta Gorniak respectively.

No UK songs were voted on in this poll and it was interesting to note that 11 contest winners didn't make the Top 100.

Four of them were from the early years of UK involvement and of the four joint winners in 1969, La Troubadour from the Netherlands didn't make it.

There was no place either for Ding Dinge Dong (Netherlands again), A Ba Ni Bi (Israel), Diggi Loo Diggi Ley (Sweden) – something to do with silly song titles? – and also two Irish songs, Why Me? and The Voice.

The only non-entrant winner from the new Millennium – it probably won't take you too long to work out that it was Everybody from Estonia!

01	1974	Waterloo	Abba	Sweden
02	1988	Ne Partez Pas Sans Moi	Celine Dion	Switzerland
03	1998	Diva	Dana International	Israel
04	1972	Apres Toi	Vicky Leandros	Luxembourg
05	1987	Hold Me Now	Johnny Logan	Ireland
06	1998	Neka Ni Me Svane	Danijela	Croatia
07	2003	Every Way That I Can	Sertab Erener	Turkey
08	2006	Hard Rock Hallelujah	Lordi	Finland
09	1964	Ho Non L'Eta	Gigliola Cinquetti	Italy
10	1979	Hallelujah	Milk & Honey	Israel
11	2004	Wild Dances	Ruslana	Ukraine
12	1965	Poupee De Cire Poupee De Son	France Gall	Luxembourg
13	1973	Tu Te Reconnaitras	Anne-Marie David	Luxembourg
14	1991	Le Dernier Qui A Parle	Amina	France
15	1993	In Your Eyes	Niamh Kavanagh	Ireland
16	1994	Rock 'N' Roll Kids	Paul Harrington & Charlie McGettigan	Ireland
17	2000	Fly On The Wings Of Love	The Olsen Brothers	Denmark
18	1971	Un Banc, Un Arbre, Une Rue	Severine	Monaco
19	1982	A Little Peace	Nicole	Germany
20	1990	Insieme 1992	Toto Cotugno	Italy
21	1994	To Nie Ja	Edyta Gorniak	Poland
22	1995	Nocturne	Secret Garden	Norway
23	2001	Die For You	Antique	Greece
24	2002	Il Faut Du Temps	Sandrine Francois	France
25	2005	Angel	Chiara	Malta
26	2005	My Number One	Helena Paparizou	Greece

27	1969	**Vivo Cantando**	**Salome**	**Spain**
28	1983	**Si La Vie Est Cadeau**	**Corinne Hermes**	**Luxembourg**
29	1985	**La Det Swinge**	**Bobbysocks**	**Norway**
30	1989	**Rock Me**	**Riva**	**Yugoslavia**
31	1998	Hemel En Aarde	Edsilia Rombley	Netherlands
32	2000	My Star	Brainstorm	Latvia
33	2001	Energy	Nusa Derenda	Slovenia

34	1966	**Merci Cherie**	**Udo Juergens**	**Austria**
35	1968	**La La La**	**Massiel**	**Spain**
36	1969	Un Jour, Un Enfant	Frida Boccara	France
37	1980	**What's Another Year**	**Johnny Logan**	**Ireland**
38	1980	Amsterdam	Maggie MacNeal	Netherlands
39	1982	Mono I Agapi	Anna Vissi	Cyprus
40	1983	Dzuli	Danijel	Yugoslavia
41	1986	**J'Aime La Vie**	**Sandra Kim**	**Belgium**

42	1987	Gente Di Mare	Umberto Tozzi & Raf	Italy
43	1988	Stad I Ljus	Tommy Korberg	Sweden
44	1988	Lied Fuer Einen Freund	Maxi & Chris Garden	Germany
45	1990	White And Black Blues	Joelle Ursul	France
46	1990	Bandido	Azucar Moreno	Spain
47	1991	**Fangad Av En Stormwind**	**Carola**	**Sweden**
48	1991	Canzone Per Te	Sandra Simo	Switzerland
49	1993	Vrede	Ruth Jacott	Netherlands
50	1994	Vechni Stranik	Youddiph	Russia

51	1995	Se Pa Mej	Jan Johansen	Sweden
52	1997	Fiumi Di Parole	Jalisse	Italy
53	1999	**Take Me To Your Heaven**	**Charlotte Nilsson**	**Sweden**
54	1999	Marija Magdalena	Doris Dragovic	Croatia
55	2000	Once In A Lifetime	Ines	Estonia
56	2001	Never Ever Let You Go	Rollo and King	Denmark
57	2001	Je N'Ai Que Mon Ame	Natasha St Pier	France
58	2002	Runaway	Sahlene	Estonia
59	2002	I Wanna	Marie N	Latvia
60	2002	Seventh Wonder	Ira Losco	Malta
61	2003	Open Your Heart	Birgitta	Iceland
62	2003	Ne Verj, Ne Bojsia, Ne Prosi	t.A.t.U	Russia
63	2004	It Hurts	Lena Philipsson	Sweden
64	2004	Lane Moje	Zeljko Joksimovic	Serbia and Montenegro

65	2004	Stronger Every Minute	Lisa Andreas	Cyprus
66	2005	Talking To You	Jakob Sveistrup	Denmark
67	2006	Tornero	Mihai Traistariu	Romania
68	2006	Invincible	Carola	Sweden
69	2006	No No Never	Texas Lightning	Germany
70	**2007**	**Molitva**	**Marija Serifovic**	**Serbia**
71	**1957**	**Net Als Toen**	**Corry Brocken**	**Netherlands**
72	1958	Nel Blu Dipinto Di Blu	Domenico Modugno	Italy
73	**1963**	**Dansevise**	**Grethe & Jorgen Ingmann**	**Denmark**
74	1964	Des Que Le Printemps Revient	Hugues Aufrey	Luxembourg
75	1967	Il Doit Faire Beau La-Bas	Noelle Cordier	France
76	1969	The Wages Of Love	Muriel Day& The Lindsays	Ireland
77	**1970**	**All Kinds Of Everything**	**Dana**	**Ireland**
78	1971	Diese Welt	Katja Ebstein	Germany
79	1972	Nur Die Liebe Laesst Uns Leben	Mary Roos	Germany
80	1974	Si	Gigliola Cinquetti	Italy
81	1975	Seninle Bir Dakika	Semiha Yanki	Turkey
82	1975	Ein Lied Kann Eine Bruecke Sein	Joy Fleming	Germany
83	1975	Tu Volveras	Sergio Y Estbaliz	Spain
84	1976	Ne Mogu Skriti Svoju Bol	Ambassadori	Yugoslavia
85	1976	Panaghia Mou, Panaghia Mou	Mariza Koch & Dimitris Zouboulis	Greece
86	1976	Mata Hari	Anne-Karine Strom	Norway
87	**1977**	**L'Oiseau Et L'Enfant**	**Marie Myriam**	**France**
88	1978	Parlez-Vous Francais?	Baccara	Luxembourg
89	1978	Questo Amore	Ricchi E Poveri	Italy
90	1979	Dschingis Khan	Dschingis Khan	Germany
91	1979	Disco Tango	Tommy Seebach	Denmark
92	1979	Colorado	Xandra	Netherlands
93	1980	Taenker Altid Pa Dig	Bamses Venner	Denmark
94	1980	Theater	Katja Ebstein	Germany
95	1980	Cinema	Paola del Medico	Switzerland
96	1980	Le Papa Pingouin	Sophie & Magaly	Luxembourg
97	1980	He He M'sieurs, Dames	Profil	France
98	1980	Autostop	Anna Vissi & The Epikouri	Greece
99	1980	Eurovision	Telex	Belgium
100	1980	Quedate Esta Noche	Trigo Limpo	Spain

Invitation Jury Vote – Favourite Eurovision Nation

Our good neighbours France wins this section comfortably, universally recognised as the long-serving nation that has consistently produced the most memorable songs of the Eurovision experience.

Most votes were naturally enough garnered during the early years, when the French language ruled and France got off to a flying start with a number of early victories.

A turn-up in second place is Germany, although they had shared 49 contests with the UK up to 2007 – maybe the Austrian influence on the voting panel played a part here?

Luxembourg, now a distant memory in Eurovision circles, came in third with Ireland – who some may have placed higher – having to settle for fourth.

Italian songs also find a place in the UK jury hearts and Sweden receives a vote of confidence, as you might expect.

Songs from Belgium and Finland, both long-standing Eurovision participants, score disappointingly.

Naturally, the newer nations will not feature prominently, although Russia sits half way which is pretty good going.

Serbia has 12 points, solely from the 2007 contest – so on a percentage basis, Maria Serifovic would have them way out front!

1	France	180 points
2	Germany	146
3	Luxembourg	124
4	Ireland	112
5	Italy	106
6	Sweden	103
7	Netherlands	95
8	Denmark	91
9	Switzerland	86
10	Spain	85
11	Norway	73
12	Monaco	57
13	Israel	56
14	Greece	47
15	Yugoslavia	42
16	Cyprus	39
17	Turkey	35
18	Russia	31
19	Croatia	30
20	Malta	28
21	Austria	27
22	Belgium	26
23	Finland	23
24	Ukraine	22
25	Estonia	21
26	Latvia	20
27	Iceland	18
	Slovenia	18
29	Poland	15
30	Romania	13
31	Serbia	12
32	Serbia&Montenegro	12
33	Portugal	6
34	Belarus	1
	Bosnia&Herzegovina	1
	Hungary	1

All other competing nations to 2007 did not poll and as the jury was UK biased there were no votes cast for United Kingdom songs.

Favourite UK entry

1	1997	Love Shine A Light	Katrina and the Waves	18
2	1998	Where Are You?	Imaani	10
3	1996	Just A Little Bit	Gina G	09
4	1967	Puppet On A String	Sandie Shaw	08
5	1976	Save Your Kisses For Me	Brotherhood Of Man	07
6	1981	Making Your Mind Up	Bucks Fizz	07
7	1994	Lonely Symphony	Frances Ruffelle	07
8	1988	Go	Scott Fitzgerald	04
9	1982	One Step Further	Bardo	03
10	2001	No Dream Impossible	Lindsey Dracass	03
11	1964	I Love The Little Things	Matt Monro	02
12	1965	I Belong	Kathy Kirby	02
13	1970	Knock Knock (Who's There?)	Mary Hopkin	02
14	1972	Beg, Steal Or Borrow	The New Seekers	02
15	1984	Love Games	Belle and the Devotions	02
16	1985	Love Is	Vikki	02
17	1968	Congratulations	Cliff Richard	01
18	1971	Jack In The Box	Clodagh Rogers	01
19	1973	Power To All Our Friends	Cliff Richard	01
20	1974	Long Live Love	Olivia Newton-John	01
21	1977	Rock Bottom	Lindsey de Paul/Mike Moran	01
22	1989	Why Do I Always Get It Wrong?	Live Report	01
23	1992	One Step Out Of Time	Michael Ball	01
24	1995	Love City Groove	Love City Groove	01
25	2000	Don't Play That Song Again	Nicki French	01
26	2003	Cry Baby	Jemini	01
27	2006	Teenage Life	Daz Sampson	01
28	2007	Flying The Flag	Scooch	01
29	1957	All	Patricia Bredin	00
30	1959	Sing Little Birdie	Pearl Carr/Teddy Johnson	00
31	1960	Looking High, High, High	Bryan Johnson	00
32	1961	Are You Sure?	The Allisons	00
33	1962	Ring-A-Ding Girl	Ronnie Carroll	00
34	1963	Say Wonderful Things	Ronnie Carroll	00
35	1966	A Man Without Love	Kenneth McKellar	00
36	1969	Boom Bang A Bang	Lulu	00
37	1975	Tonight	The Shadows	00
38	1978	The Bad Old Days	Co-Co	00
39	1979	Mary Ann	Black Lace	00
40	1980	Love Enough For Two	Prima Donna	00
41	1983	I'm Never Giving Up	Sweet Dreams	00
42	1986	Runner In The Night	Ryder	00

43	1987 Only The Light	Rikki	00
44	1990 Give A Little Love Back To The World	Emma	00
45	1991 A Message To Your Heart	Samantha Janus	00
46	1993 Better The Devil You Know	Sonia	00
47	1999 Say It Again	Precious	00
48	2002 Come Back	Jessica Garlick	00
49	2004 Hold On To Our Love	James Fox	00
50	2005 Touch My Fire	Javine	00

Least Favourite UK entry

1	2007	Flying The Flag	Scooch	22
2	2003	Cry Baby	Jemini	15
3	1995	Love City Groove	Love City Groove	10
4	2005	Touch My Fire	Javine	09
5	1989	Why Do I Always Get It Wrong?	Live Report	06
6	1966	A Man Without Love	Kenneth McKellar	05
7	1993	Better The Devil You Know	Sonia	04
8	1986	Runner In The Night	Ryder	03
9	1987	Only The Light	Rikki	03
10	2006	Teenage Life	Daz Sampson	03
11	1975	Tonight	The Shadows	02
12	1977	Rock Bottom	Lindsey de Paul/Mike Moran	02
13	1988	Go	Scott Fitzgerald	02
14	1994	Lonely Symphony	Frances Ruffelle	02
15	1999	Say It Again	Precious	02
16	2004	Hold On To Our Love	James Fox	02
17	1957	All	Patricia Bredin	01
18	1979	Mary Ann	Black Lace	01
19	1981	Making Your Mind Up	Bucks Fizz	01
20	1984	Love Games	Belle and the Devotions	01
21	1990	Give A Little Love Back To The World	Emma	01
22	1991	A Message To Your Heart	Samantha Janus	01
23	1997	Love Shine A Light	Katrina and the Waves	01
24	2001	No Dream Impossible	Lindsey Dracass	01
25	1959	Sing Little Birdie	Pearl Carr/Teddy Johnson	00
26	1960	Looking High, High, High	Bryan Johnson	00
27	1961	Are You Sure?	The Allisons	00
28	1962	Ring-A-Ding Girl	Ronnie Carroll	00
29	1963	Say Wonderful Things	Ronnie Carroll	00
30	1964	I Love The Little Things	Matt Monro	00
31	1965	I Belong	Kathy Kirby	00
32	1967	Puppet On A String	Sandie Shaw	00
33	1968	Congratulations	Cliff Richard	00
34	1969	Boom Bang A Bang	Lulu	00
35	1970	Knock Knock (Who's There?)	Mary Hopkin	00
36	1971	Jack In The Box	Clodagh Rogers	00
37	1972	Beg, Steal Or Borrow	The New Seekers	00
38	1973	Power To All Our Friends	Cliff Richard	00
39	1974	Long Live Love	Olivia Newton-John	00
40	1976	Save Your Kisses For Me	Brotherhood Of Man	00
41	1978	The Bad Old Days	Co-Co	00
42	1980	Love Enough For Two	Prima Donna	00

43	1982 One Step Further	Bardo	00
44	1983 I'm Never Giving Up	Sweet Dreams	00
45	1985 Love Is	Vikki	00
46	1992 One Step Out Of Time	Michael Ball	00
47	1996 Just A Little Bit	Gina G	00
48	1998 Where Are You?	Imaani	00
49	2000 Don't Play That Song Again	Nicki French	00
50	2002 Come Back	Jessica Garlick	00

The Favourite Eurovision Years

Sweden, through the global superstars Abba, if nothing else, is a nation strongly associated with Eurovision.

There is a clear affection for a nation that always approaches the contest positively, usually to the accompaniment of a schlager backing track.

The Swedish selection for Eurovision – the established and high-profile Melodifestivalen – is a firm favourite with diehard fans.

So it is maybe no surprise that Sweden dominates the poll to find the best contest ever.

The Millennium contest from the Globen Theatre in Stockholm emerged as a clear favourite with voters on the invitation jury.

That in itself though is something of a shock, as it is the 1985 contest in Gothenburg – hosted by the marvellous Lill Lindfors – that tends to get devotees talking for all the right reasons.

Gothenburg was actually squeezed into third place by Birmingham 1998, the Terry Wogan and Ulrika Jonsson show (can't keep the Swedes out of it!)

Dublin 1981, where Bucks Fizz were victorious, was voted fourth most popular, tying with two new century contests – Riga 2003 and, wait for it, Kiev 2005.

Of the contests up to 2007, 16 actually registered the dreaded nul points from our voters. Half of those were contests from the 1950s and 1960s so consideration should clearly be given to the fact that the early shows were always going to experience a musical credit crunch from the old memory bank.

The most recent contest to get a zero – ironically enough, given Sweden's dominance of the charts – was Malmo in 1992. I'm sure Michael Ball won't mind too much. But keep any pins away from your eyes Michael!

Of the early shows, Naples 1965 together with Luxembourg 1966 and London 1968 scored reasonably well. So to all those involved with those early contests, heartfelt congratulations – you clearly made a good impression!

1	2000 STOCKHOLM	Sweden	11
2	1998 BIRMINGHAM	United Kingdom	09
3	1985 GOTHENBURG	Sweden	08
4	1981 DUBLIN	Ireland	07
5	2003 RIGA	Latvia	07
6	2005 KIEV	Ukraine	07
7	1990 ZAGREB	Yugoslavia	04
8	2004 ISTANBUL	Turkey	04
9	2006 ATHENS	Greece	04
10	1989 LAUSANNE	Switzerland	03
11	1996 OSLO	Norway	03
12	1965 NAPLES	Italy	02
13	1966 LUXEMBOURG	Luxembourg	02
14	1968 LONDON	United Kingdom	02
15	1978 PARIS	France	02
16	1991 ROME	Italy	02
17	1993 MILLSTREET	Ireland	02
18	1995 DUBLIN	Ireland	02
19	1997 DUBLIN	Ireland	02
20	1999 JERUSALEM	Israel	02
21	2007 HELSINKI	Finland	02
22	1963 LONDON	United Kingdom	01
23	1971 DUBLIN	Ireland	01
24	1973 LUXEMBOURG	Luxembourg	01
25	1974 BRIGHTON	United Kingdom	01
26	1975 STOCKHOLM	Sweden	01
27	1976 THE HAGUE	Netherlands	01
28	1980 THE HAGUE	Netherlands	01
29	1983 MUNICH	Germany	01
30	1984 LUXEMBOURG	Luxembourg	01
31	1988 DUBLIN	Ireland	01
32	1994 DUBLIN	Ireland	01
33	2001 COPENHAGEN	Denmark	01
34	2002 TALLINN	Estonia	01
35	1957 FRANKFURT	Germany	00
36	1959 CANNES	France	00
37	1960 LONDON	United Kingdom	00

38	1961 CANNES	France	00
39	1962 LUXEMBOURG	Luxembourg	00
40	1964 COPENHAGEN	Denmark	00
41	1967 VIENNA	Austria	00
42	1969 MADRID	Spain	00
43	1970 AMSTERDAM	Netherlands	00
44	1972 EDINBURGH	United Kingdom	00
45	1977 LONDON	United Kingdom	00
46	1979 JERUSALEM	Israel	00
47	1982 HARROGATE	United Kingdom	00
48	1986 BERGEN	Norway	00
49	1987 BRUSSELS	Belgium	00
50	1992 MALMO	Sweden	00

The Roll Of Honour

Again from the invitation jury, what follows is a list of all 49 competing Eurovision nations to 2007 – and the favourite song as voted for by the panel where applicable.

Those nations in italics did not receive points from the jury, therefore the most successful song for that nation is put forward on the roll of honour.

Those nations in bold indicate songs that won the contest in that particular year.

Going down the list, there are really no great surprises until France where Amina – who lost out to Carola on a tie in 1991 – was put forward.

You can probably put that result down to the memory bank, with France putting in some samey and none too memorable entries in recent times.

I would not class the Estonian selection as a shock as I have yet to encounter any neutrals who rate the winner in Copenhagen as the finest hour for Estonia – or Eurovision for that matter.

And I'm personally pleased that Antique got the nod ahead of Helena Paparizou for Greece.

Birgitta for Iceland was a surprise but the jury restored my faith in natural justice in selecting outstanding non-winning songs for both Latvia and the Netherlands.

I found it curious that Dima Bilan, with his 2006 entry, did not win through for Russia and it could only be Abba for Sweden.

And much as I quite liked Yugoslavia's lone winner, I'm not sure it can be bracketed as a Eurovision classic!

01	ALBANIA	2004	The Image Of You	Anjeza Shahini
02	ANDORRA	2007	Salvem El Mon	Anonymous
03	ARMENIA	2006	Without Your Love	Andre
04	**AUSTRIA**	**1966**	**Merci Cherie**	**Udo Juergens**
05	BELARUS	2007	Work Your Magic	Dimitri Koldun
06	**BELGIUM**	**1986**	**J'Aime La Vie**	**Sandra Kim**
07	BOSNIA HERZEGOVINA	2006	Lejla	Hari Mata Hari
08	BULGARIA	2007	Water	Elitsa Todorova & Stoyan Yankoulov
09	CROATIA	1998	Neka Ni Me Svane	Danijela
10	CYPRUS	1982	Mono I Agapi	Anna Vissi
11	CZECH REPUBLIC	2007	Mala Dama	Kabat
12	**DENMARK**	**2000**	**Fly On The Wings Of Love**	**Olsen Brothers**
13	ESTONIA	2000	Once In A Lifetime	Ines
14	**FINLAND**	**2006**	**Hard Rock Hallelujah**	**Lordi**
15	FRANCE	1991	Le Dernier Qui A Parle	Amina
16	F Y R O M	2007	Mojot Svet	Karolina Gocheva
17	GEORGIA	2007	Visionary Dream	Sopho
18	**GERMANY**	**1982**	**A Little Peace**	**Nicole**
19	GREECE	2001	Die For You	Antique
20	HUNGARY	1994	Kinek Mondjam El Vetkeimet	Friderika Bayer

21	ICELAND	2003 Open Your Heart	Birgitta
22	**IRELAND**	**1987 Hold Me Now**	**Johnny Logan**
23	**ISRAEL**	**1998 Diva**	**Dana International**
24	**ITALY**	**1964 Non Ho L'Eta**	**Gigliola Cinquetti**
25	LATVIA	2000 My Star	Brainstorm
26	*LITHUANIA*	*2006 We Are The Winners*	*LT United*
27	**LUXEMBOURG**	**1972 Apres Toi**	**Vicky Leandros**
28	MALTA	2005 Angel	Chiara
29	*MOLDOVA*	*2005 Boonika Bate Doba*	*Zdob Si Zdub*
30	**MONACO**	**1971 Un Banc, Un Arbre, Une Rue**	**Severine**
31	*MONTENEGRO*	*2007 Ajde Kroci*	*Stevan Faddy*
32	*MOROCCO*	*1980 Bitakat Hob*	*Samira Bensaid*
33	NETHERLANDS	1998 Hemel En Aarde	Edsilia Rombley
34	**NORWAY**	**1995 Nocturne**	**Secret Garden**
35	POLAND	1994 To Nie Ja	Edyta Gorniak
36	PORTUGAL	1984 Silencio E Tanta Gente	Maria Guinot
37	ROMANIA	2006 Tornero	Mihai Traistariu
38	RUSSIA	1994 Vechni Stranik	Youddiph
39	**SERBIA**	**2007 Molitva**	**Marija Serifovic**
40	SERBIA & MONTENEGRO	2004 Lane Moje	Zeljko Joksimovic

41	*SLOVAKIA*	*1996 Kym Nas Ma*	*Marcel Polander*
42	SLOVENIA	2001 Energy	Nusa Derenda
43	**SPAIN**	**1969 Vivo Cantando**	**Salome**
44	**SWEDEN**	**1974 Waterloo**	**Abba**
45	**SWITZERLAND**	**1988 Ne Partez Pas Sans Moi**	**Celine Dion**
46	**TURKEY**	**2003 Every Way That I Can**	**Sertab Erener**
47	**UKRAINE**	**2004 Wild Dances**	**Ruslana**
48	**UNITED KINGDOM**	**1997 Love Shine A Light**	**Katrina & The Waves**
49	**YUGOSLAVIA**	**1989 Rock Me Baby**	**Riva**

Friend Or Foe

So who are the UK's friends in Eurovision – and how do you measure that friendship?

For example, the UK does not get many votes from eastern European nations – to the great delight of Johnny Foreigner.

But turn it round and – hang on a minute Johnny – the UK is not too liberal in dishing them out either to Warsaw and beyond.

So in examining that all-important handshake, whose hand actually extends the furthest.

In this section, the UK's Eurovision rivals are classified in terms of 'friend, 'neutral' and 'foe'.

A friend to the UK is a nation that has allocated a higher percentage of its top mark and also more maximum point awards than vice-versa.

This covers the UK's participation since 1957, so we go back beyond the introduction of the familiar 'douze points' in 1975.

A neutral nation is one that meets one of the two criteria but not the other. In other words, honours even.

A foe to the UK is a nation to which the UK has allocated a higher percentage of its top mark and also more maximum point awards than vice-versa.

So where does that leave our good friends Ireland and our entente cordiale with France?

Do the wartime gremlins with Germany persist and are Portugal really our oldest allies? How does the big bad growling bear that is Russia rate?

Which nations come out to bat for us when the going gets tough on the Eurovision Song Contest stage?

Let's start with Ireland. Our traditional near neighbour and a shared language but admittedly there have been political differences not so long ago. Here it's political. *Foe.*

The entente cordiale with France? Sir Terry Wogan opined in amazement when the French gave votes to the UK. They have done it more than you probably think. *Friend.*

And dear old Germany? Surely they won't like us in light of everything that has gone on before. Well, they do like us actually. *Friend.*

Our oldest allies Portugal, who have suffered greatly in the Eurovision but plough gamely on. True to form. *Friend.*

And finally Russia. It's highly unlikely they'd throw any votes at all over to the west, let alone to the UK. Well, they are more likely to back us than we are to back them. *Friend.*

Of our 48 rivals over 50 years, the United Kingdom – in a Facebook sort of way – has 25 friends.

There are 11 in the acquaintances category and 12 that are definitely not on the Christmas card list.

Not that I wish to make any sort of point, but for good measure I shall list the dirty dozen here.

In alphabetical order, please step forward: Albania, Bulgaria, Cyprus, Estonia, Greece, Iceland, Ireland, Latvia, Lithuania, Moldova, Serbia/Montenegro and Ukraine.

It is the Ukraine who have the furthest to go in extending the hand of friendship. Interestingly, Ukraine are the only one of the former Soviet nations categorised as a foe.

The UK needs to be more wary of the Baltic nations, where Estonia, Latvia and Lithuania all line up against us.

On a happier note, we do have a lot of friends out there really so the xenophobes should not get too excited.

Who would have thought it... Belarus, FYR Macedonia, Morocco, Romania, Slovakia and Turkey also number as friends of the United Kingdom.

Even Armenia and Georgia are meeting us half way, putting them on a par with Sweden.

The full list is as follows:-

FRIEND	NEUTRAL	FOE
Andorra	Armenia	Albania
Austria	Czech Republic	Bulgaria
Belarus	Finland	Cyprus
Belgium	Georgia	Estonia
Bosnia Herzegovina	Italy	Greece
Croatia	Monaco	Iceland
Denmark	Montenegro	Ireland
France	Poland	Latvia
FYR Macedonia	Serbia	Lithuania
Germany	Sweden	Moldova
Hungary	Yugoslavia	Serbia/Montenegro
Israel		Ukraine
Luxembourg		
Malta		
Morocco		
Netherlands		
Norway		
Portugal		
Romania		
Russia		
Slovakia		
Slovenia		
Spain		
Switzerland		
Turkey		
25	11	12

The Dreaded 'Nul Points'

Norway still holds the proud record for the most number of occasions that a nation has finished on the bottom rung in the Eurovision final.

And to boot, Norway's tally of four 'nul points' is also out front, although Finland, Austria, Spain and Switzerland are not far behind.

The UK and Ireland each share one last place, although in the UK's case it was accompanied by 'nul points'.

The table does not include the result of the 2008 contest, where the UK finished joint bottom with Germany and Poland.

Nation	Last Place	Nul Points
NORWAY	10	4
FINLAND	8	3
BELGIUM	8	2
AUSTRIA	7	3
GERMANY	5	2
SPAIN	4	3
SWITZERLAND	4	3
PORTUGAL	3	2
TURKEY	3	2
NETHERLANDS	3	2
MALTA	3	0
ICELAND	2	1
SWEDEN	2	1
MONACO	2	1
LUXEMBOURG	2	1
LITHUANIA	1	1
ITALY	1	1
YUGOSLAVIA	1	1
UNITED KINGDOM	1	1
CYPRUS	1	0
IRELAND	1	0
DENMARK	1	0

FLYING THE FLAG!

When it comes down to dishing out the points over the years, none have been so mountainous with their generosity than the cowbell twins of Switzerland and Austria.

The association goes back a long way obviously but both have tended to back the UK to the hilt, certainly in the days when there was a distinct western European bias.

The UK has shared the Eurovision stage 44 times with Switzerland over the 50 years, so a return of 204 points works out at an average of nearly five which is very good going.

France and Belgium form an alliance a little closer to home at the top of the tree with Ireland fifth, providing us with 177 points from 40 joint appearances – an average of little more than four.

That still isn't too bad a ratio although we've whisked back a hefty 203 in return!

Sweden and Portugal show up pretty well in this chart but we've never had much from Greece and Cyprus and Iceland, apart from one year, is pretty much a lost cause.

This tabulation favours nations of long standing in the Eurovision – there may of course be others who have made far fewer appearances who may also be really supportive.

Don't get too excited on that front is all I would say. However, on the strength of eight out of 12 possible points from her one and only Eurovision appearance in 1980, Morocco proudly tops the percentage poll!

Hungary and Malta are also up in the top ten here but further down the ranks it's really the same old story.

So when you combine the charts, you get a pretty uniform – and totally realistic – picture in respect of who have been the main supporters of the UK in Eurovision.

TOTAL POINTS GIVEN TO THE UK
(1957 TO 2007)

Rank	Nation	Points to UK
1	SWITZERLAND	204
2	AUSTRIA	188
3	FRANCE	184
4	BELGIUM	180
5	IRELAND	177
6	LUXEMBOURG	174
7	GERMANY	172
8	SWEDEN	167
9	PORTUGAL	163
10	NORWAY	152
11	NETHERLANDS	147
12	ISRAEL	142
13	FINLAND	141
14	SPAIN	140
15	DENMARK	134
16	TURKEY	120
17	ITALY	114
18	MALTA	099
19	YUGOSLAVIA	095
20	MONACO	083
21	GREECE	071
22	CYPRUS	065
23	CROATIA	060
24	ESTONIA	039
25	SLOVENIA	033
26	ICELAND	033
27	HUNGARY	032
28	POLAND	030

29	BOSNIA AND HERZEGOVINA	029
30	RUSSIA	022
31	ROMANIA	017
32	LITHUANIA	016
33	LATVIA	015
34	MACEDONIA	014
35	SLOVAKIA	010
36	MOROCCO	008
37	ANDORRA	002
38	BELARUS	001
39	CZECH REPUBLIC	000
40	GEORGIA	000
41	MONTENEGRO	000
42	SERBIA	000
43	ARMENIA	000
44	SERBIA AND MONTENEGRO	000
45	BULGARIA	000
46	MOLDOVA	000
47	ALBANIA	000
48	UKRAINE	000

PERCENTAGE OF MAXIMUM AWARD GIVEN TO THE UK (1957 TO 2007)

Rank	Country	Max points to UK	Points	Possible	award	%
1	<u>MOROCCO</u>	0	008	012		<u>67</u>
2	LUXEMBOURG	<u>9</u>	174	361		48
3	HUNGARY	1	032	072		44
4	SWITZERLAND	<u>9</u>	<u>204</u>	491		42
5	AUSTRIA	<u>9</u>	188	451		42
6	MALTA	2	099	236		42
7	ISRAEL	5	142	356		40
8	IRELAND	3	177	462		38
9	FRANCE	8	184	517		36
10	BELGIUM	<u>9</u>	180	503		36
11	PORTUGAL	4	163	457		36
12	DENMARK	3	134	375		36
13	MONACO	6	083	229		36
14	YUGOSLAVIA	3	095	269		35
15	TURKEY	2	120	348		34
16	GERMANY	4	172	<u>527</u>		33
17	SWEDEN	5	167	502		33
18	ITALY	2	114	347		33
19	CROATIA	2	060	180		33
20	FINLAND	2	141	439		32
21	NORWAY	6	152	507		30
22	NETHERLANDS	6	147	491		30
23	SPAIN	4	140	509		28
24	SLOVAKIA	0	010	036		28
25	ESTONIA	0	039	156		25
26	CYPRUS	0	065	300		22
27	GREECE	1	071	334		21
28	SLOVENIA	0	033	156		21
29	POLAND	0	030	144		21
30	BOSNIA & HERZ	0	029	156		19
31	LITHUANIA	0	016	084		19
32	RUSSIA	1	022	132		17
33	MACEDONIA	0	014	084		17
34	ROMANIA	1	017	108		16
35	LATVIA	0	015	096		16
36	ICELAND	1	033	240		14
37	ANDORRA	0	002	048		04
38	BELARUS	0	001	048		02
39	CZECH REPUBLIC	0	000	012		00
40	GEORGIA	0	000	012		00
41	MONTENEGRO	0	000	012		00
42	SERBIA	0	000	012		00

43	ARMENIA	0		000	024		00
44	SERB & MONT	0		000	024		00
45	BULGARIA	0		000	036		00
46	MOLDOVA	0		000	036		00
47	ALBANIA	0		000	048		00
48	UKRAINE	0		000	060		00

In terms of friendliness to the United Kingdom between 1957 and 2007, this is how the countries rank:-

01	SWITZERLAND
02	AUSTRIA
03	LUXEMBOURG
04	FRANCE
05	IRELAND
06	BELGIUM
07	ISRAEL
08	PORTUGAL
09	GERMANY
10	MALTA
11	SWEDEN
12	DENMARK
13	HUNGARY
14	TURKEY
15	NORWAY
16	MONACO
17	YUGOSLAVIA
18	FINLAND
19	NETHERLANDS
20	ITALY
21	MOROCCO
22	SPAIN
23	CROATIA
24	CYPRUS
25	GREECE
26	ESTONIA
27	SLOVENIA
28	POLAND
29	SLOVAKIA
30	BOSNIA/HERZEGOVINA
31	RUSSIA
32	ICELAND
33	LITHUANIA
34	ROMANIA

35	MACEDONIA
36	LATVIA
37	ANDORRA
38	BELARUS
39	CZECH REPUBLIC
40	GEORGIA
41	MONTENEGRO
42	SERBIA
43	ARMENIA
44	SERBIA/MONTENEGRO
45	BULGARIA
46	MOLDOVA
47	ALBANIA
48	UKRAINE

VOTES TO NATIONS FROM THE UK

Key

A	Number of appearances together in a Eurovision final
B	Nation
C	Total points from the UK
D	Possible points award from the UK
E	Percentage
F	Rank out of 48 in terms of UK support to the nation (composite of G and H)
G	Rank in terms of points
H	Rank in terms of percentage

A	B	C	D	E	F	G/H
02	ALBANIA	1	24	04	38	38/37
00	ANDORRA	0	0	00	39	39/39
02	ARMENIA	0	24	00	46	46/46
40	AUSTRIA	104	388	27	08	08/14
01	BELARUS	0	12	00	43	43/43
44	BELGIUM	105	411	26	09	07/15
13	BOSNIA/HERZ	4	156	03	37	35/38
01	BULGARIA	5	12	42	20	34/03
14	CROATIA	15	168	09	32	28/33
23	CYPRUS	71	276	26	16	15/16
00	CZECH REP	0	0	00	41	41/41
33	DENMARK	92	325	28	07	09/13
09	ESTONIA	49	108	45	12	22/02
39	FINLAND	64	383	17	23	17/26
48	FRANCE	113	466	24	11	05/18
01	GEORGIA	0	12	00	45	45/45
49	GERMANY	151	471	32	04	03/09
28	GREECE	81	329	25	15	13/17
06	HUNGARY	12	72	17	30	31/27
17	ICELAND	48	204	24	21	23/19
40	IRELAND	203	420	48	01	01/01
28	ISRAEL	107	327	33	05	06/07
34	ITALY	55	291	19	24	20/24
07	LATVIA	27	84	32	18	25/10
06	LITHUANIA	17	72	24	25	27/20
35	LUXEMBOURG	87	310	28	10	11/12
07	MACEDONIA	0	84	00	48	48/48

19	MALTA	75	224	33	06	14/08
03	MOLDOVA	2	36	06	36	37/36
21	MONACO	54	145	37	13	21/04
00	MONTENEGRO	0	0	00	40	40/40
01	MOROCCO	0	12	00	44	44/44
43	NETHERLANDS	86	399	22	17	12/21
45	NORWAY	92	448	21	18	10/23
09	POLAND	14	108	13	31	29/29
37	PORTUGAL	36	385	09	29	24/32
09	ROMANIA	6	108	06	35	33/35
11	RUSSIA	20	132	15	28	26/28
01	SERBIA	0	12	00	42	42/42
02	SERBIA/MONT	3	24	13	34	36/31
03	SLOVAKIA	0	36	00	47	47/47
10	SLOVENIA	10	120	08	33	32/34
47	SPAIN	61	471	13	26	19/30
46	SWEDEN	160	460	35	02	02/06
44	SWITZERLAND	146	411	36	03	04/05
29	TURKEY	63	348	18	22	18/25
05	UKRAINE	13	60	22	27	30/22
27	YUGOSLAVIA	69	231	30	14	16/11

In terms of whom the UK favours, this is how the countries rank:-

1	IRELAND
2	SWEDEN
3	SWITZERLAND
4	GERMANY
5	ISRAEL
6	MALTA
7	DENMARK
8	AUSTRIA
9	BELGIUM
10	LUXEMBOURG
11	FRANCE
12	ESTONIA
13	MONACO
14	YUGOSLAVIA
15	GREECE
16	CYPRUS
17	NETHERLANDS
18	NORWAY
19	LATVIA
20	BULGARIA
21	ICELAND
22	TURKEY
23	FINLAND
24	ITALY
25	LITHUANIA
26	SPAIN
27	UKRAINE
28	RUSSIA
29	PORTUGAL
30	HUNGARY
31	POLAND
32	CROATIA
33	SLOVENIA
34	SERBIA/MONTENEGRO
35	ROMANIA
36	MOLDOVA

37	BOSNIA/HERZEGOVINA
38	ALBANIA
39	ANDORRA
40	MONTENEGRO
41	CZECH REPUBLIC
42	SERBIA
43	BELARUS
44	MOROCCO
45	GEORGIA
46	ARMENIA
47	SLOVAKIA
48	MACEDONIA

LE ROYAUME-UNI – ANY POINT?

In the next pages, we spotlight the 48 nations that have shared the Eurovision stage with the United Kingdom.

They relate to the 50 contests the UK have appeared in between 1957 and 2007 and exclude the inaugural event in 1956 and the 1958 contest, where the UK failed to appear.

The information on each nation is standard, and the statistical section has proved to be a veritable anorak heaven!

The figure against the nation headline represents that nation's fondness for the United Kingdom, ranked from 1 to 48.

This figure is a composite of the rankings of nations in terms of total points and percentage points given to the United Kingdom between 1957 and 2007.

In terms of total points, the rankings are obviously skewed towards the old guard of nations which have made most appearances with the UK.

In terms of percentage points, the rankings are then skewed towards those nations who were most generous from few appearances – Morocco's 8 out of 12 points for the UK in 1980, the African nation's only Eurovision appearance, naturally springs to mind.

To make the overall rank more representative, a composite of these two listings was sought and this is the figure that headlines.

Maximums relate to highest number of votes granted by a nation during the course of a single contest.

Since 1975, when the 12-point maximum was introduced, this process was quite straightforward. Before that, it wasn't so simple, and on those occasions where marks were handed over on a discretionary basis, one or more nations could receive another country's top mark.

Whatever, if a top mark was granted in these circumstances, then for the purposes of this research it is recorded.

Below the headline is the French translation of the country in question – an acknowledgement that French was the founding language of the Eurovision Song Contest. How else have we all come to love the dear old Royaume-Uni?!

Below this, in italics, is the Esc-eranto translation of the nation's name, the common identifiable pronunciation of many a jury representative and contest host over the years. I give you Croaysheeur, Moltur, Belgeeum, Feenlunt for example...

Finally, in brackets, is the nation's rank of favour as decreed by United Kingdom juries and televoters over the years. You can probably guess who is at number one but the top five might hold some surprises!

The commentary on the nations is entirely personal, concentrating on perceptions and how they have influenced the UK's progress in the contest.

The shining light is the artist from the nation who has made the biggest impression on the Eurovision stage – among many eastern bloc nations, where appearances have been limited, there is often not a great deal of choice.

And finally there is my personal choice of favourite song and that chosen by the UK Invitation jury, drawn from voters far and wide.

The section about Russia suggests that they are without a Eurovision win, but of course this is not the case as they were triumphant at Belgrade 2008.

Please bear in mind, stats relate to the 1957 contest and then everyone from 1959 to 2007. The 2008 contest is therefore excluded.

For that reason, there is no mention of the participations from Azerbeijan and San Marino. The latter's swift withdrawal for 2009 could make them a one-contest wonder.

A number of other nations have flirted with the idea of entering the Eurovision. Lebanon and Tunisia both came close to registering an entry and Liechtenstein were certainly keen, although they did not meet the entry requirements set down by the European Broadcasting Union.

So here goes, from Tirana to Belgrade and Berne to Kiev, as Scooch may have sung. Let's fly the flag!

1   SWITZERLAND
Suisse
Sweetsurlunt
(3)

CONTESTS WITH THE UK	44
FIRST PARTICIPATION	1956
VICTORIES	2
1956 1988	
TOTAL POINTS TO THE UK	204
MAXIMUMS	9
1959 1960 1961 1964 1965 1967 1968 1976 1997	
POINTS AVAILABLE TO THE UK	491
AVERAGE (OUT OF 10)	4
RANK **POINTS/%**	1/4

Switzerland? Mountains, cowbells, edelweiss, cheese and the Red Cross.
Are they OK with the UK? Our biggest friend in Eurovision, with no less than nine maximums, seven in ten years between 1959 and 1968.
Switzerland's defining Eurovision moment? The first venue, the first winner and one of the biggest-name winners. That's definition!

TOTAL POINTS FROM THE UK	*146*
MAXIMUMS	*6*
1959 1961 1963 1976 1981 1982	
POINTS AVAILABLE FROM THE UK	*411*
AVERAGE POINTS (OUT OF 10)	*3*
RANK *POINTS/%*	*4/5*

SHINING LIGHT Celine Dion
PERSONAL FAVOURITE Io Senza Te (Peter, Sue and Marc) 1981
INVITATION JURY FAVOURITE Ne Partez Pas Sans Moi (Celine Dion) 1988

2 AUSTRIA
Autriche
Owstreeur
(8)

CONTESTS WITH THE UK	42
FIRST PARTICIPATION	1957
VICTORIES	1
1966	
TOTAL POINTS TO THE UK	188
MAXIMUMS	9
1960 1967 1977 1982 1992 1993 1995 1997 2002	
POINTS AVAILABLE TO THE UK	451
AVERAGE POINTS (OUT OF 10)	4
RANK POINTS/%	2/5

Austria? Mountains again, the home of Jozef Strauss, Sacher torte, right-wing politicians, Arnie Schwarzenegger.

Are they OK with the UK? Yes, very much, with only neighbours Switzerland proving more supportive. We haven't returned the love with our only maximum points to Austria coming during our first participation in 1957.

Austria's defining Eurovision moment? Udo Juergens landed the Eurovision prize with Merci Cherie in 1966. It remains Austria's only win. More recently, Alf Poier brightened up the scene in 2003!

TOTAL POINTS FROM THE UK	*104*
MAXIMUMS	*1*
1957	
POINTS AVAILABLE FROM THE UK	*388*
AVERAGE POINTS (OUT OF 10)	*2*
RANK *POINTS/%*	*8/14*

SHINING LIGHT Udo Juergens
PERSONAL FAVOURITE Weil Der Mensch Zaehlt (Alf Poier) 2003
INVITATION JURY FAVOURITE Merci Cherie (Udo Juergens) 1966

3 LUXEMBOURG
Luxembourg
Lucsemburrg
(10)

CONTESTS WITH THE UK	35
FIRST PARTICIPATION	1956
VICTORIES	5
1961 1965 1972 1973 1983	
TOTAL POINTS TO THE UK	174
MAXIMUMS	9
1960 1961 1967 1969 1973 1975 1977 1982 1989	
POINTS AVAILABLE TO THE UK	361
AVERAGE POINTS (OUT OF 10)	4
RANK POINTS/%	6/2

Luxembourg? Somewhere in the heart of Europe, a Grand Duchy close to Belgium and the Netherlands, the iconic Radio Luxembourg of bygone days, a capital city of the same name, the stage of infamous English football riots.

Are they OK with the UK? Luxembourg loves the UK, with a record-equalling nine maximums while we have been quite frugal in reply.

Luxembourg's defining Eurovision moment? There were five victories between 1961 and 1983 and some cracking winners among them too.

TOTAL POINTS FROM THE UK	*87*
MAXIMUMS	*3*
1967 1972 1973	
POINTS AVAILABLE FROM THE UK	*310*
AVERAGE POINTS (OUT OF 10)	*2*
RANK POINTS/%	*11/12*

SHINING LIGHT Anne-Marie David
PERSONAL FAVOURITE Apres Toi (Vicky Leandros) 1972
INVITATION JURY FAVOURITE Apres Toi (Vicky Leandros) 1972

4 FRANCE

France

Fraants

(11)

CONTESTS WITH THE UK	48
FIRST PARTICIPATION	1956
VICTORIES	5
1958 1960 1962 1969 1977	
TOTAL POINTS TO THE UK	184
MAXIMUMS	8
1967 1968 1972 1975 1977 1989 1995 1997	
POINTS AVAILABLE TO THE UK	517
AVERAGE POINTS (OUT OF 10)	3
RANK POINTS/%	3/9

France? The dull north and the stylish south and the offhand bit in the middle around Paris, frogs, onions, berets and striped shirts.

Are they OK with the UK? France demonstrate the entente cordiale towards the rosbifs. In spite of recent indifferent offerings, the invitation jury has rated France's songs the best.

France's defining Eurovision moment? The prominence of the French language in the early years of Eurovision set the pace.

TOTAL POINTS FROM THE UK	*113*
MAXIMUMS	*5*
1957 1960 1961 1967 1969	
POINTS AVAILABLE FROM THE UK	*466*
AVERAGE POINTS (OUT OF 10)	*2*
RANK *POINTS/%*	*5/18*

SHINING LIGHT Marie Myriam
PERSONAL FAVOURITE Je N'Ai Que Mon Ame (Natasha St Pier) 2001
INVITATION JURY FAVOURITE Le Dernier Qui A Parle (Amina) 1991

5   IRELAND
Irlande
Eiurlund
(1)

CONTESTS WITH THE UK	41
FIRST PARTICIPATION	1965
VICTORIES	7
1970 1980 1987 1992 1993 1994 1996	
TOTAL POINTS TO THE UK	177
MAXIMUMS	3
1966 1970 1997	
POINTS AVAILABLE TO THE UK	462
AVERAGE POINTS (OUT OF 10)	3
RANK POINTS/%	5/8

Ireland? The shamrock, Guinness ready and waiting, Jamesons, U2, and a welcome in song.

Are they OK with the UK? The Irish have only given the UK one maximum since 1970, that going to Katrina in 1997. The UK, however, adores the Irish, with eight maximums and top marks to four of their seven winners. The UK has consistently backed Ireland more than any other nation, so please bear that in mind when the debate comes round to neighbour voting.

Ireland's defining Eurovision moment? A record seven victories, two of them by the same artist, Johnny Logan, who then penned a winner for Linda Martin in 1992. Too many moments to choose from!

TOTAL POINTS FROM THE UK	*203*
MAXIMUMS	*8*
1967 1970 1977 1980 1987 1993 1997 2003	
POINTS AVAILABLE FROM THE UK	*420*
AVERAGE POINTS (OUT OF 10)	*4*
RANK POINTS/%	*1/1*

SHINING LIGHT Johnny Logan
PERSONAL FAVOURITE What's Another Year? (Johnny Logan) 1980
INVITATION JURY FAVOURITE Hold Me Now (Johnny Logan) 1987

6 BELGIUM
Belgique
Belgeeum
(9)

CONTESTS WITH THE UK	47
FIRST PARTICIPATION	1956
VICTORIES	1
1986	
TOTAL POINTS TO THE UK	180
MAXIMUMS	9
1965 1967 1976 1977 1988 1990 1992 1993 1996	
POINTS AVAILABLE TO THE UK	503
AVERAGE POINTS (OUT OF 10)	3
RANK POINTS/%	4/10

Belgium? A non-descript capital city, famous chocolate, cool beers, chips and mayonnaise but not many famous Belgians – Jackie Ickx, Claude Van Damme, Plastic Bertrand. Hercule Poirot, Luc Altidore?

Are they OK with the UK? Belgium has been a very good friend to the UK, joining Austria, Luxembourg and Switzerland with maximum awards in nine contests.

Belgium's defining Eurovision moment? Sandra Kim, naturally, with J'Aime La Vie in 1986, their one and only victory, but I like to think of Telex six years before and their wonderful Eurovision electro-parody as being equally noteworthy.

TOTAL POINTS FROM THE UK	*105*
MAXIMUMS	*1*
1978	
POINTS AVAILABLE FROM THE UK	*411*
AVERAGE POINTS (OUT OF 10)	*2*
RANK POINTS/%	*7/15*

SHINING LIGHT Sandra Kim
PERSONAL FAVOURITE Eurovision (Telex) 1980
INVITATION JURY FAVOURITE J'Aime La Vie (Sandra Kim) 1986

7 ISRAEL
Israel
Izrayell
(5)

CONTESTS WITH THE UK	30
FIRST PARTICIPATION	1973
VICTORIES	3
1978 1979 1998	
TOTAL POINTS TO THE UK	142
MAXIMUMS	5
1973 1976 1981 1993 1998	
POINTS AVAILABLE TO THE UK	356
AVERAGE POINTS (OUT OF 10)	4
RANK POINTS/%	12/7

Israel? The kibbutz, kosher, a volatile region, security-conscious El Al, a seething mix of modern and ancient.

Are they OK with the UK? Israel gave us five maximums between 1973 and 1998. We've usually found points for Israel, maximums for the excellent Gali Atari with Milk and Honey and for Liora's Anthem.

Israel's defining Eurovision moment? Hallelujah in 1979 remains one of the most pleasingly tuneful of Eurovision anthems; Diva, and the accompanying fanfare, remains one of the most enduring – and certainly most defining – of Eurovision winners.

TOTAL POINTS FROM THE UK	*107*
MAXIMUMS	*2*
1979 1995	
POINTS AVAILABLE FROM THE UK	*327*
AVERAGE POINTS (OUT OF 10)	*3*
RANK POINTS/%	*6/7*

SHINING LIGHT Izhar Cohen and Alpha Beta
PERSONAL FAVOURITE Diva (Dana International) 1998
INVITATION JURY FAVOURITE Diva (Dana International) 1998

8 PORTUGAL
Portugal
Portoogul
(29)

CONTESTS WITH THE UK	41
FIRST PARTICIPATION	1964
VICTORIES	0
TOTAL POINTS TO THE UK	163
MAXIMUMS	4
1976 1977 1989 1996	
POINTS AVAILABLE TO THE UK	457
AVERAGE POINTS (OUT OF 10)	3
RANK POINTS/%	9/11

Portugal? Historically the UK's oldest ally, the sunspot delights of the Algarve, the beauty of the Lisbon coast and the Douro valley, the Fado and Cristiano Ronaldo.

Are they OK with the UK? In line with the historical aspect, Portugal indeed has been a good friend to the UK with four maximum awards. We have only ever given 36 points in total to Portuguese songs.

Portugal's defining Eurovision moment? Portugal has never won the Eurovision so their defining moment is yet to come.

TOTAL POINTS FROM THE UK	*36*
MAXIMUMS	*0*
POINTS AVAILABLE FROM THE UK	*385*
AVERAGE POINTS (OUT OF 10)	*0*
RANK POINTS/%	*24/32*

SHINING LIGHT Lucia Moniz
PERSONAL FAVOURITE Playback (Carlos Paiao) 1981
INVITATION JURY FAVOURITE Silencio E Tanta Gente (Maria Guinot) 1984

9   GERMANY
Allemagne
Jurmunee
(4)

CONTESTS WITH THE UK	49
FIRST PARTICIPATION	1956
VICTORIES	1
1982	
TOTAL POINTS TO THE UK	172
MAXIMUMS	4
1970 1974 1989 1992	
POINTS AVAILABLE TO THE UK	527
AVERAGE POINTS (OUT OF 10)	3
RANK POINTS/%	7/16

Germany? The beloved Fatherland, all sorts of wurst, kaffee und kuchen, a neat and tidy nation and notoriously efficient.

Are they OK with the UK? We have shared 49 of the 50 contests with Germany and they have been pretty kind. They even gave top marks to Olivia ahead of Abba in 1974. The return vote has been solid although we didn't go a bundle on Nicole's winner, probably because we were at war with Argentina at the time. Don't mention the war!

Germany's defining Eurovision moment? The one and only victory remains a highlight but for me Germany is better remembered through the antics of Dschingis Khan, Guildo Horn and Stefan Raab.

TOTAL POINTS FROM THE UK	*151*
MAXIMUMS	*2*
1968 1986	
POINTS AVAILABLE FROM THE UK	*471*
AVERAGE POINTS (OUT OF 10)	*3*
RANK POINTS/%	*3/9*

SHINING LIGHT Nicole
PERSONAL FAVOURITE Lass Die Sonne In Dein Herz (Wind) 1987
INVITATION JURY FAVOURITE A Little Peace (Nicole) 1982

10 MALTA
Malte
Moltur
(6)

CONTESTS WITH THE UK	20
FIRST PARTICIPATION	1971
VICTORIES	0
TOTAL POINTS TO THE UK	99
MAXIMUMS	2
1971 2007	
POINTS AVAILABLE TO THE UK	236
AVERAGE POINTS (OUT OF 10)	4
RANK POINTS/%	18/6

Malta? A warm sunshine island in the Mediterranean which is popular with the Brits, a tradition of good cuisine, big on religion, the Maltese Cross, capital city Valetta.

Are they OK with the UK? They are a friendly lot, the Maltese, twice bestowing maximums upon us – the last occasion, somewhat ironically, favouring Scooch in 2007. We've also sent two by return.

Malta's defining Eurovision moment? Malta has never won the contest but Chiara, has come agonisingly close on two occasions. For me, Angel was a stronger song than My Number One in 2005.

TOTAL POINTS FROM THE UK	*75*
MAXIMUMS	*2*
1998 2002	
POINTS AVAILABLE FROM THE UK	*224*
AVERAGE POINTS (OUT OF 10)	*3*
RANK POINTS/%	*14/8*

SHINING LIGHT Chiara
PERSONAL FAVOURITE Seventh Wonder (Ira Losco) 2002
INVITATION JURY FAVOURITE Angel (Chiara) 2005

11   SWEDEN
Suede
Sweedurn
(2)

CONTESTS WITH THE UK	46
FIRST PARTICIPATION	1958
VICTORIES	4
1974 1984 1991 1999	
TOTAL POINTS TO THE UK	167
MAXIMUMS	5
1969 1973 1980 1983 1997	
POINTS AVAILABLE TO THE UK	502
AVERAGE POINTS (OUT OF 10)	3
RANK POINTS/%	8/17

Sweden? Abba, Volvo and Ikea, giants in their field; beautiful blondes and chilled chaps; a little arrogance; smorgasbord and schlager!

Are they OK with the UK? They have given us five maximums. We have given them fewer maximums but a higher percentage of the vote. And not one single point to Waterloo. What does that tell you?

Sweden's defining Eurovision moment? Abba and Waterloo, of course. However, The Herreys were more popular at Eurovision.

TOTAL POINTS FROM THE UK	*160*
MAXIMUMS	*2*
1991 1999	
POINTS AVAILABLE FROM THE UK	*460*
AVERAGE POINTS (OUT OF 10)	*3*
RANK POINTS/%	*2/6*

SHINING LIGHT The Herreys
PERSONAL FAVOURITE Waterloo (Abba) 1974
INVITATION JURY FAVOURITE Waterloo (Abba) 1974

12   DENMARK
Danemark
Denmarrk
(7)

CONTESTS WITH THE UK	35
FIRST PARTICIPATION	1957
VICTORIES	2
1963 2000	
TOTAL POINTS TO THE UK	134
MAXIMUMS	3
1965 1992 1997	
POINTS AVAILABLE TO THE UK	375
AVERAGE POINTS (OUT OF 10)	3
RANK **POINTS/%**	15/12

Denmark? The cosmopolitan and libertarian arm of Scandinavia, the Tivoli Gardens, the Little Mermaid, a dissenting voice on Europe, Carlsberg!

Are they OK with the UK? A steady ally over the years. The UK has also been reasonably kind to Denmark.

Denmark's defining Eurovision moment? Their two victories were memorable, especially the classy Fly On The Wings Of Love, and were separated by 37 years. Denmark spent many years out of Eurovision.

TOTAL POINTS FROM THE UK	*92*
MAXIMUMS	*2*
1984 2000	
POINTS AVAILABLE FROM THE UK	*325*
AVERAGE POINTS (OUT OF 10)	*2*
RANK *PTS/%*	*9/13*

SHINING LIGHT The Olsen Brothers
PERSONAL FAVOURITE Fra Mols Til Skagen (Aud Wilken) 1995
INVITATION JURY FAVOURITE Fly On The Wings Of Love (The Olsen Brothers) 2000

13   HUNGARY
Hongrie
Hunguree
(30)

CONTESTS WITH THE UK	6
FIRST PARTICIPATION	1994
VICTORIES	0
TOTAL POINTS TO THE UK	32
MAXIMUMS	1
1997	
POINTS AVAILABLE TO THE UK	72
AVERAGE POINTS (OUT OF 10)	4
RANK POINTS/%	27/3

Hungary? The famous goulash national dish, the beautiful twin cities of Buda and Pest, intriguing stamps, Ferenc Puskas, a gateway from the east.

Are they OK with the UK? A good proportion of votes down the years but we have not been so kind – again a case of the east may not be that kind to us but do remember that kindness is a two-way street.

Hungary's defining Eurovision moment? Friderika Bayer was fourth on Hungary's debut in 1994 but Hungary's finest hour had to be Magdi Rusza and her Unsubstantial Blues at the bus stop in Helsinki.

TOTAL POINTS FROM THE UK	*81*
MAXIMUMS	*0*
POINTS AVAILABLE FROM THE UK	*329*
AVERAGE POINTS (OUT OF 10)	*2*
RANK POINTS/%	*31/27*

SHINING LIGHT Magdi Rusza
PERSONAL FAVOURITE Unsubstantial Blues (Magdi Rusza) 2007
INVITATION JURY FAVOURITE Kinek Mondjam El Vetkeimet
(Friderika Bayer) 1994

14 TURKEY
Turquie
Turkee
(24)

CONTESTS WITH THE UK	29
FIRST PARTICIPATION	1975
VICTORIES	1
2003	
TOTAL POINTS TO THE UK	120
MAXIMUMS	2
1988 1998	
POINTS AVAILABLE TO THE UK	348
AVERAGE POINTS (OUT OF 10)	3
RANK POINTS/%	16/15

Turkey? The meeting place of Europe and Asia, Turkish delight, the Blue Mosque, the Grand Bazaar and of course the kebab.

Are they OK with the UK? The Turks have been pretty good to us. In return we have only given one maximum, to Kenan Dogolu in Helsinki.

Turkey's defining Eurovision moment? After many years of toil, Turkey finally made the breakthrough with Sertab's worthy winner.

TOTAL POINTS FROM THE UK	*63*
MAXIMUMS	*1*
2007	
POINTS AVAILABLE FROM THE UK	*348*
AVERAGE POINTS (OUT OF 10)	*1*
RANK POINTS/%	*18/25*

SHINING LIGHT Sertab Erener
PERSONAL FAVOURITE Every Way That I Can (Sertab Erener) 2003
INVITATION JURY FAVOURITE Every Way That I Can (Sertab Erener) 2003

15 NORWAY
Norvege
Norrway
(18)

CONTESTS WITH THE UK	46
FIRST PARTICIPATION	1960
VICTORIES	2
1985 1995	
TOTAL POINTS TO THE UK	152
MAXIMUMS	6
1963 1964 1967 1972 1976 1989	
POINTS AVAILABLE TO THE UK	507
AVERAGE POINTS (OUT OF 10)	3
RANK POINTS/%	10/21

Norway? Jahn Teigen, stunning fjords, a hugely expensive nation, clean living and A-Ha. And Jahn Teigen!

Are they OK with the UK? Yes, they have done us proud over the years with six maximums, although none since 1989. We eventually grew to like Norway in the 1980s, with two maximums in that decade.

Norway's defining Eurovision moment? The dreaded 'nul points' was synonymous with the Norwegians before the nation eventually revived its fortunes. Elisabeth Andreassen guaranteed respectability. Victory for Norway? It wouldn't be the same without them!

TOTAL POINTS FROM THE UK	*92*
MAXIMUMS	*2*
1985 1988	
POINTS AVAILABLE FROM THE UK	*448*
AVERAGE POINTS (OUT OF 10)	*2*
RANK POINTS/%	*10/23*

SHINING LIGHT Elisabeth Andreassen
PERSONAL FAVOURITE La Det Swinge (Bobbysocks) 1985
INVITATION JURY FAVOURITE Nocturne (Secret Garden) 1995

16 MONACO
Monaco
Monacoh
(13)

CONTESTS WITH THE UK	23
FIRST PARTICIPATION	1959
VICTORIES	1
1971	
TOTAL POINTS TO THE UK	83
MAXIMUMS	7
1959 1967 1968 1970 1972 1975 1977	
POINTS AVAILABLE TO THE UK	229
AVERAGE POINTS (OUT OF 10)	3
RANK **POINTS/%**	20/13

Monaco? A very rich suburb in the south of France, rolling hills, expensive boats, a rollicking casino and a haven for tax exiles and a Grand Prix which **has which has little to do with exciting motorsport.**
Are they OK with the UK? An interesting one, as the UK has actually received seven maximums up to 1977. But the UK has actually given the Prinicipality's songs a greater share of the vote.
Monaco's defining Eurovision moment? Severine in 1971.

TOTAL POINTS FROM THE UK	*54*
MAXIMUMS	*1*
1965	
POINTS AVAILABLE FROM THE UK	*145*
AVERAGE POINTS (OUT OF 10)	*3*
RANK *POINTS/%*	*21/4*

SHINING LIGHT Severine
PERSONAL FAVOURITE Un Banc, Un Arbre, Une Rue (Severine) 1971
INVITATION JURY FAVOURITE Un Banc, Un Arbre, Une Rue (Severine) 1971

17 YUGOSLAVIA
Yougoslavie
Yougoslayveeur
(14)

CONTESTS WITH THE UK	27
FIRST PARTICIPATION	1966
VICTORIES	1
1989	
TOTAL POINTS TO THE UK	95
MAXIMUMS	3
1970 1974 1975	
POINTS AVAILABLE TO THE UK	269
AVERAGE POINTS (OUT OF 10)	3
RANK POINTS/%	19/14

Yugoslavia? Now the former Yugoslavia, President Tito, the clear blue Adriatic, a fiery people and the impenetrable language of Serbo-Croat.

Are they OK with the UK? This has been an interesting relationship. The UK has fared reasonably well from the points tally but we have given Yugoslavia more maximums than they have given us.

Yugoslavia's defining Eurovision moment? For me, it was Danijel hitting the high notes in Munich, a single that I still have in my collection. Followed by victory for Riva six years later.

TOTAL POINTS FROM THE UK	*69*
MAXIMUMS	*4*
1966 1970 1983 1989	
POINTS AVAILABLE FROM THE UK	*231*
AVERAGE POINTS (OUT OF 10)	*3*
RANK *POINTS/%*	*16/11*

SHINING LIGHT Riva
PERSONAL FAVOURITE Dzuli (Danijel) 1983
INVITATION JURY FAVOURITE Rock Me Baby (Riva) 1989

18   FINLAND
Finlande
Feenlunt
(23)

CONTESTS WITH THE UK	41
FIRST PARTICIPATION	1961
VICTORIES	1
2006	
TOTAL POINTS TO THE UK	141
MAXIMUMS	2
1962 1973	
POINTS AVAILABLE TO THE UK	439
AVERAGE POINTS (OUT OF 10)	3
RANK **POINTS/%**	13/20

Finland? A good hike to Lapland, Santa Claus, saunas, twigs-a-beating, a harsh-sounding language and some excellent racing drivers.

Are they OK with the UK? No maximum from the Finns since 1973. We have given them four, the last going to Lordi. The UK has given more maximums to Finland than to Sweden. Strange but true!

Finland's defining Eurovision moment? The glazed look of the lads with the Finnish flags wandering the streets of Athens in 2006 said it all after Lordi had swept the board. A very long wait for victory, but well worth waiting for!

TOTAL POINTS FROM THE UK	*64*
MAXIMUMS	*4*
1961 1962 1971 2006	
POINTS AVAILABLE FROM THE UK	*383*
AVERAGE POINTS (OUT OF 10)	*1*
RANK *POINTS/%*	*17/26*

SHINING LIGHT Lordi
PERSONAL FAVOURITE Hard Rock Hallelujah (Lordi) 2006
INVITATION JURY FAVOURITE Hard Rock Hallelujah (Lordi) 2006

19 THE NETHERLANDS
Pays-Bas
Nethurrlunz
(17)

CONTESTS WITH THE UK	46
FIRST PARTICIPATION	1956
VICTORIES	4
1957 1959 1969 1975	
TOTAL POINTS TO THE UK	147
MAXIMUMS	6
1959 1960 1961 1973 1981 1997	
POINTS AVAILABLE TO THE UK	491
AVERAGE POINTS (OUT OF 10)	3
RANK POINTS/%	11/22

The Netherlands? Amsterdam's canals and delights, windmills, clogs and dykes, Delft pottery, Anne Frank and hagelslag!

Are they OK with the UK? Definitely a friend to the UK, they have given us six maximums, three of them rewarding our first four participations. We found 12 points for Ding Dinge Dong!

The Netherlands' defining Eurovision moment? Domination of the Eurovision with the French in the early stages and provided the contest with one of its silliest sing-along winners.

TOTAL POINTS FROM THE UK	*86*
MAXIMUMS	*1*
1975	
POINTS AVAILABLE FROM THE UK	*399*
AVERAGE POINTS (OUT OF 10)	*2*
RANK POINTS/%	*12/21*

SHINING LIGHT Teach In
PERSONAL FAVOURITE Het Is Een Wonder (Linda Williams) 1980
INVITATION JURY FAVOURITE Hemel En Aarde (Edsilia Rombley) 1998

20   ITALY
L'Italie
Iturlee
(24)

CONTESTS WITH THE UK	34
FIRST PARTICIPATION	1956
VICTORIES	2
1964 1990	
TOTAL POINTS TO THE UK	114
MAXIMUMS	2
1974 1988	
POINTS AVAILABLE TO THE UK	347
AVERAGE POINTS (OUT OF 10)	3
RANK POINTS/%	17/18

Italy? A nation with a true sense of style, pasta, ice cream, teeming vibrant cities and many Prime Ministers.

Are they OK with the UK? We have given them more maximums than they have us, but not to Volare in 1958!

Italy's defining Eurovision moment? Gigliola Cinquetti wowed her audience to put Italy on the Eurovision map in 1964. In uniting Europe, however, Toto Cotugno's hair dye made the wrong impression.

TOTAL POINTS FROM THE UK	*55*
MAXIMUMS	*3*
1957 1964 1974	
POINTS AVAILABLE FROM THE UK	*291*
AVERAGE POINTS (OUT OF 10)	*1*
RANK POINTS/%	*20/24*

SHINING LIGHT Gigliola Cinquetti
PERSONAL FAVOURITE Nel Blu Dipinti Di Blu (Domenico Modugno) 1958
INVITATION JURY FAVOURITE Non Ho L'Eta (Gigliola Cinquetti) 1964

21   MOROCCO
Maroc
Morockoh
(44)

CONTESTS WITH THE UK	1
FIRST PARTICIPATION	1980
VICTORIES	0
TOTAL POINTS TO THE UK	8
MAXIMUMS	0
POINTS AVAILABLE TO THE UK	12
AVERAGE POINTS (OUT OF 10)	6
RANK POINTS/%	36/1

Morocco? What on earth were they doing in Eurovision in the first place? a hot country on the north coast of Africa, sweetmeats, Casablanca and not too far from Spanish territory.

Are they OK with the UK? We only played together once, in 1980, but on that occasion they proved a doughty ally with eight points to Prima Donna. It was fleeting though. And we didn't return the favour.

Morocco's defining Eurovision moment? A place in the history book for Samira Bensaid in Morocco's one and only appearance.

TOTAL POINTS FROM THE UK	*0*
MAXIMUMS	*0*
POINTS AVAILABLE FROM THE UK	*12*
AVERAGE POINTS (OUT OF 10)	*0*
RANK POINTS/%	*44/44*

SHINING LIGHT Samira Bensaid
PERSONAL FAVOURITE Message d'Amour (Samira Bensaid) 1980
INVITATION JURY FAVOURITE Message d'Amour (Samira Bensaid) 1980

22   SPAIN
Espagne
Spen
(26)

CONTESTS WITH THE UK	47
FIRST PARTICIPATION	1961
VICTORIES	2
1968 1969	
TOTAL POINTS TO THE UK	140
MAXIMUMS	4
1961 1963 1965 1976	
POINTS AVAILABLE TO THE UK	509
AVERAGE POINTS (OUT OF 10)	2
RANK POINTS/%	14/23

Spain? Stylish cities and sportsmen, the Canary Islands, tapas and sangria; Seve Ballesteros, the pride of the Basques and the Catalans.

Are they OK with the UK? Three maximums in the Sixties. In return, not one maximum for Spain and only a handful of votes at that.

Spain's defining Eurovision moment? The first victory, from Massiel in 1968, saw off the challenge of Cliff Richard, but it has not been without controversy. A year later, the Spaniards joined Lulu in the contest's embarrassing four-way tie.

TOTAL POINTS FROM THE UK	*61*
MAXIMUMS	*0*
POINTS AVAILABLE FROM THE UK	*471*
AVERAGE POINTS (OUT OF 10)	*1*
RANK POINTS/%	*19/30*

SHINING LIGHT Massiel
PERSONAL FAVOURITE Vuelve Conmigo (Anabel Conde) 1995
INVITATION JURY FAVOURITE Vivo Cantando (Salome) 1969

23   CROATIA
Croatie
Croaysheeur
(32)

CONTESTS WITH THE UK	15
FIRST PARTICIPATION	1993
VICTORIES	0
TOTAL POINTS TO THE UK	60
MAXIMUMS	2
1997 1998	
POINTS AVAILABLE TO THE UK	180
AVERAGE POINTS (OUT OF 10)	3
RANK POINTS/%	23/19

Croatia? Arguably the proudest of the chest-hugging, flag-waving Balkan nations; a beautiful Dalmatian coastline currently being discovered by tourists, a warm welcome, Davor Suker, Danijela!

Are they OK with the UK? Croatia is the friendliest of the now eastern bloc to the UK. They are in the top half of the table although we have failed to reciprocate.

Croatia's defining Eurovision moment? No doubt it was the stunning Danijela's dramatic opener in Birmingham. Neka Ni Me Svane finished sixth in the invitation jury's poll, the highest-ranking song not to have won the contest.

TOTAL POINTS FROM THE UK	*15*
MAXIMUMS	*0*
POINTS AVAILABLE FROM THE UK	*168*
AVERAGE POINTS (OUT OF 10)	*0*
RANK POINTS/%	*28/33*

SHINING LIGHT Danijela
PERSONAL FAVOURITE Neka Ni Me Svane (Danijela) 1998
INVITATION JURY FAVOURITE Neka Ni Me Svane (Danijela) 1998

24 CYPRUS
Chypre
Seiproos
(16)

CONTESTS WITH THE UK	25
FIRST PARTICIPATION	1981
VICTORIES	0
TOTAL POINTS TO THE UK	65
MAXIMUMS	0
POINTS AVAILABLE TO THE UK	300
AVERAGE POINTS (OUT OF 10)	2
RANK POINTS/%	22/26

Cyprus? A distant Mediterranean island with a distinct British feel, always 12 points to Greece, the archetypal neighbour voter, a true north/south divide, vivid memories for many a British serviceman.

Are they OK with the UK? The British feel does not extend to UK votes – no maximums in there at all. In return, we have backed Cyprus more strongly.

Cyprus's defining Eurovision moment? Most would say the emergence of Anna Vissi in 1982, but others would argue that Lisa Andreas did enough in 2004. Take your pick!

TOTAL POINTS FROM THE UK	*71*
MAXIMUMS	*1*
1996	
POINTS AVAILABLE FROM THE UK	*276*
AVERAGE POINTS (OUT OF 10)	*2*
RANK POINTS/%	*15/16*

SHINING LIGHT Lisa Andreas
PERSONAL FAVOURITE Mono I Agapi (Anna Vissi) 1982
INVITATION JURY FAVOURITE Mono I Agapi (Anna Vissi) 1982

25 GREECE
Grece
Grees
(15)

CONTESTS WITH THE UK	29
FIRST PARTICIPATION	1974
VICTORIES	1
2005	
TOTAL POINTS TO THE UK	71
MAXIMUMS	1
1976	
POINTS AVAILABLE TO THE UK	334
AVERAGE POINTS (OUT OF 10)	2
RANK POINTS/%	21/27

Greece? The grimy, hot and bustling metropolis that is the ancient city of Athens, the Acropolis, the Parthenon, Mamma Mia's Skopolous and the beauty of the islands.

Are they OK with the UK? Not really, the only Greek maximum which has come our way was for Brotherhood of Man. We also didn't pay Greece much attention in the early years, probably because we couldn't see further east beyond Switzerland.

Greece's defining Eurovision moment? At one point they looked like losing the plot altogether (2002 springs to mind) but they have put together a formidable catalogue in recent years.

TOTAL POINTS FROM THE UK	*81*
MAXIMUMS	*2*
2004 2005	
POINTS AVAILABLE FROM THE UK	*329*
AVERAGE POINTS (OUT OF 10)	*2*
RANK POINTS/%	*13/17*

SHINING LIGHT Helena Paparizou
PERSONAL FAVOURITE Die For You (Antique) 2001
INVITATION JURY FAVOURITE Die For You (Antique) 2001

26 ESTONIA
Estonie
Estowneeur
(12)

CONTESTS WITH THE UK	13
FIRST PARTICIPATION	1994
VICTORIES	1
2001	
TOTAL POINTS TO THE UK	39
MAXIMUMS	0
POINTS AVAILABLE TO THE UK	156
AVERAGE POINTS (OUT OF 10)	2
RANK POINTS/%	24/25

Estonia? The most businesslike of the Baltic states, strong Nordic tendencies, the most beautiful women in Europe, home to the singing revolution and a gem of a capital in Tallinn and its dreaming spires.

Are they OK with the UK? Yet to give us a maximum and pretty cool on our offerings it has to be said. All the more galling in that we sent our maximum to Dave Benton and Tanel Padar's weak winner in 2001.

Estonia's defining Eurovision moment? I would hate to say it was the winning song. For me, the best of Estonia came in the years either side and since then they have faded away disappointingly.

TOTAL POINTS FROM THE UK	*49*
MAXIMUMS	*1*
2001	
POINTS AVAILABLE FROM THE UK	*108*
AVERAGE POINTS (OUT OF 10)	*4*
RANK PTS/%	*22/2*

SHINING LIGHT Dave Benton and Tanel Padar
PERSONAL FAVOURITE Runaway (Sahlene) 2002
INVITATION JURY FAVOURITE Once In A Lifetime (Ines) 2000

27   SLOVENIA
Slovenie
Slovayneeur
(33)

CONTESTS WITH THE UK	13
FIRST PARTICIPATION	1993
VICTORIES	0
TOTAL POINTS TO THE UK	33
MAXIMUMS	0
POINTS AVAILABLE TO THE UK	156
AVERAGE POINTS (OUT OF 10)	2
RANK POINTS/%	25/28

Slovenia? A tranquil and beautiful nation, the most western leaning of the Balkans, the capital is Ljubljana, a popular European holiday destination, a footballing surprise at the turn of the century.

Are they OK with the UK? Slovenia has given us reasonable backing but in return not a single point has gone their way from us, albeit on the strength of just three appearances.

Slovenia's defining Eurovision moment? In the absence of a victory, it has to be Nusa Derenda's Energy in 2001 which had them sitting up and taking notice, as did transvestite air stewardesses Sestre a year later.

TOTAL POINTS FROM THE UK	*0*
MAXIMUMS	*0*
POINTS AVAILABLE FROM THE UK	*36*
AVERAGE POINTS (OUT OF 10)	*0*
RANK *POINTS/%*	*32/34*

SHINING LIGHT Darja Svajger
PERSONAL FAVOURITE Energy (Nusa Derenda) 2001
INVITATION JURY FAVOURITE Energy (Nusa Derenda) 2001

28 POLAND
Pologne
Polurrnd
(31)

CONTESTS WITH THE UK	12
FIRST PARTICIPATION	1994
VICTORIES	0
TOTAL POINTS TO THE UK	30
MAXIMUMS	0
POINTS AVAILABLE TO THE UK	144
AVERAGE POINTS (OUT OF 10)	2
RANK **POINTS/%**	28/29

Poland? A good work ethic, an adventurous spirit, Pope John Paul II, Lech Walesa and Solidarnosc, beetroot soup.

Are they OK with the UK? We're in neutral territory as the Poles have yet to award the UK a maximum but are generally more supportive of us than we are of them. However we marked Edyta Gorniak's impressive debut in 1994 with 12 points.

Poland's defining Eurovision moment? It has to be that debut which scored so well. Unfortunately, Poland is one of many nations which do so well on debut and then fail to sustain their performance.

TOTAL POINTS FROM THE UK	*14*
MAXIMUMS	*1*
1994	
POINTS AVAILABLE FROM THE UK	*108*
AVERAGE POINTS (OUT OF 10)	*1*
RANK *POINTS/%*	*29/29*

SHINING LIGHT Edyta Gorniak
PERSONAL FAVOURITE To Nie Ja (Edyta Gorniak) 1994
INVITATION JURY FAVOURITE To Nie Ja (Edyta Gorniak) 1994

29   SLOVAKIA
Slovakie
Slovakeeur
(47)

CONTESTS WITH THE UK	3
FIRST PARTICIPATION	1994
VICTORIES	0
TOTAL POINTS TO THE UK	10
MAXIMUMS	0
POINTS AVAILABLE TO THE UK	36
AVERAGE POINTS (OUT OF 10)	2
RANK POINTS/%	35/24

Slovakia? One half of the former Czechoslovakia, the capital is Bratislava, Slovaks not Czechs, a stag party venue, cheap beers.

Are they OK with the UK? The Slovaks have certainly been more generous than we have in return but then that wouldn't be difficult as we have presented them with a big fat zero

Slovakia's defining Eurovision moment? Marcel Polander has been Slovakia's shining light in terms of success but there is much to build on in future years, if only to deflect from the Czech Republic's emergence.

TOTAL POINTS FROM THE UK	*0*
MAXIMUMS	*0*
POINTS AVAILABLE FROM THE UK	*36*
AVERAGE POINTS (OUT OF 10)	*0*
RANK POINTS/%	*47/47*

SHINING LIGHT Marcel Polander
PERSONAL FAVOURITE Modlitba (Katarina Hasparova) 1998
INVITATION JURY FAVOURITE Kym Nas Ma (Marcel Polander) 1996

30   BOSNIA HERZEGOVINA
Bosnie Herzogovine
Bozneeurhairtsohgoveenur
(37)

CONTESTS WITH THE UK	13
FIRST PARTICIPATION	1993
VICTORIES	0
TOTAL POINTS TO THE UK	29
MAXIMUMS	0
POINTS AVAILABLE TO THE UK	156
AVERAGE POINTS (OUT OF 10)	1
RANK POINTS/%	29/30

Bosnia and Herzegovina? A nation synonymous with the Balkans war, the televised horrors, an unwieldy name, the capital is Sarajevo, an unusual flag.
Are they OK with the UK? It's hard to tell, nothing concrete has come our way over the years and we have responded in kind.
Bosnia and Herzegovina's defining Eurovision moment? Their debut in 1993, just being there. And then Hari Mata Hari's beautiful Lejla in Athens in 2006, my favourite song of the contest and one which enabled them to feature strongly in the competition.

TOTAL POINTS FROM THE UK	*4*
MAXIMUMS	*0*
POINTS AVAILABLE FROM THE UK	*156*
AVERAGE POINTS (OUT OF 10)	*0*
RANK POINTS/%	*35/38*

SHINING LIGHT Hari Mata Hari
PERSONAL FAVOURITE Lejla (Hari Mata Hari) 2006
INVITATION JURY FAVOURITE Lejla (Hari Mata Hari) 2006

31   RUSSIA
Russie
Rusheeur
(28)

CONTESTS WITH THE UK	11
FIRST PARTICIPATION	1994
VICTORIES	0
TOTAL POINTS TO THE UK	22
MAXIMUMS	1
1997	
POINTS AVAILABLE TO THE UK	132
AVERAGE POINTS (OUT OF 10)	1
RANK POINTS/%	30/32

Russia? The Kremlin and the KGB, Red Square, Vladimir Putin and Boris Yeltsin and Mikhail Gorbachev, dolls, the Cold War and Siberia and Lenin, Trotsky, Stalin and Bilan!

Are they OK with the UK? Russia is not the most UK-hostile nation within the eastern bloc. They awarded top marks to Katrina.

Russia's defining Eurovision moment? Alla Pugacheva in Dublin? t.A.t.U getting the bird in Riga? But it was the arrival of Dima Bilan in Athens that gave the Russians real belief that victory was near.

TOTAL POINTS FROM THE UK	*20*
MAXIMUMS	*0*
POINTS AVAILABLE FROM THE UK	*132*
AVERAGE POINTS (OUT OF 10)	*1*
RANK POINTS/%	*26/28*

SHINING LIGHT Dima Bilan
PERSONAL FAVOURITE Ne Verj, Ne Bojsia, Ne Prosi (t.A.t.U) 2003
INVITATION JURY FAVOURITE Ne Verj, Ne Bojsia, Ne Prosi (t.A.t.U) 2003

32 ICELAND
Island
Icelurnd
(21)

CONTESTS WITH THE UK	20
FIRST PARTICIPATION	1986
VICTORIES	0
TOTAL POINTS TO THE UK	33
MAXIMUMS	1
1993	
POINTS AVAILABLE TO THE UK	240
AVERAGE POINTS (OUT OF 10)	1
RANK POINTS/%	26/36

Iceland? The Northern Lights, dodgy bankers, the geysers and the mud baths, the Blue Lagoon and the multi-coloured roofs of Reykjavik.

Are they OK with the UK? Not at all, points from Iceland are extremely hard to come by. We have been more benevolent.

Iceland's defining Eurovision moment? Paul Oscar's triumph of latex, fishnets and choreography in 1997 – Terry Wogan's 'Is This Channel Four' moment – was truly memorable. The last song up, following straight after Katrina, meant it got few votes. A travesty.

TOTAL POINTS FROM THE UK	*48*
MAXIMUMS	*2*
1990 1992	
POINTS AVAILABLE FROM THE UK	*204*
AVERAGE POINTS (OUT OF 10)	*1*
RANK POINTS/%	*23/19*

SHINING LIGHT Selma
PERSONAL FAVOURITE Minn Hinsti Dans (Paul Oscar) 1997
INVITATION JURY FAVOURITE Open Your Heart (Birgitta) 2003

33   LITHUANIA
Lithuanie
Litooayneeur
(25)

CONTESTS WITH THE UK	8
FIRST PARTICIPATION	1993
VICTORIES	0
TOTAL POINTS TO THE UK	16
MAXIMUMS	0
POINTS AVAILABLE TO THE UK	84
AVERAGE POINTS (OUT OF 10)	1
RANK POINTS/%	32/31

Lithuania? Capital city Vilnius, as yet not a Eurovision destination, a rebel to Soviet rule, a flag of rainbow colours, Vitas Gerulaitis.

Are they OK with the UK? Can't say that they are, and the UK has tended to be marginally more generous in return.

Lithuania's defining Eurovision moment? It has to be in Athens with the gimmicky and bold We Are The Winners ... of Eurovision, from LT United. In the end, they lost out to the awesome Lordi but provided arguably the contest's second-most memorable song.

TOTAL POINTS FROM THE UK	*17*
MAXIMUMS	*0*
POINTS AVAILABLE FROM THE UK	*72*
AVERAGE POINTS (OUT OF 10)	*2*
RANK POINTS/%	*27/20*

SHINING LIGHT LT United
PERSONAL FAVOURITE We Are The Winners (LT United) 2006
INVITATION JURY FAVOURITE We Are The Winners (LT United) 2006

34   ROMANIA
Roumanie
Rohmayneeur
(35)

CONTESTS WITH THE UK	9
FIRST PARTICIPATION	1994
VICTORIES	NIL
TOTAL POINTS TO THE UK	17
MAXIMUMS	1
1998	
POINTS AVAILABLE TO THE UK	108
AVERAGE POINTS (OUT OF 10)	1
RANK POINTS/%	31/34

Romania? The horrors of Ceaucescu, Transyllvania, the Cheeky Girls, Steaua Bucharest and when did Rumania become Romania?

Are they OK with the UK? We have received a smattering of votes from Romania down the years and they even awarded us top marks 1998. In return, the percentage vote is miniscule.

Romania's defining Eurovision moment? Some half-decent songs. Mihai Traistariu's Tornero hit the high notes and the nation's high point in Athens and certainly deserved a higher placing.

TOTAL POINTS FROM THE UK	*6*
MAXIMUMS	*0*
POINTS AVAILABLE FROM THE UK	*108*
AVERAGE POINTS (OUT OF 10)	*0*
RANK POINTS/%	*33/35*

SHINING LIGHT Mihai Traistariu
PERSONAL FAVOURITE Tornero (Mihai Traistariu) 2006
INVITATION JURY FAVOURITE Tornero (Mihai Traistariu) 2006

35 MACEDONIA
Macedoine
Masurdohneeyur
(48)

CONTESTS WITH THE UK	7
FIRST PARTICIPATION	1998
VICTORIES	0
TOTAL POINTS TO THE UK	14
MAXIMUMS	0
POINTS AVAILABLE TO THE UK	84
AVERAGE POINTS (OUT OF 10)	1
RANK POINTS/%	34/33

Macedonia? A mouthful if you add the 'Former Yugoslav Republic' bit, the flag is rather striking, an intriguing and strategic position in the south Balkans, capital city of Skopje, interesting history.

Are they OK with the UK? There have been some points from Macedonia but nothing to write home about. In return, we have yet to send Macedonia a single point in seven appearances.

Macedonia's defining Eurovision moment? It came with the late Tose Proeski and all those hands but as a nation they haven't yet taken off in spite of a remarkably good record in qualification.

TOTAL POINTS FROM THE UK	*0*
MAXIMUMS	*0*
POINTS AVAILABLE FROM THE UK	*84*
AVERAGE POINTS (OUT OF 10)	*0*
RANK POINTS/%	*48/48*

SHINING LIGHT Tose Proeski
PERSONAL FAVOURITE Ninanajna (Elena Risteska) 2006
INVITATION JURY FAVOURITE Mojot Svet (Karolina Gocheva) 2007

36 LATVIA
Lettonie
Latveeur
(18)

CONTESTS WITH THE UK	8
FIRST PARTICIPATION	2000
VICTORIES	1
2002	
TOTAL POINTS TO THE UK	15
MAXIMUMS	0
POINTS AVAILABLE TO THE UK	96
AVERAGE POINTS (OUT OF 10)	1
RANK　　　　　POINTS/%	33/35

Latvia? Another Baltic gem of a capital in go-ahead Riga, a Germanic influence, mixed cultures, Brainstorm, the maroon and white.

Are they OK with the UK? Interest in UK songs has been fleeting and Latvia comes in as the least friendly of the Baltic states. In return, we have given Latvia a fair chunk of points.

Latvia's defining Eurovision moment? For me, it was the wonderful debut song from Brainstorm in Stockholm. Marie N's choreographed winner in Tallinn was just reward for a strong introduction on the Eurovision stage and a good show followed in 2003.

TOTAL POINTS FROM THE UK	*27*
MAXIMUMS	*0*
POINTS AVAILABLE FROM THE UK	*84*
AVERAGE POINTS (OUT OF 10)	*3*
RANK　　　　　POINTS/%	*25/10*

SHINING LIGHT Marie N
PERSONAL FAVOURITE My Star (Brainstorm) 2000
INVITATION JURY FAVOURITE My Star (Brainstorm) 2000

37 ANDORRA
Andorre
Andorah
(39)

CONTESTS WITH THE UK		4
FIRST PARTICIPATION		2004
VICTORIES		0
TOTAL POINTS TO THE UK		2
MAXIMUMS		0
POINTS AVAILABLE TO THE UK		48
AVERAGE POINTS (OUT OF 10)		0
RANK	POINTS/%	37/37

Andorra? A tiny nation squeezed somewhere between France and Spain, domination by the Pyrenees, a thorn in the side of English football, home city Barcelona, Anonymous!

Are they OK with the UK? They gave two points to Daz Sampson's Teenage Life in Athens so the outlook is promising. They have yet to reach the final, so the UK has not been able to send across any votes.

Andorra's defining Eurovision moment? It has to be the travesty that boy band Anonymous did not make the 2007 final, as the Eastern bloc dominated proceedings in Helsinki.

TOTAL POINTS FROM THE UK		*0*
MAXIMUMS		*0*
POINTS AVAILABLE FROM THE UK		*0*
AVERAGE POINTS (OUT OF 10)		*0*
RANK	*POINTS/%*	*39/39*

SHINING LIGHT Anonymous
PERSONAL FAVOURITE Salvem El Mon (Anonymous) 2007
INVITATION JURY FAVOURITE Salvem El Mon (Anonymous) 2007

38 BELARUS
Bielorussie
Bellahruce
(43)

CONTESTS WITH THE UK	4
FIRST PARTICIPATION	2004
VICTORIES	0
TOTAL POINTS TO THE UK	1
MAXIMUMS	0
POINTS AVAILABLE TO THE UK	48
AVERAGE POINTS (OUT OF 10)	0
RANK POINTS/%	38/38

Belarus? White Russia, loyal to the old guard, the nation throws lots of money at the Eurovision, a depth of sporting pride, capital city is Minsk.

Are they OK with the UK? They gave a point to James Fox in Istanbul, which was something of a surprise. Nothing back in return, we couldn't even work our magic for Dmitri Koldun.

Belarus's defining Eurovision moment? Koldun succeeded in reaching the 2007 final with a song likened to a James Bond theme. Tipped as a possible winner, it failed to live up to the hype.

TOTAL POINTS FROM THE UK	*0*
MAXIMUMS	*0*
POINTS AVAILABLE FROM THE UK	*12*
AVERAGE POINTS (OUT OF 10)	*0*
RANK: *POINTS/%*	*43/43*

SHINING LIGHT Koldun
PERSONAL FAVOURITE Work Your Magic (Koldun) 2007
INVITATION JURY FAVOURITE Work Your Magic (Koldun) 2007

39   CZECH REPUBLIC
Republique Tscheque
Chekreepublic
(41)

CONTESTS WITH THE UK	1
FIRST PARTICIPATION	2007
VICTORIES	0
TOTAL POINTS TO THE UK	0
MAXIMUMS	0
POINTS AVAILABLE TO THE UK	12
AVERAGE POINTS (OUT OF 10)	0
RANK POINTS/%	39/39

Czech Republic? Tourist trap capital Prague, a popular destination for young and old, the sights and sounds of the stags and hens, an undoubted spirit of independence, Czechs not Slovaks.

Are they OK with the UK? Not a lot to go on either way but no points so far and don't hold your breath. The UK has to date not had the chance to vote for a Czech song in the final.

Czech Republic's defining Eurovision moment? The instrumental opening from Kabat promised more than what was actually delivered when the vocal kicked in. Rock bottom on debut was an undesirable outcome so the defining moment is yet to arrive.

TOTAL POINTS FROM THE UK	*0*
MAXIMUMS	*0*
POINTS AVAILABLE FROM THE UK	*0*
AVERAGE POINTS (OUT OF 10)	*0*
RANK POINTS/%	*41/41*

SHINING LIGHT Kabat
PERSONAL FAVOURITE Mala Dama (Kabat) 2007
INVITATION JURY FAVOURITE Mala Dama (Kabat) 2007

40   GEORGIA
Georgie
Jawjeeur
(45)

CONTESTS WITH THE UK	1
FIRST PARTICIPATION	2007
VICTORIES	0
TOTAL POINTS TO THE UK	0
MAXIMUMS	0
POINTS AVAILABLE TO THE UK	12
AVERAGE POINTS (OUT OF 10)	0
RANK POINTS/%	40/40

Georgia? An almighty recent spat with big brother Russia, the capital city is Tbilisi, another footballing dynamo, not to be confused with Georgia in the United States, a flag which adheres to the cross of St George so they do strike a chord with a legion of patriotic Englishmen.

Are they OK with the UK? Only one appearance to go on and no points either way. So difficult to say.

Georgia's defining Eurovision moment? A strong debut in Helsinki where Sopho warbled about her visionary dream.

TOTAL POINTS FROM THE UK	*0*
MAXIMUMS	*0*
POINTS AVAILABLE FROM THE UK	*12*
AVERAGE POINTS (OUT OF 10)	*0*
RANK POINTS/%	*45/45*

SHINING LIGHT Sopho
PERSONAL FAVOURITE Visionary Dream (Sopho) 2007
INVITATION JURY FAVOURITE Visionary Dream (Sopho) 2007

41 MONTENEGRO
Montenegro
Monteenaygro
(40)

CONTESTS WITH THE UK	1
FIRST PARTICIPATION	2007
VICTORIES	0
TOTAL POINTS TO THE UK	0
MAXIMUMS	0
POINTS AVAILABLE TO THE UK	12
AVERAGE POINTS (OUT OF 10)	0
RANK POINTS/%	41/41

Montenegro? A scenic nation at the foot of the Balkans, hidden beauties, prised itself away from Serbia to stand on its own two feet, like Serbia two name checks in the Eurovision charts, capital city is Podgorica.

Are they OK with the UK? Nothing much to go on as there has only one shared contest.

Montenegro's defining Eurovision moment? To date the debut from Stevan Faddy, who has Caledonian connections, which failed to get anyone too excited and failed to reach the final in Helsinki.

TOTAL POINTS FROM THE UK	*0*
MAXIMUMS	*0*
POINTS AVAILABLE FROM THE UK	*0*
AVERAGE POINTS (OUT OF 10)	*0*
RANK POINTS/%	*40/40*

SHINING LIGHT Stevan Faddy
PERSONAL FAVOURITE Ajde Kroci (Stevan Faddy) 2007
INVITATION JURY FAVOURITE Ajde Kroci (Stevan Faddy) 2007

42 SERBIA
Serbie
Serbeeur
(42)

CONTESTS WITH THE UK	1
FIRST PARTICIPATION	2007
VICTORIES	1
2007	
TOTAL POINTS TO THE UK	0
MAXIMUMS	0
POINTS AVAILABLE TO THE UK	12
AVERAGE POINTS (OUT OF 10)	0
RANK POINTS/%	42/42

Serbia? A nation craving acceptance by the European fraternity, an unlikely role model in Marija Serifovic, a strong sporting heritage in basketball and tennis in particular, a bellicose past, war-torn Belgrade.

Are they OK with the UK? Just one contest with Serbia, so it is hard to gauge. Can't blame the Serbs for failing to back Scooch in 2007, more of a surprise was the UK not notching a single point for Molitva.

Serbia's defining Eurovision moment? Serbia definitely hit the ground running with victory on debut in 2007, backing up the general view of the pundits in Helsinki with the stirring and striking Molitva.

TOTAL POINTS FROM THE UK	*0*
MAXIMUMS	*0*
POINTS AVAILABLE FROM THE UK	*12*
AVERAGE POINTS (OUT OF 10)	*0*
RANK POINTS/%	*42/42*

SHINING LIGHT Marija Serifovic
PERSONAL FAVOURITE Molitva (Marija Serifovic) 2007
INVITATION JURY FAVOURITE Molitva (Marija Serifovic) 2007

43   ARMENIA
Armenie
Arrmayneeur
(46)

CONTESTS WITH THE UK	2
FIRST PARTICIPATION	2006
VICTORIES	0
TOTAL POINTS TO THE UK	0
MAXIMUMS	0
POINTS AVAILABLE TO THE UK	24
AVERAGE POINTS (OUT OF 10)	0
RANK POINTS/%	43/43

Armenia? A distant part of the old Soviet bloc, not far from Turkey and Iran, capital city of Yerevan, not keen on Azerbeijan, nestled between the Black Sea and Caspian Sea.

Are they OK with the UK? No points so far so nothing to suggest that they are. No points going the other way either.

Armenia's defining Eurovision moment? Has to be on debut in 2006 when Andre proved to be a hit with most of the boys. His song, Without Your Love, put on a very good show in finishing strongly behind all-conquering Lordi.

TOTAL POINTS FROM THE UK	*0*
MAXIMUMS	*0*
POINTS AVAILABLE FROM THE UK	*24*
AVERAGE POINTS (OUT OF 10)	*0*
RANK POINTS/%	*46/46*

SHINING LIGHT Andre
PERSONAL FAVOURITE Anytime You Need (Hayko) 2007
INVITATION JURY FAVOURITE Without Your Love (Andre) 2006

44 SERBIA AND MONTENEGRO
Serbie et Montenegro
Serbeeuramontaynaygro
(34)

CONTESTS WITH THE UK	2
FIRST PARTICIPATION	2004
VICTORIES	0
TOTAL POINTS TO THE UK	0
MAXIMUMS	0
POINTS AVAILABLE TO THE UK	24
AVERAGE POINTS (OUT OF 10)	0
RANK POINTS/%	44/44

Serbia and Montenegro? Not a lot to be said that hasn't already been said about Serbia and Montenegro as separate entities. A brief union and they get two name checks each in the Eurovision directory.

Are they OK with the UK? No points from Serbia and Montenegro and no more to follow. We did despatch a few votes for Zelkjo Joksimovic in 2004 for the surprise package that was Lane Moje. That counts as friendship!

Serbia and Montenegro's defining Eurovision moment? Lane Moje in Istanbul was certainly their finest hour.

TOTAL POINTS FROM THE UK	*3*
MAXIMUMS	*0*
POINTS AVAILABLE FROM THE UK	*24*
AVERAGE POINTS (OUT OF 10)	*1*
RANK POINTS/%	*36/31*

SHINING LIGHT Zelkjo Joksimovic
PERSONAL FAVOURITE Lane Moje (Zelkjo Joksimovic) 2004
INVITATION JURY FAVOURITE Lane Moje (Zelkjo Joksimovic) 2004

45 BULGARIA
Bulgarie
Bulgaireeur
(20)

CONTESTS WITH THE UK	3
FIRST PARTICIPATION	2005
VICTORIES	0
TOTAL POINTS TO THE UK	0
MAXIMUMS	0
POINTS AVAILABLE TO THE UK	36
AVERAGE POINTS (OUT OF 10)	0
RANK POINTS/%	45/45

Bulgaria? An emerging cheap sunspot destination, reputedly dodgy wines, surnames that end in 'ov' or 'ev', capital city Sofia, Balkans fringe.
Are they OK with the UK? No, they have not given us a single point. In return, we gave the Bulgarians solid support in their first final.
Bulgaria's defining Eurovision moment? The surprising success of the booming, screeching Water.

TOTAL POINTS FROM THE UK	*5*
MAXIMUMS	*0*
POINTS AVAILABLE FROM THE UK	*12*
AVERAGE POINTS (OUT OF 10)	*4*
RANK POINTS/%	*34/3*

SHINING LIGHT Elitsa Todorova and Stoyan Yankoulov
PERSONAL FAVOURITE Water (Elitsa Todorova and Stoyan Yankoulov) 2007
INVITATION JURY FAVOURITE Water (Elitsa Todorova and Stoyan Yankoulov) 2007

46 MOLDOVA
Moldove
Moldoveeur
(36)

CONTESTS WITH THE UK	3
FIRST PARTICIPATION	2005
VICTORIES	0
TOTAL POINTS TO THE UK	0
MAXIMUMS	0
POINTS AVAILABLE TO THE UK	36
AVERAGE POINTS (OUT OF 10)	0
RANK POINTS/%	46/46

Moldova? Strongly allied to Romania in the heart of eastern Europe, I say Moldavia and you say Moldova, capital city is Chisinau, home to some good-looking women, neighbours the Ukraine.

Are they OK with the UK? Not a single point to the UK. In return we have given Moldova a couple of points but they have barely registered.

Moldova's defining Eurovision moment? A madcap group graced the Kiev stage in 2005, singing about grandma banging her drum. Scored well in the novelty stakes but haven't hit the heights since.

TOTAL POINTS FROM THE UK	*2*
MAXIMUMS	*0*
POINTS AVAILABLE FROM THE UK	*36*
AVERAGE POINTS (OUT OF 10)	*0*
RANK POINTS/%	*37/36*

SHINING LIGHT Zdob Si Zdub
PERSONAL FAVOURITE Boonike Bate Toba (Zdob Si Zdub) 2005
INVITATION JURY FAVOURITE Boonike Bate Toba (Zdob Si Zdub) 2005

47   ALBANIA
Albanie
Albayneeur
(38)

CONTESTS WITH THE UK	4
FIRST PARTICIPATION	2004
VICTORIES	0
TOTAL POINTS TO THE UK	0
MAXIMUMS	0
POINTS AVAILABLE TO THE UK	48
AVERAGE POINTS (OUT OF 10)	0
RANK POINTS/%	47/47

Albania? The most secretive nation of the old Soviet bloc, some great names to conjure with, a weird and wonderful fascination with the veteran English comedian Norman Wisdom, the capital is Tirana, less than 72 kilometres from Italy.

Are they OK with the UK? The figures say it all, not a single point for Blighty to date. We've given them one point in the past.

Albania's defining Eurovision moment? It has to be the strong debut song from Anjeza Shahini in Istanbul. That apart, they have struggled to make any sort of impact.

TOTAL POINTS FROM THE UK	*1*
MAXIMUMS	*0*
POINTS AVAILABLE FROM THE UK	*48*
AVERAGE POINTS (OUT OF 10)	*0*
RANK POINTS/%	*38/37*

SHINING LIGHT Anjeza Shahini
PERSONAL FAVOURITE The Image Of You (Anjeza Shahini) 2004
INVITATION JURY FAVOURITE The Image Of You (Anjeza Shahini) 2004

48 UKRAINE
Ukraine
Youcren
(27)

CONTESTS WITH THE UK	5
FIRST PARTICIPATION	2003
VICTORIES	1
2004	
TOTAL POINTS TO THE UK	0
MAXIMUMS	0
POINTS AVAILABLE TO THE UK	60
AVERAGE POINTS (OUT OF 10)	0
RANK **POINTS/%**	48/48

Ukraine? Dinamo Kiev and Shakhtar Donetsk, the Orange Revolution, gas wars with Russia, capital city is Kiev, Odessa and the Black Sea.

Are they OK with the UK? They most certainly are not. They may share the first two letters with the UK but that's far as any solidarity goes. No points in five attempts, bottom of all the ranks.

Ukraine's defining Eurovision moment? Since becoming a member of the Eurovision family, Ukraine has provided one winner and some excellent entries.

TOTAL POINTS FROM THE UK	*13*
MAXIMUMS	*0*
POINTS AVAILABLE FROM THE UK	*60*
AVERAGE POINTS (OUT OF 10)	*2*
RANK *POINTS/%*	*30/22*

SHINING LIGHT Ruslana
PERSONAL FAVOURITE Danzing Lasha Tumbai (Verka Serduchka) 2007
INVITATION JURY FAVOURITE Wild Dances (Ruslana) 2004

And finally...
UNITED KINGDOM
Royaume-Uni
Younydedkingdurm

FIRST PARTICIPATION	1957
VICTORIES	5

1967 1969 1976 1981 1997

SHINING LIGHT Brotherhood Of Man

PERSONAL FAVOURITE Just A Little Bit (Gina G) 1996

INVITATION JURY FAVOURITE Love Shine A Light (Katrina and the Waves) 1997

BETWEEN 1957 AND 2007, THE UK HAS TO DATE GIVEN NO POINTS TO:
Andorra, Armenia, Belarus, Czech Republic, Georgia, FYR Macedonia, Montenegro, Morocco, Serbia and Slovakia

MADE MOST EUROVISION APPEARANCES WITH:
Germany (49)

POTENTIALLY BEEN ABLE TO GIVE THE MOST POINTS TO:
Germany and Spain (471)

AWARDED MOST POINTS TO:
Ireland (203)

GIVEN THE HIGHEST PERCENTAGE POINTS AWARD TO:
Ireland (48 per cent)

GIVEN THE MOST MAXIMUM POINTS TO:
Ireland (8 awards) followed by Switzerland (6), France (5), Finland and Yugoslavia (4) and Italy and Luxembourg (3)

INSTITUTION

I consider myself very fortunate to have been able to travel Europe in the last ten or so years in pursuit of that weird and wonderful institution that is the Eurovision Song Contest.

The contest appeals to my Europhile instincts and the essence of gentle competition, a concept that flings nations from all over Europe into an artistic battle while at the same time bringing them ever closer together.

It is not something for the Little Englander who looks down in disdain at anyone or anything that does not have roots on the tiny island pointing away from the French mainland.

It is for someone willing to recognize and appreciate that there is a continent and a world beyond Dover, someone willing to learn more about our continental neighbours and explore the architectural, cultural and scenic delights of this diverse paradise.

Proud that I am to be English first and British second, I am also proud to be a European citizen.

And for this reason primarily, I look forward to the annual odyssey that is a visit to the world of Eurovision.

My first excursion was rather close to home, a short hop across the Irish Sea to Dublin in 1995.

Ireland's domination of the contest in the 1990s was on the wane but this represented my first visit to the fair capital city which certainly lived up to expectations.

Such friendly people the Irish, a land of song and bonhomie and such a laid back attitude it's unbelievable.

Next year it was Oslo, arriving in the country on the Norwegian national day and then being greeted by biting cold, sleet and snow on the day of the final.

A memorable visit, in that good old Gina G was representing the UK with one of my favourite songs Just A Little Bit – great tune, great hook and one to make you feel good.

I missed out on a return to Dublin in 1997, just a couple of days after Tony Blair's landslide election victory.

But I was back the following year, when Eurovision returned to the UK after an absence of 16 years.

Birmingham was the venue, just up the M6 from Northampton, and to this day a fond recollection of good friends and a good time in England's second city.

Dana International's victory topped off a sparkling night and Terry Wogan and Ulrika Jonsson did a good job in hosting the event.

Author Andy Roberts with old ESC friends Christian Dufresnes (left) and Patrick Racine, whose photographs in this book demonstrate l'entente cordiale!

Limited space prevented me from attending Jerusalem in 1999 but my extended tour of Scandinavia and the Baltics began with the new Millennium.

Stockholm it was in 2000 and it felt good to be in Abba-land for what turned out to be another storming contest.

This year marked the debut of the Eurovision Song Contest CD, which these days you can actually get prior to the event, even in UK music stores which otherwise feign disinterest.

And a victory here for the Olsen Brothers, who hit exactly the right note and gathered crucial momentum as the week played out.

Denmark 2001, and the Danes were keen to put on a Eurovision show like no other.

Copenhagen's Parken stadium accommodated 38,000 visitors on finals night and the emerging Estonia clinched a surprise victory which charted Eurovision progress into the Baltics.

Lindsay Dracass had the unenviable job of appearing in this vast arena – she didn't quite pass the test but gave it her all, and her friendly demeanour throughout won her a lot of friends.

On to Tallinn, the following year, and what an absolute joy the Estonian capital was to behold.

Then still largely undiscovered, happy memories of mooching around the old town and checking out some pretty cool bars. One day I must return, it is certainly one of my favourite Eurovision haunts.

The baton passed to Riga as Latvia ended the night victorious – one thing Eurovision definitely helps with is knowledge of obscure European flags, currencies and capital cities.

While Estonia was rapidly advancing into the electronic age, the Latvian capital presented itself as a chic, go-ahead and cosmopolitan city, something I was quite unprepared for.

I loved Riga too, but here we took a large geographical leap as Turkey stepped forward to claim its first title – a result which sent the delegation of Turkish officials and fans into rhapsody.

I was also quite unprepared for Istanbul in 2004, what a fascinating city but one which certainly has a dark side.

My day exploring the metropolis, straddling as it does Europe and Asia, will live with me forever. So much to see, so much to take in and so much to look out for, in particular the omnipresent hustlers and shady characters on city centre trams.

Istanbul gave rise to a hop back into the former Soviet republics, this time down south to the Ukraine.

Kiev I am not so sure about, a city with wide streets, underground shopping malls and imperious architecture.

Some of its architecture though was crumbling and certainly in 2005, not too long after the famous Orange Revolution, the Ukrainian capital appeared to be finding it difficult to move out of the Soviet age.

The people were friendly enough and seemed to enjoy the attention and opportunities that arrived with Eurovision. But I would not hurry to go back there, it has to be said.

In marked contrast, courtesy of Greece's victory, was the visit to Athens the year after.

I'd heard much about the chaotic and dirty streets, the stunning old and the ugly new and the overpowering traffic fumes.

I left Athens with the impression of a vibrant, disorganized city, bursting with history and beautiful buildings and monuments and chaos, yes, but a wonderful chaos.

At the end of it all, a good show, a powerful winning song from Finland's monsters of rock and the prospect of completing the Millennium circle back in northern Europe in 2007.

Helsinki emerged as the latest city to tick off on Eurovision tours and it did leave me a little underwhelmed.

Very clean and healthy, as has already been said, but it was tiny and not at all distinctive. Don't get me wrong, it was pleasant enough but there is no pull to return any day soon.

The sequence of Eurovision victories since Ireland's domination has seen no nation win the contest two years running, each year since 1996 yielding a different winner.

The winners, consecutively, have been Ireland, United Kingdom, Israel, Sweden, Denmark, Estonia, Latvia, Turkey, Ukraine, Greece and Finland.

In 2007, the sequence was maintained as Serbia – performing at Eurovision for the first time in her own right – rubber-stamped a ticket to Belgrade.

Now that was an eye-opener, as the taxi driver ferrying me from the airport into the city centre disdainfully pointed out the many buildings which still bore the scars of the Balkans war in the early 1990s.

Belgrade certainly had an edge to it but it was more interesting than Helsinki and I definitely preferred it to Kiev.

The police and inhabitants were required to be on their best behaviour and there was a tiny sense of unease in not quite knowing how the locals would react to Eurovision's massive gay following.

It wasn't a problem as it turned out – the Serbs I encountered were polite, respectful and helpful.

The United Kingdom, having been routinely charged with not taking Eurovision seriously enough in recent years, certainly laid that bogey to rest in 2009.

We should be serious every year, playing our part to bond together Europe via the platform of entertainment while working hard behind the scenes to ensure that a modern Eurovision Song Contest becomes completely inclusive, as it should be. It won't be over until the attractive lady from east London sings?

Or as I might have put it amid the excitement of a bathtime with Abba regatta, it won't be over until the fat red boat sinks.

Oh happy days.

Printed in the United Kingdom by
Lightning Source UK Ltd., Milton Keynes
142040UK00001B/117/P